HARD TO BELIEVE
TOO OLD AT SIXTEEN

TO JACK — HOPING
THIS BRINGS BACK
HAPPY MEMORIES OF
HIS TIME IN THE
ROYAL ELECTRICAL AND
MECHANICAL ENGINEERS.
WITH VERY BEST
WISHES.

Peter Horsfall

Hard To Believe
Too Old At Sixteen

by

PETER HORSFALL

Peter Horsfall

The Memoir Club

© Peter Horsfall 1999

First edition 1999
Reprinted 2008

The Memoir Club
Arya House
Langley Park
Durham
DH7 9XE

British Library Cataloguing in
Publication Data.
A catalogue record for this book
is available from the
British Library

ISBN: 978-1-84104-190-2

Typeset by TW Typesetting, Plymouth, Devon
Printed by Biddles Ltd, King's Lynn

In Memory of the

27th Colonel Coldstream Guards
Lieutenant General The Honourable
Sir William Rous, KCB, OBE
'General Willie'

Who Always Led From The Front

Contents

List of Illustrations

Acknowledgements

WITHOUT QUESTION the person to thank for this book is my wife Mary. Not only has she encouraged and cajoled me into pressing on with the writing of it – she has typed every word; some sections several times and checked and corrected my spelling and other aspects of poor English.

The wonderful Eva Nicholas who was the Senior Clerical Officer in my office in the Lords for several years told me on a number of occasions that I should write a book – having typed some of my articles for publishing in the 'Coldstream Gazette'.

I am indebted to The Lord Denham for giving me permission to use his brilliant description of the ceremonial on the State Opening of Parliament – copied from his book 'Black Rod'. Similarly, the late Charlie Chester for his most moving poem 'Which is the road to contentment'. How sad that this really great character is not here to see it published.

My publishers have been terrific and for a first time writer it has been a pleasure to work with them. Their advice has been invaluable and the finished article is ten times better than Mary and I envisaged.

I hope that the marvellous staff, police, security and works departments in the Lords will feel that I have done them justice. It goes without saying that the Peers were a delight to work for and their thoughtfulness and hospitality beyond belief.

The real inspiration behind the book has been our fine sons Terry and Bob, our lovely daughter-in-law Judi and beautiful grand-children Jemma, Megan and Jack. Hopefully they will have something to show their own families in the next century.

Finally, I cannot thank Lady Rous enough for allowing me to dedicate the book to General Willie. He epitomised everything good about the Regiment and a modern day General. If he is looking down on us now I hope he approves of Boy Horsfall's efforts.

Foreword

WHEN CHOOSING A TITLE for a biography, some authors choose fact and others choose fiction.

For example, Gerald Kersh, who wrote about the Coldstream Guards during the Second World War, called the book, 'They died with their boots clean'. This was a statement of fact, as Guardsmen did clean their boots prior to going into action.

Ted Willis (later to become Baron Willis of Chislehurst) called his autobiography 'Whatever Happened to Tom Mix?'. When questioning his mother about what he should call his life story, she suggested the title. When he failed to understand this, she told him that whenever he arrived home from the Saturday morning (penny entrance fee!) cinema, having seen the serial of the 'cowboy of the day', Tom Mix, he impersonated him for the rest of the weekend. Fiction of course?

I have gone for fact. I was turned down for both the West Yorkshire Regiment and the Royal Marines because, having had my 16th birthday, I was too old. Indeed it was the latter who wrote to me suggesting that I apply to the Brigade of Guards, as they accepted Drummer Boys at the grand old age of 16. It is questionable whether the Royal Marines' loss was the Coldstream Guards' gain. Readers of this book can judge for themselves.

Note on the Illustrator Bill Tidy

BILL TIDY'S FIRST LOVE is drawing although he appears regularly on radio and television and, over four decades, has written and illustrated more than 60 books.

Along with scriptwriting, plays, stage and costume design, after-dinner speaking and the use of the occasional innovative ventriloquist's dummy, he potters (in the garden), totters (to the Rose & Crown) and is produced and directed by his wife, Rosa.

In spite of a Lancastrian upbringing, he is delighted to be involved in the telling of a Tyke's life story and grateful that he got out of the Army when he did (1952-55), narrowly avoiding Horsfall and his ferocious moustache.

CHAPTER 1

The Horsfall Family

As I LOOKED DOWN from the window of the residence of the Staff Superintendent in the House of Lords, I could hardly believe that a lad from a Leeds working class family could be in such a prestigious building. It was the 29th March, 1980 and it was my first night on duty – but more about that later.

I was born in Leeds on the 24th January, 1930. My brothers were Tony, born 25th April 1925 and Terry, born 3rd October, 1928. My only sister was Pauline, born several years later.

Dad (Chris) was born on Christmas Day, 1900 and Mother (she liked to be called Mam) was born on the 6th May, 1897. Her first name was May and her maiden name Chapman. Dad was one of 11 children – his father and several of his brothers were military men, and some were musical. Mam had two brothers, Fred and Arthur, and one sister called Doris. She was the eldest child and outlived them all, dying on the 24th February, 1997, 10 weeks before her 100th birthday! Grandad Chapman was described on Mother's birth certificate as a Bookbinder/Journeyman. The Chapman family could be called gentle folk, whereas the Horsfalls were sterner – but

1

with a great zest for enjoying life. Both sides of the family had a sense of fun.

Dad had a remarkable life in many ways. His father had a cobbler's shop and young Chris had to leave school at 11 to help his Dad run the shop when he was ill.

At 14 he joined the West Yorkshire Regiment as a Band Boy and served in India with the regiment from 1914 until 1916. After the Great War he left the Army to help in the family business, which was unfortunate as he would have loved to be a regular soldier.

Between the Great War and the 1939-45 War he had several jobs: insurance agent, tram and bus conductor, tram and bus driver. He was even unemployed for a while and it was amazing how he and Mother brought up four children reasonably well. The main interest in his life, however, was the Territorial Army. For many years he was the Bugle Major of the 8th Battalion Leeds Rifles, based in Carlton Hill Barracks, Leeds. Not only was he very smart, although only 5'6" tall, but he was an excellent musician. He had a flair for arranging band and bugle marches and he once told me that he was paid 6d. as a 'royalty' on certain occasions when one of the marches he had arranged was played. He liked a pint (or two!) and bought Terry and me our first pints of shandy when we were about 14 or 15 – with strict instructions not to tell Mam!

The 8th Battalion (Leeds Rifles) West Yorkshire Regiment in the mid-1930s. The Bugle Major is the author's father, Chris Horsfall. Like father – like son!

When war broke out in 1939, Dad was called up into the Royal Artillery (Anti-Aircraft) as a Battery Sergeant Major. Due to his age he was not allowed to go abroad, but served all over the United Kingdom in various Anti-Aircraft units – towards the end of the war as Regimental Sergeant Major. When the Guards Chapel in London was bombed, he was one of the first on the scene. He said it was horrendous!

Until the 1939-45 War it was the exception rather than the rule for women to work. Nevertheless Mother was made to work in a factory – quite long hours at times. She did not work full-time after the War, mainly due to the fact that Dad disagreed with women working!

Brother Tony is the cleverest in the whole family and won a scholarship to Leeds Technical College. I have never understood why he joined the Army as an Apprentice Tradesman in the RAOC in 1939, at the age of 14. He served for 26 years, initially in the RAOC and, from 1943, on the forming of that Corps, in the REME. He became a WO2 (Armourer Artificer) but would have risen much higher if it had not been for his sporting ability.

Tony was an outstanding all-round sportsman. Before joining the Army, he represented Leeds schoolboys at cricket. In the REME he gained Corps Colours at cricket, hockey, rugby union and, towards the end of his service, golf. He always put his sport before his career and refused courses that would have gained him promotion. He served about seven years in Germany and four in Hong Kong – all to the detriment of his military career.

In 1996 I met a retired General, late REME, who had served with Tony in the 1950s, and he was amazed that Tony never went to the very top in the Corps (The Major General became the Director of REME!). On completion of his military service, Tony became a teacher at Ashford (Kent) Technical College and retired at 65. He has two sons, Tony and Keith, and two daughters, Avril and Sharon. He married Anne in 1945 in London.

Brother Terry was, by common consent, a beautiful baby, a very handsome man, and extremely popular throughout his life, dying at 65 after illnesses lasting about four years. He was a natural leader even when a boy at school. He was the 'cock' of Sheepscar School and as tough as they came. He always looked after his weedy young brother (me!) both in and out of school. At the age of 16, he was in theory a co-driver of a furniture van. However, it was not uncommon for him to drive it – on one occasion to London and back – although he was only just 17 at the time! Mother nearly died when she heard of this – afterwards. Dad was away in the Army at the time.

Terry and Gladys' wedding day, 1947.

Terry served for about three years in the REME, becoming a Sergeant in less than a year and a Driving Instructor at Bordon. He would have made a terrific soldier but missed Gladys (whom he married in 1947) and family too much to be away from home for long. After his military service he had several jobs, almost always ones in which his leadership qualities were to the fore. Towards the end of his working life he was in charge of a butchery department in ASDA, Leeds. He had one daughter, Denise. She and her husband Peter have two sons, Lee and Luke.

Mother says that she went in for a fourth child because she was determined to have a daughter. This she did, giving birth to Pauline. Apart from 14 months in New Zealand (1956/7), Pauline has remained in Leeds, Dewsbury and Huddersfield. She married Roy Fox in 1964. They have one son, Chris. Pauline was a shorthand/typist/secretary. Roy is mad on all sports, especially cricket.

Mam and Dad were wonderful parents. After Dad died in 1982, Pauline was a source of strength to Mam and it was due to her, Roy and Chris that she enjoyed her last 15 years.

The family, and many friends, took the news of Mam's death in February 1997 very badly. She had only been ill for seven weeks and would have been 100 the following May. Amongst the many messages of condolence, was a lovely letter from Buckingham Palace on behalf of the Queen.

CHAPTER 2

Childhood and Children

NOWADAYS IT DOES NOT SEEM to be 'politically correct' to refer to the working class. This is ridiculous because so many successful people whom Mary and I have met are proud that they came from that background. That is certainly so in my case.

Because it was 'not the done thing' prior to the 39-45 War, married women did not work. This meant that the man of the house had to earn enough to keep the whole family. In the case of the Horsfall family, there were four children, with a span of just over ten years in ages, to be fed and watered.

As explained in Chapter 1, Dad's job was not highly paid! Nevertheless we were kept well and enjoyed life to the full. We were content with the simple things. Older brother Tony — apart from being an outstanding sportsman — would disappear for a full day at a time to go fishing. Even in

Mam, baby Peter, Terry and Tony at Scarborough in 1931.

his early teens it was common for him to be out from first to last light, not something that could happen nowadays, due to certain 'funny people'.

The fact that Terry and I were just 16 months apart in age spurred us on. We were right little tearaways and accident-prone. We competed with 'Our Gang' in the *Dandy* comic in our adventures. It was common to be always climbing trees, scrumping apples or rhubarb. Along with other little terrors, we would spend hour after hour kicking a ball about or playing a form of cricket with a piece of wood and a home-made 'ball'. Terry, being the tough guy, nearly always won whatever game we played and I was an 'also-ran'.

Both of us were fire bugs and later on I will tell of my own exploits in this regard. When Terry was quite tiny – about five or six, I believe – he started a fire (intentionally!) in a cupboard in the living room. Fortunately Dad appeared in time to put it out before too much damage was done.

We seemed to be forever moving house. The memory dims, but I can certainly remember living in at least six houses before joining the Army at 16. A couple of times we moved at night. In old age I asked Dad if these were what were commonly called 'moonlight flits'. This was a common practice amongst the working classes as a way of avoiding paying bills. Dad never admitted this, but neither did he deny it! He simply laughed, but Mam never forgave me and thought I was naughty to suggest such a thing.

Schooling during the war was a joke. Due to the shortage of teachers, many of whom were away in the services, the routine was that in alternative weeks we would attend school either in the morning or in the afternoon. The size of the classes was enormous and the teachers must have had a terrible time trying to control us. Strangely enough, most of our age-group seemed to do reasonably well at school.

The teacher who made the most impression on us was the one who had us for about the last 18 months of our time at school, from about twelve-and-a-half to fourteen. This was an elderly man who came out of retirement to teach when the younger teachers went off to War. His name was 'Buggy' Shaw.

'Buggy' was very strict and he had to be! He used the cane regularly and needed to. One of his favourite tricks, if a boy was misbehaving, was to hit him with a piece of chalk – even if he was at the back of the class! He should have played for Yorkshire. He would have been terrific at hitting the stumps and running out batsmen.

A boy called Butterfield was an absolute menace and sometimes got the whole class in trouble. He used to throw ink pellets at the blackboard (and miss!). He was forever, and deservedly, being caned. This was always on the hand and I wonder if this caused him trouble in later life.

On one occasion Butterfield passed water in a milk bottle and hid the bottle behind the blackboard. When 'Buggy' found the bottle he went berserk. When he had got over his initial temper, he addressed the class in these terms: 'Someone, some boy, has left the room in a milk bottle'. He repeated this several times and although a lot of the boys were giggling, remained absolutely poker-faced until eventually Butterfield owned up to the offence. Needless to say, he got six of the best!

I have often wondered whether Buggy lived to a great age and if so, whether he 'dined out' on such stories. He was certainly a terrific teacher despite, or because of, his strictness. During our last term there was a stream of potential employers visiting the school vetting us for jobs. HOW TIMES HAVE CHANGED! I was offered three jobs, all in factories, before leaving school at Easter 1944.

When we were very young, Terry and I would do anything to earn a few shillings. We both had newspaper rounds. At one time Terry thought of the following wheeze. When we lived at Sheepscar, there was a number of derelict houses. We took timber from these, chopped and tied it into uniform bundles, and went around the houses selling it. It seems ridiculous now but the prices charged were one penny for a small bundle and twopence for a larger one. Mind you, it has to be remembered that during the War, coal, the only means of heating, was rationed.

We were expected to go to church on Sundays – sometimes twice. Firstly there would be the normal family service and then Sunday school. On a

Pauline and Roy's wedding day, 1964.

Sunday we wore our best clothes the whole day (I had Terry's pass-ons until I grew taller than he at about 13). If we had visitors, we were to speak only when spoken to. We said our prayers prior to going to sleep each night – and included a special prayer for Dad when he was away.

Pauline was a very placid child and when Dad was on leave from the Army, we would baby-sit when he and Mam went out. She was no trouble at all and one way and another we were a very happy family. Just before the War Tony joined the Royal Army Ordnance Corps despite being only 14. He was an Apprentice Tradesman at Arborfield. Terry and I missed him badly as he was the ideal 'older brother'. He was a terrific example to us and always very kind. When he came on leave, we were 'spoilt rotten'.

There is one incident that now sounds amusing, but at the time did not amuse Tony. In the summer of 1938 the *Yorkshire Evening Post* was awarding a cricket bat weekly to the schoolboy who had put up the most outstanding performance on the cricket field. By chance Tony won this, with a wonderful bowling performance, the week prior to the England-versus-Australia Test match at Headingley. He was invited to Headingley to meet the teams and to be presented with the bat. The bat was signed by all the Australian team.

After Tony had joined the Army, he came on leave with the intention of taking the bat back to his unit. This proved to be pointless – Terry had sawn about four inches off the bottom of the bat so that he and I could play with it. As stated above, Tony was not amused!

In our younger days sport played a big part in our lives. Dad would take us to Elland Road to see Leeds United and to Headingley to see Leeds playing rugby league or Yorkshire playing cricket. Goodness knows how he afforded this, even though the admission charge for some games was as little as threepence! At football we never saw Dad during the actual game. In those days children were passed over the top of adult spectators and stood in a group at the front of the crowd.

Both our parents were very heavy smokers and before the War Tony helped Dad to save cash on cigarettes. It was possible to purchase tiny packs of Woodbine cigarettes from a machine outside the local newsagents. Alternate packets contained either two or three cigarettes. Occasionally Dad gave Tony a pile of one penny coins with instructions to buy all the cigarettes possible. Each packet cost one penny, so Tony would ensure that he ALWAYS got packets of three by waiting for other people to put a coin in and getting a pack of two. What patience, initiative and loyalty!

Although Dad and Mam did not help in our education, it was made clear to us that when we left school we would have to work hard and contribute to the housekeeping – but more about that later. Despite a shortage of cash, our childhood can be described as idyllic. None of us can ever remember being smacked, and yet obviously we deserved it at times. This is living proof of the fact that in a proper loving family it should not be necessary.

CHAPTER 3

The Formative Years or Preparing for Life

WHEN CONSIDERING WHAT 'prepares you for life' it is something of a mystery to decide what makes the biggest impression. It is strange to think that not long after the 1939 War started, Terry and I were evacuated to Retford – and hated it even though the married couple we lived with were quite nice. Later in life our only real memory of our time there was beans, beans, beans and more beans! After a few months there Mam and Dad came to collect us and took us back to Leeds.

In a previous chapter I have mentioned the firebug incident and there will be more about that later. On one occasion Terry and I had a fire going in the garden and we were kneeling down on opposite sides blowing to make it go better. Then I stopped blowing and you can imagine the result. I tried to hide the burns on my leg by pulling a long sock over them, but unfortunately the blisters grew rapidly and the Leeds Infirmary had a customer.

As a kid I was always mad about the Army and used to follow 'my Dad's' band for miles. He was Bugle Major of the Eighth Leeds Rifles. I proved the point that I was keen when I was about eight years old. Incredible as it seems now, I cut the sleeves off my Dad's best Service Dress jacket in an effort to make it fit. That in itself was bad enough, but unfortunately he never discovered it until just before he was due on parade. You should have seen the speed with which I left the house, pushing Pauline in a pram, when I suddenly realised that my 'master stitching' had been discovered.

In 1941, when Terry was 12 and I was 11, we cycled over 200 miles from Leeds to Swindon to visit my Dad, who was stationed there as a BSM in the Royal Artillery. To digress a bit: like all younger brothers, I got all Terry's second-hand 'pass-ons' and for this ride I had a very old Raleigh bike, whereas he had Wigfalls brand new one (with 3-speeds). We were so saddle-sore that we travelled back by train. Dad kept the old Raleigh, and as we learned, many years later, raffled it off – for charity of course!

Whilst at Swindon we were given beds in the tented ration stores. This lasted precisely two days – which was as long as it took for the Rations NCO to catch us with our hands in the dried fruit bin – just counting the currants and raisins, we said!

The only holiday we had as youngsters was an annual one in August, usually to Bridlington or Scarborough, and always travelling by train or coach. On one occasion Dad borrowed a small car, I believe an Austin Seven, and I recall having to push it up a hill at least once. Life was fun, nevertheless.

We were never coached at any sport but both Terry and I were adequate cricketers and soccer players. I took quite a lot of wickets with what were kindly referred to as 'donkey drop' leg breaks. When I joined the Army I was told that only Len Hutton bowled slower than I. I think that the reason batsmen got themselves out was because they grew weary of waiting for the ball to arrive at their end of the pitch.

Terry was a lion on the soccer field, nearly always at the centre of the defence. He made the tackles by 'Bite-Your-Legs' Hunter (Leeds United) and 'Chopper' Harris (Chelsea) appear like kindergarten stuff! Terry never shirked a tackle and brought down players twice his size. This was due to the training on the local recreation ground, in which we sometimes used a stone as a ball. I once made the mistake of heading this 'ball' and have a scar where my parting *was* to prove it.

While our amateurish efforts continued, Tony progressed on his way, producing high quality performances in sports of all kinds. He represented Leeds at schoolboy cricket on a number of occasions.

At 13, having lied about my age (saying I was 14), I joined the West Yorkshire Regiment Cadets. Remarkably, within nine months I had passed both Parts I and II of what was then known as Certificate A. I was Drum Major before I was 15, despite fierce competition. If proof were needed that soldiering was in the genes, this was it.

When I became Drum Major, I was constantly being asked who taught me to throw and swing the mace. I never had a lesson and Dad had never had a full-size mace, as Light Infantry Regiments equip their Bugle Majors with a smallish 'cane'. Mind you, I did use this 'cane' to master certain movements and used it for exhibitions and for showing off.

I was 14 on the 24th January 1944 and left school on the following Good Friday, starting work as an Apprentice Electrician at the Yorkshire Switchgear immediately after Easter. The Manager, a Mr Schofield, seemed to like the look of me and put me in the Maintenance Team immediately. The other two boys who joined on the same day went on to normal factory work – very boring.

My weekly pay was seventeen shillings and sixpence (about 86 pence in modern currency) and within six months Mr Schofield had increased this by five shillings a week, but he made me promise not to tell the other two apprentices! I handed all my wages over to Mam and she gave me five shillings a week as spending money. Riches indeed!

The Team boss was Martin Stapleton and the Electrician I worked with was Bill. They were terrific and taught me everything about maintenance-type electrical work. Even to this day I can remember lots of what they taught me over a period of about two years. Bill was a bit of a dirty old man and one of his sayings was: 'It's not the size of the weapon that counts, it's the strength of the thrust'. The first few times I heard this I thought it was an electrical saying. Children/teenagers were very naive in those days – no bad thing.

All my Dad's family had served in the County regiment – the West Yorks. It was therefore ironical that not only was I in the Cadets of the Regiment, but also that I was based in Carlton Hill Barracks, which had a great affiliation with the Regiment. It was also noteworthy that Dad had been stationed there when he served with the Leeds Rifles. It therefore follows that all Dad's mates made a very big fuss of me – particularly when I became Drum Major. They used to challenge me to throw the mace higher and treated me to a pint (shandy of course!) if they thought I had done well. They never once told me that I was as smart as my Dad; which did not surprise me, as he was always immaculate.

DO ANYTHING FOR A PINT OF SHANDY!

Our social life, even after I joined the Army, revolved around the Sergeants' Mess in Carlton Hill Barracks or the Commercial Club, a great place for entertainment in central Leeds.

So in one way or another this was good training for what was to follow – the Coldstream Guards, seeing the world and finally becoming Staff Superintendent in the House of Lords.

CHAPTER 4

Caterham, Pirbright and 'The Smoke'

As soon as I was 14, I wanted to join the Army but Mam, whose husband and eldest son were both away in it, would have none of it. This was not surprising, as with a war on, and constant news of casualties and prisoners of war and losses, the future did not look promising.

I therefore put everything into enjoying the Army Cadet Force. We had two parade evenings per week and quite often a Sunday parade as well. However, at 16 (Dad now being demobbed from the Royal Artillery), Mam relented and signed the appropriate form allowing me to join the Army. As explained in the Foreword, I was turned down by both the West Yorkshire Regiment and the Royal Marines as – it is hard to believe – 'too old at 16'! As soon as I received the letter from the Marines, I went to the Recruiting Office in Leeds. The Sergeant (who turned out to be a Coldstreamer, although I did not know this at the time) welcomed me with open arms. He sat me down to take the 'entrance exam'. This consisted of some *very* simple arithmetic, reading about two or three pages from a book, and writing a one-page letter. I also had a medical and passed with flying colours. How could I fail? Five feet nine inches tall and weighing 138 pounds (dripping wet of course!).

Before I knew what was happening, I had signed on the dotted line for nine years with the Colours and three years on the Reserve. My service would start from the age of 18 and my regiment would be the Coldstream Guards. Within three weeks I arrived at the Guards Depot at Caterham. The journey from Leeds on the 2nd September, 1946 was highly interesting, to say the least. The Recruiting Sergeant put an 'adult' who was joining the Coldstream in charge of me with instructions to get to Caterham. Neither he nor I had ever been to London, so it was the 'blind leading the blind' on the journey south.

The next twelve days are vague in the extreme. I was the only Boy so was kept in the Receiving Room, where I seemed to spend most of my time cleaning my kit or polishing the floor. The adult recruits only seemed to spend a few days in the Receiving Room before being squadded and posted to a Company. I think the adults were amazed to think that this weedy looking character (chest 34"!) was being allowed into the élite Guards. I recall my Dad, when seeing me off in Leeds, asking me if I knew what I was letting myself in for. When I asked what he meant, he said something along the lines of: 'They're a pretty tough lot, y'know'.

After 12 days I was made to dress up in what was known as Change of Quarter Dress. This consisted of a large pack, small pack, water bottle, ammunition pouches, web belt and braces. It weighed a ton. Fortunately, the Sergeant in charge of the squad leaving Caterham for Pirbright took one look at me and made me travel in the baggage vehicle. The squad MARCHED from the Guards Depot to Caterham railway station. On arrival at Brookwood, they also MARCHED to Pirbright camp. Dad's words came back to me: 'Do you know what you are letting yourself in for?' WHAT HAD I DONE?

On arrival at Pirbright, I joined another 35 boys who were to become Coldstream Drummers. 33 of these had been in for almost a year and the other two new boys and I were made to feel very inferior. Fortunately my cadet training stood me in good stead and I quickly caught up with most of the other boys in all aspects – especially drill and cleaning kit.

In the same spider-like huts were boys going to the other four Regiments of Foot Guards, the Grenadiers, Scots, Irish and Welsh Guards. I had a stroke of luck. One of the Grenadier boys came from Leeds and knew that I had been Drum Major. They soon had me doing exhibition-type stuff – usually with a broom handle but occasionally with the Drum Major's cane. The other two new boys had a miserable time as they had not been in the Cadets.

To give some idea of the type of boys we had, these two tales are worth relating. One Sunday afternoon 'Tich' Davies (he was 4'11" when he joined with his BIG brother who was 5'3"!) came into the barrack room and collapsed on his bed absolutely hysterical with laughter. Nothing would induce him to tell us what he was laughing at. We should have guessed. A short while later we heard a tremendous explosion from the direction of the ranges. We learned later that he had got hold of some gun cotton and detonators and had caused a small range hut to disappear off the face of the earth. However, it shows the remarkable loyalty amongst us in those days that despite being bombarded with questions by Warrant and Non-Commissioned Officers, the culprit was never caught.

The other quite remarkable story is that one morning, just after joining the Training Battalion, I woke up when reveille sounded and jumped out of bed (you had to in those days or you got literally thumped by the NCO in

Waiting). Instead of there being thirty-six Coldstream Boys in the room, there were only three! ALL the others had gone AWOL. At first I honestly thought they must be on blanket shaking or PT, and that three of us 'had missed the boat'. Most of them were caught within a couple of days but Gordon Carter (later to become Drum Major) was away for about ten days and took the rap for the lot. In passing, it is worth recalling how Carter became known as Oggie: he once scored THREE Own Goals (OG) when playing for the Drums against the KOYLI Band in Malaya and in no time at all he was stuck with a new name.

The reason for the 33 boys going AWOL was quite simple. They had been bullied by a couple of Non-Commissioned Officers for several months. The three new boys had missed most of this. It was quite common for us to be woken very late at night and made to start cleaning the toilets etc. We would be called into the Sergeants' bunk one at a time and made to say which of the Sergeants was the most handsome, smart, best musician or what have you. No matter which answer was given, you were on a loser, as you would get thumped – usually on the muscle in the upper arm.

After the absentees returned, an enquiry was held and the NCOs concerned disappeared. We assumed that they had been charged with these bullying offences but many years later I met one of these Sergeants (Lawrence – Scots Guards) and he said that all that happened was that they were returned to their parent unit. HE SHOWED NO SHAME OR REMORSE.

After about a month in the Scots Guards Training Battalion, the Coldstream boys joined the 2nd Battalion at Pirbright. They had just returned from Italy. Many of these soldiers had been abroad for long periods during the War and had chests full of medals. The ones I got to know were terrific guys – more about that later.

We only had to move a few hundred yards to join the 2nd Battalion, as they were also in Pirbright Camp. They were preparing for duties in the Royal Palaces, the Tower of London and the Bank of England. A Boy's pay was fourteen shillings a week (70 pence in modern currency), of which we were allowed to draw five shillings a week. One shilling a week had to be placed in a Post Office Savings Bank, and we had to produce the book weekly to the Drum Major to ensure the cash had been paid in!

When the Battalion returned from Italy, all the soldiers' webbing was scrubbed, and bleached almost white. To prepare for the move to London, all webbing had to be blancoed a light green. I, along with a number of other Boys, earned £1 a set by blancoing and polishing the brasses for various

NCOs and Guardsmen. I believe I cleaned four or five sets – riches indeed! We had an idea that the Drum Major knew of this (illegal) practice but conveniently closed his eyes to it.

The Lance Corporal who taught us how to clean kit was called Martin. His nickname was 'Rubber' and when we enquired (not of him of course) why 'Rubber'? we were told that he was always rubbing and 'spit and polishing' his boots. His own kit was brilliant. On an evening we would sit cross-legged on our beds cleaning kit, whilst 'Rubber' Martin taught us regimental history and told war stories. We were spellbound. Although he was very strict, he was always fair – a great lesson.

The date we moved to London is fairly imprinted on my mind because it was bonfire night, the 5th November 1946. We moved into Wellington Barracks and our barrack room overlooked St. James' Park. I can remember how sick we all were, seeing the fireworks outside barracks and the sky illuminated and yet not being allowed out to enjoy the fun.

Our Drum Major was Tom Birkett, who, historians of military music will tell you, is possibly the greatest Drum Major in living memory. There were smarter men but musically he was the tops. Some of the marches composed by Tom Birkett are still played regularly by Corps of Drums everywhere. 'Hazelmere', named after his wife Hazel, is included in virtually every display given by Drum and Flute bands. At the age of 77 he wrote a march called 'The 27th Colonel' to honour Lt. General Sir William Rous when he took over the Coldstream Guards.

During the winter of 46/47 the 11 Drummer Boys did lots and lots of practice, and in most cases improved very quickly. I can remember how proud I was when taking my place in the third rank of the 'Corps' for the Changing the Guard ceremony, less than three months after joining the regiment. Admittedly it was on the cymbals, but I could not care less – talk about trickles up and down the spine! What a great thrill, never to be forgotten.

By February 1947 I was on all parades with a side drum. Surprisingly, by the summer of that year I was occasionally in the front rank – no mean feat when you consider there were about 11 side drummers, mostly old soldiers and very experienced. Undoubtedly what told in my favour was my Cadet training and the fact that my kit was always of a high standard. Also I stuck to the music as written, which pleased the great T.B., whereas some of the Drummers tried to improvise and were too 'flashy'. The one I copied was our superb Leading Side Drummer, 'Trixie' Nockall. He always stuck to the written music and was what could be called 'traditional'. A nice guy too!

Readers will wonder what happened to the 12th Boy. The one who was

The 2nd Battalion Coldstream Guards, Escort to the Colour on the Queen's Birthday Parade, 1947. R.S.M. Arthur Ramsden M.C. is on the left with his sword drawn.

unsuccessful at music was employed in the Tailor's Shop. In our case this was Dave Dyer, later nicknamed 'Zeke' for some unexplainable reason. This was thought of as a demotion by us Boys, but Dave had the last laugh – he was promoted to Sergeant and became the Master Tailor of the 2nd Battalion as a VERY young man.

1947 saw the first Trooping the Colour after the War and was in khaki. The Band and Drums wore Service Dress and the remainder of the parade were in Battle Dress. The quite immaculate Regimental Sergeant Major, Arthur Ramsden MC, wore Service Dress and Puttees as per pre-war. The Escort to the Colour, trained by Arthur Ramsden, was outstanding and for many years a photograph of this Escort had a place of honour in the 2nd Battalion Sergeants' Mess. I was so proud to take part in this parade.

Arthur Ramsden was the most wonderful 'man manager' and the Battalion would have done anything for him. Some of his Warrant and senior Non-Commissioned Officers were not very good so he needed to be special – which he was! His wife Ann was always kind to the Drummer Boys, and if we made a delivery of coal – yes, coal – to her married quarter, there was always a cup of tea and a biscuit for us.

I recall being at an All Ranks Dance with a number of other Boys when the Regimental Sergeant Major came and had a chat with us. He told the Bar Steward to give us a pint of beer each and said to us, 'Don't tell the Drum Major'. Many years later I reminded Arthur of this and he laughed and said 'Why not?' I also told Tom Birkett but he did not believe me as Boys and Drummers under 18 were not allowed to drink alcohol. Shades of Dad buying brother Terry and me pints with orders not to tell Mam!

The Cadet unit I served with did me an enormous favour – perhaps unwittingly! In 1947 and 1948 the 1st Battalion West Yorkshire Regiment asked the Battalion if I could be loaned to them for their summer camp in the rank of Drum Major – even while wearing the rank and uniform of a Coldstreamer. On each occasion, at the end of the attachment, I was 'recommended' and attended Commanding Officer's orders to be given a large pat on the back. This obviously put me 'one up' on the other Boys and young Drummers.

The first intimate royal occasion I can remember concerns HRH Princess Margaret. In those days the Boys sang – for want of a better word – in the choir in the Guards Chapel. One Sunday morning the Senior Chaplain to the Brigade of Guards told us to be on our best behaviour as the Princess would be in the congregation (he was a great man and always had a twinkle in his eye, but must have known he had made an impossible request!). It was just my luck to be seated in the end seat of the choir stalls nearest to the front pews where the princess sat. I was terrified and not once did I dare to look in her direction. In fact I never even saw her, although she was only about eight feet away. Throughout the service the Boys on my left were trying to make me laugh (easy to do in those days). What made it worse was that I have always been a poor singer (my sons will vouch for this) and normally would only open and close my mouth and go through the motions of singing. However, for such an important occasion, and with Drum Major Birkett watching me, I felt duty bound to sing. How we all failed to be locked up I shall never know.

My first error of judgment was in 1947 and was to do with a 'slashed cap'. Like most good Drummers, I had a floating peak in my forage cap which, when on parade, was pulled out, and when walking out, was pushed in. Having got away with this for several months, I bumped straight into the Drum Major as I was leaving Wellington Barracks one Saturday afternoon. He took the cap off me and literally jumped up and down on it. I was placed in open arrest for the weekend and on Monday morning awarded four extra drills by the Adjutant. Fortunately, the Drill Sergeant (Wilson) was an ex-drummer and I didn't do drills but spent the next four walking-out afternoons whitewashing the cookhouse walls.

I mentioned earlier what a wonderful musician Tom Birkett was (is!). His Corps of Drums, which included some professional musicians from civilian life, was superb and far in advance of its time. We regularly formed a circle – similar to the Regimental Bands, and played music from the London musicals, Gilbert and Sullivan music and operatic music. Some examples are 'In a Monastery Garden', 'Oklahoma', 'Bless the Bride', 'Poet and Peasant', 'Orpheus in the Underworld' and numerous concert marches. T.B. also wrote several marches and also arranged ten marches, by various composers, for use by all the Corps of Drums in the Brigade of Guards. Many of these are used to this day when Massed Drums are on parade.

Our two piccolo players (Corporal Frank Brooks and Boy Bill Perris) were out of the top drawer and their rendition of 'Stars and Stripes' by Sousa regularly drew applause – unusual on military parades in those days.

To give one example of Tom Birkett's short fuse and brilliant musicianship: Boy Peter Kirk – later to become the Senior Drum Major of all the Foot Guards – kept repeating the same mistake in Poet and Peasant. This was in the Practice Room and T.B. got hotter and hotter under the collar. It should be borne in mind that this is a very difficult piece of music and Peter was on the second Bb flute. Eventually it all became too much for the Drum Major. He went around all the music stands and tore every piece of music to shreds. Unbelievably – by the next day Tom had rewritten all the music and we proceeded to practice and play it perfectly. What a lesson for us all!

I had often wondered why the old soldiers referred to London as 'The Smoke'. The winter of 1947/48 soon taught me the reason. Thick fog and smog occurred regularly and we performed the ceremony of Changing the Guard in real 'pea soupers' at times. It was also a terrible winter for thick snow. I recall several occasions when the whole Battalion – less those due to go on Guard – assisted in clearing snow from the barrack square in Wellington Barracks to enable the parade to take place. Returning from week-end leave in mid-winter took over 10 hours from Leeds to Kings Cross – normally a four-hour journey. This made me AWOL for a few hours but fortunately I obtained a 'certificate' from the rail authorities, so I was not charged with the absence.

A few points about the so-called administrative arrangements. We were not issued with sheets for the beds until 1947 or pyjamas until 1948. This meant sleeping in the nude or in daytime underwear – I chose the latter!

There were eight wash-hand basins and four lavatories between about 50 soldiers. Unless you were amongst the first into the ablutions you had to wash and shave in cold water and have a long wait for a loo. I quickly learnt to get up early and be in the ablutions soon after reveille.

There was one place in barracks where soldiers could have a bath and this was controlled by an old soldier Corporal. The Boys were marched to the bath-house twice a week. Each Boy was given about five minutes to have a bath and re-dress. The Corporal recorded this fact in a book. Unbelievably, some Boys boasted that they did not take a bath, but wet their hair to give the appearance of having bathed! As we were only issued with two towels, it can be imagined the state they got into.

What a relief to go on to man's service at the age of seventeen-and-a-half. This meant that you could leave barracks every day from after duty until midnight – and in civilian clothes! The civilian clothes were inspected by the Adjutant and, if he approved them, a permanent pass was issued stating what the clothes looked like. Many of us regularly walked out in uniform, which at that time was khaki battledress. This was easier than trying to get past the Drum Major and Adjutant.

The second half of 1947 and 1948 were blissful in many ways. The facilities for playing sports were almost non-existent, but I was regularly able to watch top-class football in winter and first-class cricket at the Oval and Lords in summer. Interestingly, this was in pre-television days, so the grounds were invariably full and VERY cheap!

What joy I had watching Middlesex in 1948, when Denis Compton and Bill Edrich broke numerous batting records, supported by a wonderful team! Little did I know that in the 1980s I would become a personal friend of the brilliant Denis Compton. Later in life I also met Ted Drake, who was the Centre Forward at Chelsea in the 1940s. A terrific guy and very amusing.

1948 ushered in one of the greatest sporting highlights in the UK for many years, the Olympic Games at Wembley Stadium. The massed bands of the Brigade of Guards were in the opening ceremony. I can remember how very hot it was and it was one of the first occasions on which full dress uniform was worn after the War. This was a great thrill and despite the heat, thoroughly enjoyable.

A point that will interest past and present side drummers. In the days that I was in the Drums we did 'stick lifting' when on the march – unless in greatcoat order. Why isn't that the case nowadays?

One or two NCOs bullied the Boys and it was surprising that Drum Major Birkett did not seem to know of this. Corporal 'Ming' Simmonds was the worst offender. During bugle practice, if a Boy or young Drummer made a mistake, Simmonds hit him on the knuckles of the right hand which held the bugle. As I was a poor bugler, I was regularly struck. This was compensated for by the fact that we also had some really nice NCOs: Woodlands, Brooks and Morris come to mind. 'Dolly' Knight was nice enough but a very poor NCO. The senior NCO was Sergeant Simpson and he was a horror, ruling with a combination of fear and rudeness. There will be more about him later. The NCO in the side drummers was Ted Dade, an ex-prisoner of war who was very quiet and impossible to get to know. It was interesting that Trixie Nockall, a Drummer, was the Leading Side Drummer.

The young Drummers and Boys took their turn at being the Drummer on duty at St James Palace, Buckingham Palace, the Tower of London and the Bank of England. I was nearly always on Buckingham Palace and St James Palace, presumably because these were in the public eye and I was considered to be smart and well turned out. Between late 1946 until September 1948 I was recommended for my turnout – when on duty or Changing the Guard, at least 20 times. On each occasion I was marched in front of the Adjutant and given a long week-end pass. Because of a shortage of cash, I sometimes spent these in camp! One of my sources of income was to clean the drum belonging to a Drummer in the Welsh Guards band, for which he paid me £1. This was more than a week's wages. I also earned five shillings (25 pence) a week for cleaning Corporal Morris's kit.

The Battalion was very strong in numbers due to Conscription/National Servicemen and excellent recruiting of regulars. I was on a public duty guard about once every 10 to 12 days. NCOs and Guardsmen only performed a duty about once a month. This meant that the Drummers/Boys became experts on ceremonial procedures and it was commonplace for NCOs and Guardsmen to seek advice from them. I memorised every aspect of the Guards orders. This was to relieve boredom. There was no television or radio in the guardroom.

Homosexuals were virtually unheard of in the late 40s and 50s. However, a number of 'queers' hung around Guards barracks in the hope of picking up soldiers. Some were beaten up for making improper approaches to some of our very tough Guardsmen! Four of the young Drummers had regular male friends. They always said that there was nothing sexual in the relationships. After their 18th birthday, soldiers could stay out overnight until 8.00 am. One morning a Drummer returned to barracks with £26, having been given this for just being a friend. Eventually, the friend of one

Drummer paid him to leave the Army. Nothing would be thought unusual about that nowadays.

Amongst the regular haunts of these 'queers' were the 'Bag o' Nails' and 'Shakespeare' public houses and 'Katinis' cafe. Bill Perris and I became experts at allowing one of these men to buy us a drink or two and then doing a disappearing act. Similarly Katinis cafe sold the most marvellous sausage sandwiches and meat pies and we were occasionally bought these. They were sixpence ($2^1/2$ pence) each and a pint was about tenpence in old money.

The most famous – or is it infamous (?) – of these strange men was 'Boris, Queen of the Guards'. He was the first man I ever saw wearing lipstick and I thought he was repulsive. Some of the Guardsmen used to take the mickey out of him but he seemed to revel in this. Incidentally, it was many years before I heard the word 'lesbian'. What a changing world we live in!

The Battalion was given a hell of a shock in August 1948. We were told that we were sailing for Singapore, and then on to Malaya, within a few weeks, to perform an 'Emergency Tour'. The old soldiers, especially those who had been in the War, were furious, as many of them were waiting to be demobbed. We younger soldiers were most excited, even thrilled, at the thought of an operational tour. Mind you, we were given the impression that we would be back in England by Christmas.

We were immediately sent on embarkation leave and when we returned were fitted out with jungle green clothing and tropical kit. We were initially issued with stiff type bush hats but later these were withdrawn and we wer~ issued with jungle green floppy hats. These hats were worn with a Coldstream Star in the front and two red stripes on the side to indicate Second Battalion.

So it was that the Battalion formed up in Wellington Barracks, dressed in Field Service Marching Order and khaki battledress, ready to march to Waterloo Station en route to the Far East. One of my most vivid memories of that day was the large crowds lining Birdcage Walk and Westminster Bridge. The other outstanding memory is playing the march 'Radetsky' when marching under the bridge leading to the railway station.

A day later we sailed for Singapore on the troopship *Empire Trooper*. What an adventure that was to be, certainly different to 'The Smoke'! Dad had taken the news of our tour philosophically, having been in India at the age of 14. Mam, on the other hand, took it very badly. Who could blame her?

My 22 months in London had matured me beyond recognition. Mixing with some rough and tough soldiers in the Battalion made me grow up quickly. Also, I soon became 'street-wise' and the following true story illustrates this. As a young Drummer on St Jame's Palace Guard duty I was ordered by the officer on guard to go to his Club, off Piccadilly, with a message. I was in full dress uniform in greatcoat order with forage cap. As I passed a young attractive lady, she said 'Hello soldier'. I don't think that I replied. On the return journey the lady was still there and as I went by, she again passed the time of day and pressed a piece of white paper in my hand, giving me a huge smile. It was only when I got back to the Guardroom that I realised it was a £5 note. Even then I had to be told that my charitable friend was a 'lady of the street'.

I wondered if the Far East would be as good a lesson on 'life'. I was soon to find out.

CHAPTER 5

Who'd be a Sailor –
or Far East Here We Come!

THE MODERN SOLDIER has no idea what travelling overseas was like prior to air trooping. To say that it was 'uncomfortable' is a gross understatement. I have no idea how many people were on the *Empire Trooper*, but it must have been at least 2,000. On board were the 2nd Battalions of the Coldstream and Scots Guards, Brigade Headquarters, some service families and, of course, the crew.

Each troop deck accommodated about 200 men on three-tier bunks. Apart from being packed in like the proverbial sardines, the ablutions were minimal. The majority of personal kits was held in the ship's hold and each man lived out of a sea kit bag and a small pack. Personal hygiene had to be of the highest order and to ensure this was so, the ship's Skipper inspected every nook and cranny each morning on what was called 'Captain's Rounds'. To say the least, everywhere and everything gleamed.

The only training carried out was basic physical training and occasionally firing at targets lowered off the back of the troopship. Being in the Corps of Drums was of great benefit, as we were able to practice regularly and entertain the troops, families and the crew. Tom Birkett revelled in this and ensured that we played very popular music from the shows in London.

The only other entertainment was boxing (both the Coldstream and Scots Guards had some outstanding boxers), bingo and the odd film shown on a tiny screen in the Mess Hall. Fortunately the food was excellent and beer was easily obtained at a reasonable price.

The troopship called at several ports en route for the Far East. Several of us drummers went ashore each time and always returned somewhat tipsy. At every port several duty Guardsmen arrived back very drunk, sometimes escorted by the Military Police, and spent a day or two in the cells.

A daily sweepstake was held on how many miles the troopship would cover during the following 24 hours. The Captain gave an estimate – usually between 250 and 310 miles – and it was remarkable how accurate this was, even when the sea was rough and there were strong winds.

Needless to say, we were very pleased when the journey ended after 35 days at sea.

Our first three weeks in the Far East were spent in Nee Soon Camp on Singapore Island. Bearing in mind that the Battalion had come from ceremonial duties in London, this was a critical period of training for the rifle companies in particular. We drummers continued to practice our music, carry on with physical training and a small amount of weapon training. As I look back now, we were the ideal subject for the Leslie Thomas book *Virgin Soldiers*! We were not remotely ready to take on the Communists in the jungle. Fortunately, the 2nd Battalion had quite a number of excellent soldiers who had fought with the Regiment during the 1939-45 War. The only problem was that that was was not fought in the jungle!

At the end of about three weeks we travelled by train to Tapah on the Malayan Peninsula. Temoh Hill Camp was tented on the side of a hill and was very basic, to say the least. Our first task was to dig monsoon ditches around each tent. The drummers were lucky as most of our time was spent in camp. Including the NCOs, there were only 16 of us, so the only duties we were required to do were camp guards or escorts to vehicles/convoys.

The Corps of Drums regularly visited platoons on detachment and did marching displays in the local villages. When walking out, we had to be in 'pairs' and always carry our Lee Enfield .303 rifles and belts of ammunition containing 50 rounds. This served as a constant reminder that we were 'On Active Service'. Nobody was allowed to stay out of camp overnight.

Entertainment in camp was almost non-existent, consisting of an occasional film on a very small screen in the NAAFI. The Chah Wallahs were very popular since they provided better 'teas and wads' than the NAAFI. They also allowed purchase on tick, which was essential as our pay was so poor. Remarkably, they were well informed and seemed to know well in advance of the soldiers when an operation was to take place. It came as a shock one morning when our Chah Wallah woke us and told us that the drummers were to take part in an operation. This proved to be correct!

This short operation, three days in the jungle, was a nerve-racking experience for all the drummers, as we were poorly trained and very inexperienced. Led by the Adjutant, a European civilian policeman and a guide, we were tracking a Communist gang by day and lying in ambush by night. As it got dark in the early evening, the nights seemed to last for ever – especially when lying in ambush and not being allowed to move or have lights of any kind. Peter Kirk and I shared an ambush position and although in theory one man at a time could sleep, I don't think we slept at all! How the rifle companies spent six weeks at a time in virgin jungle I shall never know.

This operation did me a bad turn from the aspect of health. I was bitten by a leech on the left leg below the knee and this developed into an ulcer. Prior to the operation, I already had a boil in an 'unmentionable place' and this developed into an ulcer also. The Medical Officer had no option but to put me into the tented Casualty Reception Station (CRS) in our own camp. I was really quite poorly with a fever.

Whilst in the CRS I witnessed a terrible event. The private soldiers in the Royal Army Medical Corps (RAMC) were issued with revolvers. Lying in my sick bed half awake, I was aware of two medical attendants playing 'cowboys and indians' around the inside and outside of the tents. They were shouting 'bang bang' and laughing and giggling. Suddenly there was a real explosion and one of the medics fell to the ground – DEAD! The soldier who had fired the shot went berserk, rushing around and screaming until brought down by an NCO. I heard later that he had shot his best friend. He disappeared from the camp, so I can only assume that he was posted back to the UK.

After several days of unsuccessful treatment, I was transferred to the British Military Hospital (BMH) in Ipoh. This was about 30 miles from my unit. During my short time there, a doctor asked me if I had 'been with a woman'. Naively I said yes – meaning a girlfriend in England. He obviously misinterpreted this as meaning I had been with a lady of ill repute, as I was transferred to the BMH in Kuala Lumpur. For the first two days there I was dressed in pyjamas, even when walking around the grounds, in the Special Treatment Centre (STC) which dealt with cases. It took them two or three days to convince themselves that I had not got the dreaded 'lurgy'. When I complained, the Doctor said that it was my fault for saying I had been with a woman.

On being transferred to the Dermatology Ward it took them about 10 weeks to find a cure for my two ulcers. One of the treatments they tried gave me terrible mouth ulcers and I was in agony. During my three months in hospital I had only one visit from a Coldstream officer and my mail sometimes took weeks to get to me. Being in hospital so long meant that I was able to help the medical staff with some patients. I am sure that they were sorry to see me go when I returned to my unit.

During the time I was in BMH Kuala Lumpur (KL) I saw another terrible sight. A party of Grenadier Guards had been ambushed by a terrorist gang and I saw six dead Guardsmen arrive at the hospital. Ironically, about

50 years later, during a visit to Malaya, I saw the graves where some of these men were buried just outside KL. The only nice part of this story is that the cemetery is beautifully maintained by two Malayan brothers. R.I.P.

My period in hospital did not seem to be held against me, as on my return to Tapah I was appointed as the Leading Side Drummer and sent on a Drill Course to be promoted Lance Corporal.

The Drill Course was hard work in every sense of the word. Although I was good at foot drill, being a Drummer, I was not trained in rifle drill. In fact, despite hours of practice, I was hopeless at the latter. Drill Sergeant Fred ('Tug') Wilson who instructed the course, was, fortunately(!), an ex-drummer. On one occasion I was making a poor attempt at teaching the Squad the Slope Arms when 'Tug' told me to fall in with those being taught with the words, 'Bugger me, Corporal, your rifle drill is worse than mine.' Surprisingly, I came third from top out of twenty-four on the course!

During my time in hospital my best friend, Barry Rockett, shot himself through his foot with his own rifle. This was quite intentional and was an attempt to get himself posted back to the United Kingdom. He was in hospital, in Malaya, for several months and was NOT returned home. Possibly, the reason that he was never court-martialled for a 'self inflicted wound' was that the authorities thought he had suffered enough with the wound itself. The Regiment never forgave him and he only achieved Sergeant, despite being very well educated and a first-class musician. The only defence he put up for the shooting was that he wanted to get home to his 17-year-old wife, Nicky. It was no surprise to hear, several years later, that he had become a Warrant Officer Class One in the RAOC.

Another trick, which worked, was played by Drummer George Broad. He poured ice-cold water into his ears and after a while was classified as medically 'non tropical' and returned to the UK. These were the only two cases I have proof of, but rumour had it that a number of soldiers in the rifle companies tried, and succeeded, in being posted back to the UK. George Broad was not missed in the Drums as he was a poor musician. We also found out – via letters from home – that he wrote exaggerated stories to his wife about what active service in Malaya was like. Obviously this caused lots of worry to the loved ones in the UK.

Sport played a large part in our lives in Tapah. Reveille was at 0600 hours, first parade at 0645 hours, followed by breakfast, then a full morning of military duties and tiffin (lunch) at 1300 hours. If clear of guards or road escorts, the rest of the day was devoted to sport. It was quite common to play three games between about 1400 hours and 1800 hours, cricket, football and badminton. I have never been so fit in my life (except for my stint in hospital). My football – at inside or outside right – was reasonable and my badminton very good. Being the only spin bowler in the Drums, I was always in the side and my batting was fair. Amazingly, on one occasion I carried my bat throughout an innings and scored 10 not out (all singles) in a total of 26. I even took 7 wickets for 12 runs against a Chinese teenager XI. Possibly it was the first time they had ever seen slow donkey drops!

To continue the theme of sport: the 2nd Battalion had some outstandingly talented sportsmen. This was in part due to the number of conscripted/national service men. The Battalion cricket team had many top-class players, and if it had not been for operations taking the best players away quite regularly, they would have won everything in sight. Amongst those worth a special mention were the opening pair, Major Pelly and Guardsman 'Sleepy' Lees, an outstanding middle-order left-handed bat, Sergeant Jimmy Cliff from Scarborough, a right-handed batsman called Thompson, whose late cut was an absolute delight. Possibly the fastest bowler I have EVER seen was a huge Guardsman called Margeson. I only batted against him a couple of times and was absolutely terrified! The Drums had several very good players, including all-rounders Gordon Carter and Johnny Haylet, who was out of the top drawer as an accurate and successful fast bowler.

We had a number of really good boxers and especially Sergeant Dave Huggins and Lance Sergeant 'Punchy' Roberts, who became Far East Land Forces (FARELF) champions at heavyweight and middleweight respectively. The latter was as stylish and effective as any boxer I have ever seen. Sergeant Wally Metcalfe was the champion hammer thrower of FARELF. It is worth mentioning that at that time tens of thousands of troops were in the Far East in the late 1940s, which shows just how good these guys were – great, great champions.

The Battalion also had excellent rugby union and soccer players, some of which had played for top civilian teams. Badminton was very popular, but most competitions were held within the Battalion. This latter sport played a sorry part in my career as a junior non-commissioned officer, but I would have preferred that it hadn't! Having served for almost a year, less than about all the ex-Boys, there was some jealousy when I was promoted Lance Corporal. Carter and Dave Redstone possibly had a point of grievance, as they were both technically better side drummers than I. However, Tom Birkett considered them far too 'flashy' for a military band and selected me as the Leading Side Drummer. Like Trixie Nockall before me, I was a traditional drummer and played the parts as the Drum Major wanted.

Anyhow, back to badminton. Soon after my promotion, I was in charge of a party of Drummers making a badminton court – not easy for amateurs! At one stage I ordered/asked Gordon Carter to get some more shingle to put on the new court. Instead of doing so, he gave me a load of backchat including using an eight-letter swear word. I would have taken no notice but unluckily for Gordon this was overheard by a Sergeant, who then told the Drum Major. He ordered me to charge Gordon with 'using obscene language to an NCO and failing to comply with an order (etc.)' This meant that he had to attend Adjutant's Orders the next day and was 'confined to barracks' for seven days. Although I did not like what had happened, it had the desired effect: nobody ever answered me back again. I was 19 at the time and Gordon was about six months older. Strange to think that Gordon Carter later became an outstanding Drum Major in the Regiment. He was a first-class musician and a terrific all-round sportsman.

The dance band, 'Lloyd's Hotshots', provided by the Corps of Drums, was very popular and gave concerts in the Officers' and Sergeants' Messes and the NAAFI. Tom Birkett (leader) played the saxophone, Frank Brooks the trumpet, Eddie Morris the piano and Dave Redstone the drums. At Christmas the most wonderful pantomime was produced by members of the Battalion. This was most professionally done in every way and it would be unfair to select names for a mention. Suffice it to say that some of the most 'macho' type men in the battalion made delightfully attractive 'young maidens' (or was it that we had been away from women for too long?).

It is only when one gets old and looks back that one appreciates what a great battalion 2CG was in Malaya. The mixture of wartime-experienced soldiers and numerous 18- and 19-year-old keen Guardsmen was ideal. Once they had mastered jungle warfare, the soldiers were superb. They were led by (initially) Colonel Dickie Gooch and then by Colonel Victor Fitzgeorge Balfour. The latter subsequently became a full General – more about him later. All the Company Commanders and the Adjutants (Lloyd and Pemberton) were wartime soldiers who had all seen action. The Quartermaster, 'Jungle' Jim Sawden, had served in Burma throughout the War. Finally, and possibly the most important point, the Battalion was blessed with having Regimental Sergeant Major Arthur Ramsden MC – a Warrant Officer of the highest order.

The Battalion won many individual gallantry awards but paid a high price, with six soldiers killed and a number badly wounded. Looking back, it was an honour to serve in this battalion in Malaya and it was interesting to note that for many years after the Malayan tour, most of the senior ranks *throughout the Regiment* came from those who had served with 2CG between 1948-50.

In 1949 the Drummers were very sad to lose Tom Birkett on his promotion to Company Sergeant Major. Harold Simpson took over and proved to be poor, despite being a reasonable musician. He was far too boastful and insincere, and would never listen to advice. If he had not had some very good NCOs, he would not have lasted five minutes. As I was in charge of the stores when he took over, I suffered more than most from his tantrums. Unfortunately by this time Eddie Morris and Frank Brooks – both outstanding musicians and Lance Sergeants – had been demobbed. We certainly missed them!

Military history has shown that 2CG was the first battalion to carry out patrols in the jungle lasting up to six weeks. Companies relied on air drops for rations, changes of clothes, ammunition and every type of equipment. That was no mean feat. Also, Colonel Fitzgeorge Balfour initiated the idea of moving locals out of their villages into sealed 'compounds' to cut them off from the Communist terrorists, nicknamed 'bandits'. This meant that the 'bandits' could not intimidate villagers into supplying them with food and other provisions. These operations took place at first light, when it was easy to place cordons in place, surround the villages and round up the inhabitants. The locals hated us for this at the time, but later did the Regiment the honour of calling the newly created village 'Kampong Coldstream'. In the 1990s a party of us, with wives, visited this village and it was both a joyous and moving occasion. We were made to feel like very important people and fêted like royalty.

Throughout our tour in the Far East, rumours regularly spread that we were about to return to the U.K. It was therefore with great relief that we set sail on the troopship *Orbita* in September 1950. The going home voyage seemed never-ending but in fact was two days less that the outward one, 33 days as opposed to 35.

So ended the most fascinating two years imaginable. Certainly it moulded all of us young soldiers into good ones and prepared us for every aspect of life. Interestingly, many members of the Battalion have remained close friends into old age, as has been proved by the frequency of the reunions both at home and in the Far East.

Was London ready for us? Would it be boring after 'seeing the world' at the expense of the Government? Only time would tell.

There is a very nice postscript to this chapter. Early in the Malaysian tour the members of the Corps of Drums were given lessons on twin Vickers machine guns, mounted on armoured cars. These were given by Sergeant Jimmy Cliff, the Sergeant Instructor Musketry for 2 CG. For some unexplained reason Drummer Alan Coleman and I became the permanent 'escorts' when the Commanding Officer travelled by staff car to the Cameron Highlands – a winding lengthy route and real 'ambush' country! I would be in the leading scout car and Alan in the rear. Fortunately, our prowess on the guns was never tested. This seemed to develop a special bonding between the then CO and Drummer Horsfall because long after he became General Sir Victor, he always made a beeline for me at Coldstream events and we shared many happy and humorous occasions. He died in 1994 and is badly and sadly missed by us all. R.I.P.

CHAPTER 6

The Winds of Change

BEFORE STARTING TO WRITE about the next twenty years, it is necessary to mention some of the factors that were to influence everyone and everything. India had been given its independence in the late 40s, and this was to cause trouble on that continent destined to continue for many a year. There were wars in Korea and Vietnam. British forces were heavily committed in the former but, thank goodness, not in the latter.

The Middle East was a constant problem both militarily and politically. There will be more about Yemen and Aden later on. Indeed, it is a fact that almost without a break, British forces have been committed in about 50 countries in the same number of years! The 'Cold War' between East and West went on for over 40 years after the end of World War II. Without question, if it had not been for the nuclear deterrent, there would almost certainly have been an all-out war between the USSR and the Western powers. The mind boggles at the thought!

On the home front, the United Kingdom still depended on America and in many ways 'Marshall Aid', started during the War, ceased with very little warning. Nevertheless we still needed help – even with grain; which is surprising when we thought of ourselves as an agricultural country. Rationing of some items still existed in the early 50s and some examples of weekly rations per person per week are: 3 oz. bacon/ham, 1^1/2 oz cheese, 7 oz. butter/margarine, 2oz. cooking fat, 10 oz. sugar and 2 oz. chocolate/sweets. I believe that the last items to be rationed were bacon and meat, which came back on to the open market in July 1954. Fortunately, being a soldier, I was not affected too much by these stringent rations and there was always fish and chips at a reasonable price to fall back on!

Until 1955 the BBC had a monopoly in television but in that year Independent Television (ITV) was allowed to set up in opposition. With hindsight, one wonders if this is a good or bad thing – in view of the fact that both the visual and written media seem to CREATE NEWS rather than REPORT it. Also, one wonders whether swearing and sex scenes would have become so commonplace if there had been only one television station.

Anyhow, back to the subject of a young soldier returning from the Far East. After 33 days at sea, it was great to be back on dry land, initially at Pirbright, where we were kitted out with full dress uniform and then sent back to Wellington Barracks in London. Before returning to serious peace time duties, I remember having a wonderful disembarkation leave in Leeds, naturally with my family and a couple of friends. Brother Terry was by then a Sergeant in the REME, despite being a National Serviceman – and we were on leave together at times, which was great fun, to say the least. Dad still had very close ties with the Leeds Rifles in Carlton Hill Barracks, so we were able to use their Sergeants' Mess and drink at ridiculously low prices. Bear in mind that entertainment was in very short supply with the cinema, the occasional dance and football and rugby matches, which were only played on Saturday. Even bingo-tombola was very popular, as for some people this was their only bit of fun in life. Live theatre was a luxury many people could not afford.

Something happened in late 1950 that was to change my life dramatically for the better. My best friend in the Corps of Drums was Barry Rocket, who married a lovely London girl called Nicolette (Niccy). Her father, Bill Cox, was a really terrific East-Ender with a great sense of fun and a very generous disposition. Barry was not all that keen on sport, whereas Bill and I were 'football crazy'. As Bill was a supporter of Queen's Park Rangers, it became the normal practice for us to go to all their home matches and after the game, WALK to Edgware Road (quite a distance) to 'The Poppy' public house. This was Bill's favourite pub and soon became mine, not because of the beer, though incidentally it was very good. Rather it was because I had taken a fancy to the young lady barmaid. Bill teased me about this.

The strange thing was that when I was in uniform the barmaid spoke to me, but when in civvies, she didn't. As Barry was married, Johnny Haylett had become my boozing partner by this time, and The Poppy became our regular 'watering hole'. I was determined to walk this young lady home but she was never there at closing time. Eventually I had a stroke of luck. I fell into conversation with a very nice guy who was going out with the other barmaid. He told me that the lady I had my eye on finished each evening at 9.30 pm as she started earlier than the other members of staff. Sunday was the exception, when she stayed until closing time. He and I 'stage managed' a meeting for the following Sunday evening. At closing time we waited outside the pub for both barmaids to appear and he then introduced me to both of the young ladies. Then he said: 'We go this way – good night, see

Mary, 1951.

you soon' (or words to that effect). This left me with Mary, the girl who was to become my wife.

The relationship quickly developed into a courtship and Mary and I saw a lot of each other. She lived in Kilburn, which was populated by a very Irish community. It seems strange to think that I was always made to feel at home there, despite being seen regularly in my uniform, both in pubs and the 'Bamba' dance hall, where nearly all the members were Irish. One evening, in uniform, I joined in the singing in a pub and it was pointed out that some of the songs were Irish rebel ones. Nobody, least of all myself, could care less, and the singing continued. I wonder if the same could happen now. It is doubtful because of the bigotry on both sides of the religious/political divide! This is sad.

During our courtship I had my first major disappointment as a professional soldier. Although I was the Leading Side Drummer and senior storeman, the Drum Major, Simpson, a big-headed, loud-mouthed Yorkshireman, was forever picking on me and putting me on a charge, which meant me being marched in front of the Adjutant and punished. A simple example was on my 21st birthday. My Mam and Dad sent me a 'silver' key about 15 inches long and I placed this in the two slots at the base of my large pack on top of my locker. My barrack room was always immaculate and, as ever, the Drum Major could not find anything wrong on his daily barrack room inspection. After the Changing of the Guard ceremony, Simpson sent for me and told me that I was on a charge for my own kit being in BAD ORDER but would not explain why. The next day on Adjutant's Orders he gave evidence about 'the key' and what a bad example this was to the drummers in my room. The Adjutant had no option but to award me a Reprimand. This might not sound much, but in those days it meant me having to be in barracks by 10 pm and reporting to the Drill Sergeant In Waiting for 14 nights. Our courtship suffered somewhat for that two weeks. (Note from Mary: it also meant that he didn't miss the last train and have a long walk (about four miles) back to barracks every night.)

There are numerous incidents that I could relate, but they would just sound like sour grapes. Most of the junior NCOs and the Drummers were upset, as they saw what was happening. I was very worried as I knew that I was in the zone for promotion to Lance Sergeant (the Guardsman who was top on the same Lance Corporals' course as I was already a Lance Sergeant and I had come third on the course).

Things came to a head in 1951. The Corps of Drums was due to change barrack blocks in Wellington Barracks. During music practice one morning, the Drum Major gave the junior NCOs a task to perform for the move. Joe Kibble, a really smashing guy from Bristol and the senior Lance Corporal, was to hand over the old block and I was to take over the new accommodation. I should have smelt a rat because none of the Lance Sergeants or other Lance Corporals were given tasks.

A couple of days after the move had taken place I was sent for by the Drum Major and he shouted and screamed at me about the old barrack block being left in bad order etc. etc. I tried to explain that Corporal Kibble was detailed for that task but he would not listen and said that I would be on a charge the following day. Joe (Kibble) also went to see Simpson and told him that the old block handover was his task. Simpson would never admit he was wrong so the charge against me stood.

I was charged with 'Disobeying a lawful command' (or similar words) which meant the Adjutant had to remand me for Commanding Officer's Orders – especially as I offered no excuse. In no way was I going to 'cart' the excellent Joe Kibble. When I arrived back in the barrack room after Adjutant's Orders, I was met by Joe, who was horrified to hear that I was remanded for Commanding Officer's Orders at 12 noon. Once again he went to the Drum Major and told him that he was the one who was at fault. Simpson, in his normal ignorant manner, refused to listen.

I had never attended Commanding Officer's Orders except to be congratulated for my performances at Cadet camps or on being promoted. It goes without saying that I was very nervous and offered no excuse once again. The acting Commanding Officer, Major Robins, asked me several times what I had to say in my defence, but I would not mention Corporal Kibble.

Eventually Major Robins said that he had no alternative but to reduce me to the rank of Drummer. As the Regimental Sergeant Major marched me out of the Commanding Officer's office, I was absolutely stunned. I do not think that anyone, including the Drum Major, expected such a severe punishment.

When 'orders' were over, Sergeant Major Ramsden dismissed everyone except me and I was convinced that he was going to give me an almighty telling off. Instead he put one hand on my shoulder and said, 'Well boy, this must feel like the end of the world to you.' 'Yes sir' I replied. 'Don't worry boy, it will come right very soon. Now fall out and continue your good work.' If he had not said these words, I am sure that my standards would have fallen and I would have gone to pieces. As it was, I continued as the Leading Side Drummer and as the senior storeman. Also, from that day on Simpson stopped picking on me.

Joe Kibble, a wartime solder with battle service, was demobbed with an 'Exemplary' record. This would not have been the case if he had been charged with the same offence as I was. I never regretted not 'carting' him with the Adjutant and Commanding Officer. However, I never forgave Drum Major Simpson. Many years later I thought of him when reading an article in the *Daily Telegraph* sports pages. This was by Michael Parkinson, who wrote: 'Being a Yorkshireman, I am allowed to say this. There are two

kinds of Yorkshiremen, a bloody-minded Yorkshireman and a VERY bloody minded Yorkshireman and Geoff Boycott is one of the latter.'

Five months after being reduced to the rank of Drummer, I attended Adjutant's Orders to be promoted again. Standing in the line-up waiting to be marched in, Sergeant Major Ramsden came up to me and in a very quiet Yorkshire accent said: 'I told you you'd be alright, boy – well done.' One thing is certain: Arthur Ramsden MC was a Tyke of the highest order and second to none in fact. What an honour to serve under him! Within two and a half years I had whistled up through the ranks and was a full sergeant at the age of 24.

The most difficult thing about being reduced to the rank of Drummer was breaking the news to my Dad. There were no telephones so this had to be by letter. I cannot remember how I worded this, but recall receiving by return of post a quite emotional letter. There was not a word of criticism but one sentence really struck home. This read along the lines of: 'Even if you had committed murder, you know that Mam and I would have stood by you.' Truly a good example of blood is thicker than water!

Being a Coldstreamer obviously meant a lot to Mam. Even when I became a Major Quartermaster, and later the Staff Superintendent in the House of Lords, she always introduced me as a Coldstream Guardsman.

The 1950s were a happy time. Mary and I were not particularly well off, but nevertheless went to the cinema and theatres quite often and had a fairly active social life. Our favourite theatre was the Metropolitan in Edgware

Road, where we saw most of the stars of the day (Max Miller, Tommy Cooper, Max Bygraves and the big bands of the day, including Billy Cotton, Ted Heath and Joe Loss) and many other wonderful artists.

Needless to say, money being tight, we often went for the cheapest seats – usually 'the gods', thus named because the top balcony was nearest to heaven. Television being almost unheard of then, there were always enormous queues at the cinema, but this only added to the sense of occasion.

Eating out was almost unheard of, for us anyhow(!), and our idea of a treat was fish and chips – takeaways mostly. I remember that a special treat for Mary was a banana split or a 'knickerbocker glory'. Many of these social events, and goodies would have been beyond our means if Mary had not had TWO jobs – a full time one as a shorthand-typist and a part-time one as a barmaid.

After Mary left the Poppy public house, she moved upmarket to the Swiss Cottage Hotel at St John's Wood. There was one amusing incident that sticks out in my mind. Bill Cox and I were in the saloon bar after a football match and we were quite 'peckish'. The buffet prices were very high, e.g. a salmon sandwich was five shillings – a huge amount for those days, and my pay then

The author's wedding day.
Left to right: Ken Braine, the author, Mary, Barry Rocket, Tony Williamson.

was about £5 a week. Bill looked the chef straight in the eye and remaining poker-faced, asked him if he had a bit of dry bread and stale cheese as we were so hungry. This was not forthcoming so we settled for a bag of crisps each!

On the 7th June 1952 Mary and I were married in the church of The Sacred Heart of Jesus, Kilburn. This was the most wonderfully happy occasion, despite my massive hangover from my stag party the previous night. Modern grooms have the sense to have their bachelor party several days ahead of the wedding day.

As I was not a Catholic, I had to attend three 'lessons' with the Roman Catholic priest, Father Toland. He was a wonderful man and these caused no problem. He also carried out the marriage ceremony. Barry Rockett was the best man and he, several other Coldstream Guards Drummers and I, were in full-dress uniform. Mary was in white and looked beautiful. My Mam and Dad attended, as did Mary's Dad and sister Bridget.

Mary and I paid for our own reception at a restaurant in Kilburn. Over 50 attended and it was great fun. Eddie Morris, a most wonderful pianist, entertained us throughout the afternoon. Indeed, Mary felt we were 'missing out' by leaving relatively early for our one-night honeymoon in Brighton. Mary's Dad, Jim Ryan, had given Mary some cash as a present, otherwise we would have been broke after the wedding!

Mary was the first of her family to marry out of the Catholic faith. Also, marrying a British soldier was unheard of. However, from the first time I met her family in Southern Ireland, I was made to feel at home and to be one of the family. The Ryan family are what I call 'gentle folk' and are inclined to think well of everyone. This is in part due to their absolute faith in God. Some of the family are much travelled, having lived in America, Kenya and Australia in addition to the UK.

I was promoted to Lance Sergeant on the 23rd September, 1952 (Mary's birthday), and life took on a turn for the better in every way. The social life improved and also my pay went up (ironically, I still did not earn as much as Mary – with her having two jobs). As mentioned earlier, meat was still rationed, and although it sounds shameful now, I occasionally bought small amounts of meat from the battalion butcher, Corporal Alfie Farmer. Mary sometimes had a meal at the pub she worked in, which meant that I could have more than my ration of meat and other goodies. I needed this as I only weighed about ten and a half stone (soaking wet!).

The next few years absolutely flashed by and it would be impossible to list many of the events that affected Mary and me. In late 1952 and early

1953 I had an unaccompanied tour in Munster, Germany, with the 2nd Battalion. Acting on the advice of the Adjutant and Orderly Room Quartermaster Sergeant, I left the Corps of Drums to 'further my career'.

Before leaving the Drums, I had to attend a Tactics Course with the 1st Battalion Irish Guards at Düsseldorf. The officer in charge of the course was Captain the Lord Monteagle (more about him later) and the Sergeants were Jimmy Doggart and George Murphy. Jimmy was the best Weapon Training Instructor I ever met. During the course, three days were spent at Winterburg learning to ski. On day one George Murphy told us there was nothing difficult about skiing. On day two he broke his leg and it had to be put in plaster! The same evening several of us celebrated my 23rd birthday and George had to take an enormous amount of 'flak'. Being a good 'Mick', he took all this 'in his stride'. (No pun intended!)

The Tactics Course was physically very demanding. I was the only non-duty NCO on the course, and it nearly killed me. I think that the instructors on the course had a certain amount of sympathy for me and gave me a 'B' grading. Nobody on the course, of about 30 NCOs, got an 'A' grading and two duty NCOs from the 2nd Battalion Coldstream Guards got 'C's'. When I was marched in front of the Commanding Officer for the course report, he said that my future was at duty. In many ways this broke my heart as I had always wanted to be the Drum Major of the 2nd Battalion.

The good news connected with the foregoing was that I was posted to the Guards Training Battalion at Pirbright in Surrey. This meant that I would be able to remain in the Army Hiring Accommodation with Mary in Kilburn. She was well established in London and it would have been crazy to move to Pirbright. Apart from the financial aspects, we had some wonderful friends in 'The Smoke' and enjoyed the whole lifestyle. We attended occasional military functions at Pirbright, and in London had the use of the Sergeants' Mess in Wellington Barracks.

Apart from our Army friends, we saw a lot of Bill Cox, Fred and Rose Edwards and their son Peter, Agnes Kelly and several other very nice people. Even in those days we had a party at the slightest excuse (nothing changes!). Rose Edwards, a tiny cockney woman, caused a great deal of hilarity on one occasion. We had about 20 people in our small flat and Mary had made a huge pile of sandwiches. Nobody wanted to be the first to eat, so Rose in a very royal (cockney) voice, said loudly and clearly: 'I know I'm not the hostess but – blah blah blaah.' She took a long time to live that one down, especially with husband Fred and son Peter, but she took it very well.

Anyhow, her announcement did the trick – the sandwiches were gobbled up quickly.

Fred was a rascal and a mischief rolled into one. Bill and I disowned him at times at football. He would purposely get in amongst the opposing side's spectators and goad them by insulting their players loudly and clearly. How he never got himself thumped I shall never know.

Militarily I must have been doing quite well as my annual confidential reports were outstanding. Also, the Royal Army Ordnance Corps at Blackdown asked me to transfer to them to be their Drum Major. I took this seriously and applied to the Company Commander (Major, later to be Major General, Ronnie Buckland) for permission to transfer. He was not best pleased! There is a remarkable twist to this story.

A few days after my transfer request, there was a dance in the Sergeants' Mess to which the officers were invited. The Company Commander and Company Sergeant Major Charlie Grimett cornered Mary and me in the bar and convinced us that I had a great future in the Regiment. I therefore withdrew my transfer request. ONE WEEK later I was promoted to full Sergeant! This despite being the sixth senior Lance Sergeant in the Company. One wonders how my career would have gone if I had transferred to the Ordnance Corps.

Two years in the Guards Training Battalion set me up nicely for a career at duty. The first year was as a section commander and the second as a platoon Sergeant. With National Service at its height, platoons were about 50 strong plus several NCOs. This meant that both the administration and the instruction had to be of the highest order. Also, by watching another great Coldstreamer as the Regimental Sergeant Major, 'Dusty' Smith DCM, I learnt a lot. Not only was Dusty terrific on the barrack square, but his man management, sense of fun and enjoyment of soldiering were a wonderful example to us 'youngsters'. There will be more about this later when I write about royal occasions.

When I returned to the 2nd Battalion in Germany, Mary accompanied me. She soon became the shorthand typist in the Orderly Room, being on battalion strength as a 'three-star Guardsman'. She also worked for the Commanding Officer and Second in Command, Colonel Arthur Fortescue and Major Jackie Younger, two really nice gentlemen and excellent soldiers. Son Terry was born on the 3rd September, 1955.

Regrettably, I missed the birth due to being away from home with the Battalion, on a Brigade exercise. The Company Quartermaster Sergeant being unfit, I was acting on his behalf in No. 4 Company cooker truck.

During the exercise my left hand was badly burnt when the No. 1 burner had a 'blow back' as I was trying to re-light it. According to the Medical Officer, the Mess Hand, Guardsman Reg Pountain, prevented the burns from being much worse. As soon as he saw the accident, Reg smothered my hand in butter and dipped it in a large container of flour. Although the hand still blistered badly, the flesh did not come away from the bones. When I visited Mary in hospital, I had a very grubby dressing on the hand and looked pretty unsightly, as I had not been able to shave either. Needless to say we were overjoyed at Terry's arrival and celebrated in proper style.

The Battalion returned to Chelsea Barracks in London and I continued as the senior Platoon Sergeant in 4 Company. We had a very strict Company Sergeant Major, Brian Buckley, and became known as the 'Penal' Company due to having nearly all the hard men in the battalion posted to us. They had committed some sin and were returning to duty after serving a spell in detention. Having a reputation for toughness, most of these guys seemed to be in my platoon. Strangely enough, none of them gave me any trouble.

The exception to this was a conscripted man who was a professional boxer, Tommy Gibbons. His Section Commander reported to me that Gibbons was virtually refusing to soldier and wanted to put him on a charge.

I told this NCO that I would have Gibbons in my bunk and give him a 'talks fatherly' and if he accepted what I said to him, that he would not be charged on this occasion. Nobody else was present when I gave Gibbons a real dressing down. He got hotter and hotter under the collar and kept clenching and unclenching his fists, which were by his sides. I expected him to hammer me into the ground at any time – he was about 13 stone of solid muscle and I was still only about 11 stone – soaking wet! Finally, in frustration, I told him that I would have him posted out of my platoon if he did not behave properly. This did the trick as all his mates were in my platoon. He never gave the other NCOs or me any trouble after that. He went on to become a very successful boxer and ran a hugely popular pub in the East End of London. I only saw him once after his demob. and he told me that he was within an ace of hitting me. Without question it would have been NO CONTEST!

In 1956, along with the rest of the armed forces, 2nd Coldstream Guards got caught up in the Suez Canal drama. Reservists were recalled and the Battalion moved to Pirbright to carry out some very hard training. For most of that year I seemed to be acting Company Sergeant Major or Company Quartermaster Sergeant – one or the other of them always seemed to be unfit or away. I did not mind this as the Company was commanded successively by outstanding officers, Major Harbord-Hamond (later to be The Lord Suffield) and Major Mayes (later to be a Brigadier). The Battalion advance party actually left for the Middle East and sat at sea on a troopship for several weeks. Our reservists behaved themselves but we heard that the 3rd Battalion and a Grenadier Battalion had a great deal of trouble with their reservists.

My nine-year engagement was due to end in January 1957 and I had every intention of finishing. However, ORQMS Frank Betts 'chatted me up' to sign on with the promise of a posting to Bermuda with a Coldstream Company from the 2nd Battalion. It goes without saying that I was most unhappy when the Bermuda posting fell through, due to the Suez crisis, just after I had signed on! The Suez affair also changed our plans for a second child. We had planned to wait three years after Terry was born. When it looked certain that we would 'go to war' we brought this forward. Bob was born in May, 1957. We have NO regrets.

On returning from Germany in late 1955, we were given the option of a very antiquated married quarter in Chelsea or an Army Hiring in Wallington in Surrey. We chose the latter and had a very nice comfortable upstairs flat. Our landlady was Miss Goodman, a middle-aged spinster, who lived in the downstairs flat. Initially, she seemed a bit formidable, but after a while we realized she was very nice and we got on well together. After Bob arrived on the scene, she needed to be very patient and understanding.

In September 1956 I was posted to the Guards Depot at Caterham as a Superintending Sergeant. The Sergeants in the Coldstream Company were notoriously smart and the competition very fierce. However, I came top of the drill course and this gave me lots of confidence – or was it hope that I might do well? The Sergeants were Badham, Bostock, Clements, Howells, Tyas and Wilkins. I found my first squad very difficult but Cliff Bostock gave me tremendous support and it passed out O.K. Fortunately, I quickly got into the Pace Stick team and we beat the Royal Military Academy Sandhurst – no mean feat! The two and a half years at the Depot absolutely flew by, probably because there were over 20 Coldstream squads in the Company most of that time and many of these consisted wholly of conscripted men. The best drilled squad I ever saw were all national servicemen. Lance Corporal Rapson was the instructor and the Commandant commended the whole squad on their passing out parade in week 12.

Early in 1988 I was asked to provide an article for a book being written

Winners of the Inter-Company Pace Stick Competition, 1958. Standing, left to right: Sgt H. Clements, Sgt W. Ramsden, the author. Sitting: Major A.R.S. Tower.

about the Guards Depot at Catherham. I took great delight in writing the following:

'Late in 1958, towards the end of my tour at the Guards Depot as a Superintending Sergeant, I was told that I was to be one of the two Sergeants who would train the Brigade Squads forming early in 1959. There can be no greater honour for a Non-Commissioned Officer than to carry out the initial training of those destined to be officers in his own, and other, Regiments. In my case the recruits were for six of the seven regiments in the Household Division.

'When the new recruits arrived in early January, they were formed into two Squads. Mine were earmarked for the Grenadiers and Coldstream. Those in Sergeant Rudd's (SG) Squad were for the remaining four Regiments. Regrettably, this format only lasted a few days for the following reason:

'Unbeknown to the Sergeant in charge of each Squad, it had become a 'tradition' for the recruits to be taken on the obstacle course by the P.T. Instructors during the first weekend at the Depot, the theory being that this would improve their fitness! In the case of Sergeant Rudd's and my Squad this had disastrous results. The ground on the obstacle course was bone hard due to a very severe frost. At least one third of both Squads had ankle, leg and feet injuries, some quite bad.

'To say the least, the P.T. Instructors were not popular with the Squad officer, Captain Trevor Dawson SG, or with the Administrative Sergeant, George Nash, Grenadier Guards. Within a few days several of the recruits left the Depot for good. Not all of these were due to injury; some were simply sickened at the treatment received on the obstacle course. Due to these casualties, the two Squads were formed into one at the end of the first week's training. Sergeant Rudd, very unhappily, was returned to his normal duties with the Scots Guards company.

'Remaining to train were Recruits J. Ashton, R. Bruce, C. Constable Maxwell, T. Cotterall, M. Heseltine, D. Jarratt, P. Johnson, C. Lawrence, C. Madden, H. Myddleton, A. Pearson, G. Rees, J. Rickett, H. Rush, R. Saunders, The Hon S. Scott, The Hon J. Skeffington, The Hon T. Tollemache, H. Wait, J. Willis and T. Wills. There were no 'Micks', for some reason that was hard to understand – both then and now.

'To assist with the training were two outstanding Weapon Training Instructors – Sgts. Tait and Mason, a first class PT Instructor, Sergeant Stokes and two terrific Barrack Room Trained Soldiers, J. Fisher and B. Thorpe. The two Trained Soldiers, who had a real influence on each individual

The author's Brigade Squad, Guards Depot, March 1959. Back row, left to right: Gdsn. H. Myddelton, M. Rush, Tpr. R. Saunders, L/Sgt. D. Stokes (P.T. Instr.) Tpr. J. Ashton, Gdsn. C. Lawrence, M. Wait. Middle row: Gdsn: C. Madden, G. Rees, J. Rickett, The Hon. T. Tollemache, Tpr. A. Pearson, Gdsn:The Hon. S. Scott, P. Johnson, M. Heseltine, The Hon. J. Skeffington, Tpr. T. Cotterell, Gdsn: C. Constable Maxwell, R. Bruce. Front row: Gdsn. D. Jarratt, Sgt. H. Tait (W.T. Instr.), T/S J. Fisher, Sgt. G. Nash (Admin Sgt.), Capt. H.H.T. Dawson, the author, T/S B. Thorpe, L/Sgt. W. Mason (W.T. Instr.) Gdsn. M. Wills.

49

recruit, were both Coldstreamers and I knew them well. Similarly, 'Perry' Mason and Derek Stokes were both in my Regiment, and backed up well by 'Spud' Tait, we made up a first-class training team.

'Any NCO involved in training future officers for his Regiment must put out of his mind that within a few months the young men he has trained will be commanding him in certain situations. I can honestly say that in my case this did not influence me in any way and I treated the members of the Brigade Squad exactly the same as any other recruit. Indeed, at times I found myself being tougher with these recruits. This had to be the case if only because Brigade Squads had just eight weeks to achieve the same standard as a 'normal' Squad in twelve weeks. It was no easy task.

'The Squad of 21 were housed in two very old-fashioned huts with primitive ablutions. T.S. Fisher was in charge of one hut and T.S. Thorpe the other. The day consisted of nine periods of 45 minutes each with 15 minutes between each period. Brigade Squads were usually nicknamed the 'flyers', due to the speed with which they marched around barracks and the time taken to change clothing between periods. The latter was due to the two Trained Soldiers and me yelling continually at the recruits.

'Horsfall's Flyers' quickly became well known throughout the Depot and were picked on continually by senior ranks. The worst 'offender' at this (as it wasted valuable time needed for genuine training) was Drill Sergeant Pugh, Gren. Gds. He found fault where there was none!

'Shining parades each evening lasted about two hours. In addition to cleaning their kit, each recruit in turn was expected to give five-minute lecturettes to his mates in the same barrack room. In the early days each recruit could pick his own subject but later on Captain Dawson or myself picked the subject. Recruit Heseltine excelled at these and I was always interested in his talks and regretted that only five minutes were allowed (I let him and some others go on longer if they were confident and happy to do so). This was to prepare the young men for the ordeal of the Regular Commissions Board (RCB) in Westbury. Life was hectic to say the least.

'Recruits were not allowed to walk out until after 'passing off the square' during the 4th week inspection by the Adjutant. This inspection consisted of foot drill, picquet drill and saluting collectively and individually.

The Squad did well on the 4th week inspection. This was something of a miracle because several of the Squad had missed numerous drill periods due to the injuries suffered on the obstacle course during the first weekend at the Depot. The fact that their kit was immaculate helped and was due to the work put in by Trained Soldiers Thorpe and Fisher. They 'led by example' as their own kit was of the very highest order. I learnt in later years that it was common practice for members of the Squad to be still cleaning kit well after the 2215 hours Lights Out – in the ablutions/toilets, of course.

'After the 4th week inspection, there was the difficult job of selecting four Squad Leaders from the members of the Squad. There were at least six really good contenders, including Rickett, who was too quiet, and Tollemache, who was slightly immature. In the event, (in alphabetical order) Bruce, Heseltine, Madden and Wills were selected. If Heseltine had not missed so much drill due to a leg injury, I suspect he would have been the front runner for one of these appointments. It was at about this time that Willis disappeared from the course. Whether he was pushed or left of his own accord, I do not know. He was very poor in every way anyhow and was not missed.

'In about weeks six or seven all the Recruits went to Westbury for the RCB. Captain Dawson was rather pessimistic and thought several would fail. In the event he had a pleasant surprise, or was it shock, when the results came through. Only one (Skeffington) had failed and one (Wait) had a 'deferred watch'. At that time this was a record, but I do not know if it stands to this day. I understand that Wait returned to Westbury a few months later and passed at his second appearance. There were some terrific characters in the Squad and the RCB results did not surprise me one bit.

'Many years later, at a Squad reunion, John Skeffington told me that the best thing that ever happened to him was FAILING the RCB. Until that time he had had a very 'cushy' life and failing RCB – and letting his father down – made him start to work hard and learn about life. I was amazed how friendly he was/is to me, as I chased him more than any other member of the Squad. The rest of the Recruits always thought he deserved this.

'On the subject of 'chasing': I did not believe in taking recruits' names and marching them in front of the Squad Officer. Not only did I think this wasted valuable training time, but I did not think it helped a potential officer to have black marks on his record so early in his service. The nearest I came to this was when one of the Trained Soldiers found a brass knuckle-duster in the kit of one of the recruits. I went absolutely 'bananas' over this as I found it hard to believe that a future officer could behave so foolishly and in so undisciplined a way. If Captain Dawson had found out, I'm sure that the (unnamed!) recruit would have been kicked off the course, despite being a good natural leader.

'If the Squad was idle, I marched it down to the old deserted NAAFI in the Fox Lines. There I would drill them in very quick time until satisfied that they were all working for ME. As the period went on I would dismiss them one at a time as I thought they were up to standard. I was not proud of this tactic, but knew that if they were going to pass out with flying colours, I had to be 'cruel to be kind'! Regrettably, I have to report that almost always the last recruit to be dismissed on these occasions was a certain Coldstreamer. He became a good officer!

'Towards the end of the course, I was in my married quarter in C Block quite late at night and heard a fracas outside the house. It was obvious that a party of soldiers had been out 'on the town' and had been drinking. I told Mary that I would go outside and sort the offenders out. Imagine my surprise and my embarrassment when it turned out to be several members of my Brigade Squad! Instead of 'sorting them out', I took them into my quarter and Mary provided them with tea and sandwiches. Some of those involved still talk about this incident to this day. They say that it was the first time they realised that Sergeant Horsfall was human. As to having a wife and children – NEVER!

'The 8th week inspection, which was also the Squad's passing out parade, was a joy. Thorpe and Fisher had done their stuff and the Commandant, Colonel Erskine Crum (later to become a General), told the Squad that it was the best turnout he had ever seen. Praise indeed! I did not think the drill was all that good but the Commandant and Regimental Sergeant Major ('Jolly' Roger, Scots Guards) seemed delighted. They obviously allowed for the shocking weather during January–March, injuries on the obstacle course and the wonderful RCB results. Who was I to grumble when it made my name?

'I have followed the careers of the Squad and it has been interesting to say the least. Michael Heseltine became Deputy Prime Minister; Brigadier Johnny Rickett commanded the 1st Bn Welsh Guards in the Falklands and has been an outstanding soldier; Timothy Tollemache is now a Lord; John Skeffington is now The Viscount Massereene and Ferrard; Peter Johnson was a Colonel in the Scots Guards and is serving as a Gentleman at Arms; Tom Wills runs a large estate in Gloucestershire and is an officer in the Queen's Bodyguard of the Yeomen of the Guard. I believe that every member of the Squad has been successful in his chosen career.

'Unfortunately Trevor Dawson, Ashton, Jarratt and Rush have died, R.I.P. Thanks to Tom Wills, there have been several superb reunions – the last one in February 1999 – the 40th anniversary. Michael Heseltine made a brilliant unscripted speech at the latter about me. It was highly amusing and I didn't even blush!

With Michael Heseltine in the Grand Committee Room in the Commons when he was Secretary of State for Defence, 1983.

'It was a privilege to be part of an outstanding team that contributed to the training of so many fine young men. Although some of those in the Squad only served in their regiments for a relatively short time, they emphatically say it helped to shape their lives in large measure. This must be a tribute to the old Guards Depot at Caterham.'

Other highlights of my tour at the Depot included spending several months in the Company Pay Office as the Sergeant responsible for the pay of the staff and recruits. As the Company was about 500 strong, this was a most demanding task. Mary quite often helped me – well into the night – completing the Acquittance Rolls, pay books, barrack damages, quartering and other related subjects. Also, serving under three outstanding Regimental Sergeant Majors (Clutton and Drouet, Grenadiers and Rogers, Scots Guards) was highly educational and instructive for my future career. The Quartermaster was also a Grenadier, Lieutenant Colonel Arthur Spratley. Not only was he terrific at his job but his personality and man management were a wonderful example for all who served at the Depot.

CHAPTER 7

Kenya and Aden – Peace and War

O N LEAVING THE GUARDS DEPOT in March 1959, I returned to the 2nd
Battalion Coldstream, who were at Lydd in Kent preparing to go to
Kenya. Initially, there was no married quarter available for us, so Mary and
the boys stayed at Caterham. This coincided with us almost losing son Bob
when he contracted meningitis.

In late April he became tired and listless and made it obvious to his Mum,
by indicating with his hands, that he wanted to stay in his cot. When the
doctor visited him, he did not tell Mary of his suspicions but went away to
seek advice from a colleague. He returned and immediately had Bob
admitted to Queen Mary's Hospital at Carshalton, a superb childrens'
hospital.

Visiting Bob in hospital was heartbreaking. His weight went down by
about half in a little over a week. Also, because he continually pulled the
various 'tubes' out, he had to be tied down to the four corner posts of his
cot. Then his kidneys stopped working and he could not pass water. In fact
the surgeon was within an ace of operating on Bob's kidneys when
suddenly he started passing water again. Each day he had massive doses of
penicillin pumped into his thighs. The 'pock' marks from the needles still
showed years later.

Remarkably, after about ten days, he started to improve and three weeks
to the day after being admitted to hospital, we were able to bring him
home. This was on his second birthday, so the nurses put a party on for Bob,
with a beautiful ice-cream cake, before handing him back into our care. We
shall be eternally grateful to our own doctor and the wonderful staff of the
hospital, to say nothing of the modern medicine penicillin.

Mary and the boys joined me at Lydd and we had a few weeks together
before I went off to Kenya with the Battalion. The Commanding Officer
and his wife, Lieutenant-Colonel and Mrs Sweeting, made it very plain to
us all that families were not wanted in Kenya. Only about a dozen wives
and a few children travelled to Kenya on the troopship with the main
party.

As soon as we arrived in Kenya, 'Kiwi' Clements and I started searching

Terry and Bob. Butter wouldn't melt . . .

for accommodation for our families. We were very 'chuffed' to say the least when Mary, Betty and our children were able to fly out and join us twelve weeks after we had arrived. Initially, Mary and the boys lived in the Midland Hotel in Nakuru – very expensive and way beyond our means! Several other families were also in this hotel and unfortunately some of the wives of our senior ranks 'wore their husbands' rank'.

After a few weeks we moved into tiny hut-like 'houses'. We soon found out that these were converted cowsheds. To put it mildly, these huts were shocking and certainly not fit for humans. A South African family, the Engelbrets, were the owners and they must have made a fortune out of our soldiers, who were desperate for accommodation. There were about a dozen families living in these huts, some for about a year.

We had a major stroke of good fortune after a short period in our cowshed home. Mary heard that a local farmer, Mr Upton, was willing to let his house to a service family at a reasonable rent. We moved in as quickly as possible and despite having to buy some furniture and kitchen fittings/utensils etc., we were soon very comfortable.

The soldiering for me personally was in two distinct halves. For a reason I will explain later, I was only in Kenya for about 18 months. For the first half of this period I was in No. 1 Company as a Platoon Sergeant. To begin with, the Company Commander was Major Pollard, who was an excellent soldier, but far too finicky over unimportant details and casual over the things that really mattered. For example, he failed to see that his Company Sergeant Major drank too much and his man management was pathetic.

Regrettably, when Major Pollard returned to the UK, he handed over to Major Hills. I say regrettably, because he was a really good guy but with such a weak CSM, the Company went down hill quickly. This was a pity because there were some good soldiers in the Company and they deserved better leadership. The Second-in-Command was Captain Cadge and the Platoon Commanders Lieutenants Barnet, Forster and Tollemache – all first-class officers.

The second half of my tour was great. I volunteered to join No. 4 Company when it reformed after being in 'suspended animation'. The Company Commander was Major Willoughby, the CSM was Cliff Bostock and the CQMS was Jack Collier, a terrific team and my type of soldiers. In no time at all No. 4 Company became the best Company in the Battalion. The soldiers, both NCOs and Guardsmen, worked hard and played hard. They particularly excelled in the field.

At Battalion level there was a drama. The Commanding Officer was sacked and sent back to England. The final straw that caused his sacking was when he was caught in an out-of-bounds area in Nairobi by the Royal Air Force Police. This is a sad story as Colonel Sweeting's reputation as a wartime soldier was of the highest order, but he had proved to be a poor Commanding Officer.

The temporary Commanding Officer was Major Alan Pemberton and the new permanent one was Lieutenant-Colonel Julian Paget. The Battalion improved considerably under these two fine officers. The Quartermaster was Captain Norman Duckworth and the Regimental Sergeant Major was Stanley Blake. These two high-grade Coldstreamers must have been horrified at the way Colonel Sweeting had let the Regiment down.

Although the Battalion had missed the Mau Mau 'war', it spent a lot of time on exercise in the field or in the desert. This was tough soldiering in many respects, not least because of the fluctuating temperatures. For example, in the desert in the north it was swelteringly hot with the temperature above 100 degrees and very high humidity levels; by contrast in the Ngong Hills, near Nairobi, at night it was very cold, wet and miserable.

Mary and the boys loved Kenya. The first houseboy, Kimani, proved to be dishonest and unreliable. We then employed Debbie, a lovely young lady, educated by the missionaries, as our 'Girl Friday', and she adored Terry and Bob and they loved her in return. We once gave her a lift home to the village where her parents lived. All the villagers turned out and we were treated like national heroes. On our return journey, Debbie told us that many of the locals had never seen a white person before!

Mary found herself a really good job with the Kenya Police at Gilgil. This helped to raise our quality of life and provide some 'goodies', including a second-hand car. Talking about cars reminds me: I managed to wreck our first car, a Ford Sierra, in the early hours of 1st January 1960. Luckily, although turning the car over several times, I came out unscathed except for a badly damaged nose! In our second car, a Ford Anglia, we went on leave to Mombasa – over 370 miles EACH WAY. It was just as well that we had visited Carr Hartley's Game Farm and had seen lots of animals, as we saw none at all during the journeys to and from Mombasa. Hard to believe but true.

In about the middle of 1960 we were informed that we would be allocated one of the first married quarters that were being built, due to be completed in early 1961. The reader can imagine our feelings when, without warning, I was marched in front of the Commanding Officer to be told that I was to report to the Royal Military Academy Sandhurst (RMAS) as an Instructor on the 5th January 1961. Sergeant Tony Bullock had been caught taking bets from Officer Cadets and been sacked by the Commandant. I tried everything to get out of this posting, including seeing the Commanding Officer several times. This was to no avail and we left Kenya in December.

Being (literally!) homeless, the four of us descended on my brother Terry and his dear wife Gladys and their lovely daughter Denise, who was about 10 at the time. Despite the house being a terraced one, 'two up, two down', they made us very welcome. Mary, Terry and Bob stayed on there when I reported for duty at the RMAS in early January. I found two rooms in a local house in College Town, where Mary and the boys stayed for a few weeks. This was most unsatisfactory, rough and cold, but much better than being apart.

At this point I seriously considered leaving the Army and the Company Commander of Headquarter Wing, RMAS, Colonel Arthur Spratley, found out about this and sent for me to discuss it. When he heard the facts, he got cracking and found us a smallish but reasonable married quarter in the Academy grounds. He had heard by then that Sergeant Bullock, who left the RMAS in disgrace, had moved into 'my' new quarter in Kenya. Rather ironic to say the least!

The one good thing that came out of the speedy posting from Kenya was that it encouraged Mary and me to buy our first house (in Len Hutton country) in Pudsey, Yorkshire! What a shame that Terry and Bob were not born there. They would have qualified to play for Yorkshire at cricket!

Although I had not wanted to go to Sandhurst, it proved to be the best thing that could possibly have happened to me from the point of view of my career. I was surrounded by the most fabulous soldiers at various times during my three-year tour. These included General Sir John Mogg (ex Coldstream Guardsman); Colonel Lloyd Owen of the Long Range Desert Group; Major – later to be General – Farrar Hockley of the Glorious Gloucesters; Major Denis O'Flaherty, a double DSO from the Gunners; Captain (later to be the General commanding our forces in the Falklands War) Jeremy Moore; two really first-class Coldstream Regimental Sergeant Majors, Rose and Wilkinson; Company Sergeant Major Peter Clifford, and finally, and most importantly, Academy Sergeant Major John Lord, late Grenadier Guards.

The last named had the greatest influence on my life and I used many of his instructional techniques, written and verbal, for the rest of my military service. 'Jackie' Lord was a perfectionist in every way and was probably the finest Warrant Officer the Army had ever had. I was lucky enough to attend

Lieutenant-Colonel Christopher Keeble D. S. O. who commanded 2 Para in the Falklands after Lieutenant-Colonel 'H' Jones had been killed. Colonel Keeble had been an officer cadet in Blenheim Company R.M.A.S. – the author's squad.

three 6-week drill courses with him, the first one as a student and the other two as his Superintending Sergeant. Proof of the impression he made on me was brought home to me about 10 years after I had served under him. I was approached by Dick Alford, who was writing a book about John Lord, and asked to write a chapter for it. One Saturday morning I made a tape-recording from memory about the great man. Dick published this EXACTLY as I recorded it and the article takes up six full pages. What a tribute to a great Grenadier!

My three-year tour flew by and when I returned to the 2nd Battalion I was an expert on Colour drill, sword drill and virtually every aspect of ceremonial drill. More important than that, I knew how to deal with officers, both senior and junior, and had made life-long friends from many regiments and corps. This has benefited me ever since.

Mary worked for the Staff Quartermaster and the two boys made a good start at local schools. All four of us had bicycles and the roads were so quiet at that time that we were able to go out together on public roads. We purposely did without a car from late 1959 until late 1965 as we needed the cash to buy the house in Pudsey.

Space does not permit me to write much about the tour at Sandhurst but this needs recording. John Lord was in hospital with cancer for the last few months I was at Sandhurst in 1963. The Instructors were taking bets that he would not come back to duty. Not only did he come back, but he performed his normal STRENUOUS duty on the Sovereign's Parade on the 1st August. This is about a two-hour parade and the Academy Sergeant Major plays a big part in it, including handing over the Colour and other physical drills. WHAT A LEADER, WHAT A MAN, WHAT AN EXAMPLE TO ALL WHO SERVED WITH HIM!

So once again I rejoined the 2nd Battalion, this time in Wellington Barracks, London. As I had been promoted to Colour Sergeant at Sandhurst several months earlier, I was posted to Headquarter Company as Company Quartermaster Sergeant (CQMS). The previous CQMS was very poor at his job and all the books were in bad order. On 'paper' several rifles, bearskins, tunics and numerous smaller items were deficient. Having sent for every man in the company and finding out what kit and weapons he possessed, each of the 'deficient' items (and more) were accounted for. This did not stop the Regimental Quartermaster Sergeant (RQMS) putting the CQMS in front of the Commanding Officer for inefficient accounting.

After a few weeks I was posted to Number 3 Company as CQMS. This suited me, even though it meant more public duties, guards and Guards of Honour. In 1964 the battalion moved to Windsor to carry out training in preparation for a one-year unaccompanied tour in Aden. If Kenya and the RMAS had been peacetime soldiering, we were about to find out that Aden was WAR by comparison. The training at Okehampton and Otterburn was very tough, which was just as well. Even then, although we did not know it at the time, our stamina, fortitude and 'fitness to fight' would be tested to the full in Aden and the Radfan mountains.

A very odd thing happened to me at Okehampton. I knew that the CSM of 3 Company (Peter Blaby) was determined not to go to Aden for various reasons. It was no surprise to hear that he was being posted to Chepstow with a training unit. I was told to attend Commanding Officer's orders but had no idea what this was for. These orders were held in the 'middle of nowhere', with the Commanding Officer, Colonel Toler, seated behind a 6-foot table. I was the only case for CO's orders. When I was marched in front of the CO, he said with no hesitation: 'Congratulations! As far as I know, you are to first person to be promoted in the field since the War, and you will take Number 3 Company to Aden as Company Sergeant Major. WELL DONE!'

Needless to say I was both surprised and delighted at this elevation to Warrant Officer. However, there was no time for celebrations as within weeks Mary and the boys had moved into married quarters at Pirbright and I was on embarkation leave. During my time as CQMS I had become relatively unfit, so during my embarkation leave I went on nightly runs on my own on the roads around Bisley. This stood me in good stead when we arrived in Aden, as the whole tour was physically demanding and I was determined to 'lead from the front'.

It was heartbreaking to leave the family behind, especially as the boys were seven and nine. Mary had quite often been left to cope for shortish periods, but the thought of 12 months was horrifying. I honestly believe that it was worse for the wives than the soldiers. They go off with their mates whereas the wives may have nobody to turn to when problems arise. In the event they coped admirably and I had no need to worry on this account.

Number 3 Company Group of the 2nd Battalion was over 100 strong and included some drivers from the Royal Corps of Transport and some Royal Signals. Numbers 1, 3 and 4 Company Groups were about the same and all three sub-units worked separately. For some extraordinary and inexplicable reason, 'trouble' seemed to follow 3 Company about. In part this may be explained by the fact that this Company spent over seven months of the 12 up country (Radfan/Dhala), which was far more than the other two.

Some idea of the operational aspects of the tour can be gained from the following facts:

Of the 12 awards for gallantry received within the Battalion, seven went to members of 3 Company and one to an Officer (2/Lt Heywood) and one to a Sergeant (Hilling) who were frequently attached to the Company on operations. The awards were: Captain Barnet – MBE, Sergeant Goddard and Guardsman Nicholson – MM, CQMS Pell, Lance Sergeant Connell and Guardsman Snape – BEM and 2/Lt Wardle – the Queen's Commendation.

(Richard Heywood and Johnny Wardle became Brigadiers and the former commanded the Regiment for six and a half years.)

The casualties in 3 Company were:

Name & Date	Where Wounded	By What	Place
L. Sgt. Taylor 1.12.64	Head wound	Small arms	Wadi Qatana
Gdsm. Clarke 1.12.64	Face and arm wounds	Small arms	Wadi Qatana
Sgmn. Raines 2.2.65	Rocket wounds	Rocket launcher	Dhala
Gdsm. Edge Gdsm. Reynolds Gdsm. Wilkins 20.3.65	Killed	Mortar bomb	Ad Dimnah
L. Sgt. Hill 20.3.65	Back and arm wounds	Mortar shrapnel	Ad Dimnah
Major Corrigan 20.3.65	Foot, arm, Stomach wounds	Mortar shrapnel	Ad Dimnah
CQMS Pell 20.3.65	Phosphorous burns	Mortar bomb	Ad Dimnah
Gdsm. Johnson 20.3.65	Wrist wound	Mortar shrapnel	Ad Dimnah
Gdsm. Norton 27.3.65	Foot, leg, back, bottom	Grenade shrapnel	Ad Dimnah
L. Cpl. Wilkinson 3.4.65	Bruised back, leg and foot wounds	Rocket blast	Ad Dimnah
Sgt. Cockroft 5.65	Lost finger, also leg and foot wounds	Rocket blast	Little Aden
Gdsm. Hughes 12.5.65	L. Calf, upper arm, bottom, thigh	Grenade shrapnel	Little Aden
Gdsm. Dales 12.5.65	Back and head wounds	Grenade shrapnel	Little Aden
L. Cpl. Thackray 10.6.65	Shoulder and buttocks		Dhala
Gdsm. Snape 10.6.65	Head wound		Dhala
Gdsm. Tate 10.6.65	Leg wound		Dhala
Gdsm. Tolson 10.6.65	Shoulder and foot wounds		Dhala

The company's first tour up country was for five weeks at Blairs Field. We were fired on virtually every evening at sunset by dissident tribesmen, fortunately from a very long distance and with many rounds falling short of our sanger positions or more or less spent when they landed within our area.

The whole Company, less a small number left behind to guard our area, were on patrol when Lance Sergeant Taylor and Guardsman Clarke were wounded at Wadi Qatana. 2/Lt. Wardle, Sergeant Goddard and Guardsman Nicholson received their awards in that action. Ad Dimnah was awful. We were caught in low ground and ten enemy mortar bombs fell in the Company area. Edge (20), Reynolds (18) and Wilkins (17) were killed when there was a direct hit on one of our two mortar pits. Ironically, none of these three soldiers would normally have been in that pit. They were covering for three men who were away for various reasons. The three killed were single and those three who were away were all married. God acts in mysterious ways!

Dhala was a different kettle of fish. We frequently came under fire and at

Paying the locals who carried out menial tasks at Blairs Fields, Radfan, near Yemeni border, December 1964.

times were convinced we were subject to 'friendly fire'! The local 'army' was an undisciplined lot and opened fire at anything that moved or made a noise. Their camp was only a few hundred yards away, so we feared them as much as the dissidents. Lance Sergeant Connell and Guardsman Snape thoroughly deserved their British Empire Medals for actions they took during a night-time patrol. I was always disappointed that Lance Sergeant Bensey, who was in charge of our 81 MM Mortars, never received an award of any kind. His meticulous work at Dhala, Blair's Field and other places played a major part in the success of 3 Company Group. Indeed, I always reckoned that he saved the lives of the members of Lance Sergeant Connell's patrol by bringing down fire within yards of the patrol whilst they made their escape after a close-quarter gunfight.

I RECOMMEND THE 81 MM. SHEEPS' EYES!

There were numerous amusing incidents during the tour but too many to mention. However, one at Dhala stands out. The Company Commander (the superb Major Paul Adair) and I were invited to a 'Fuddle' hosted by the local Sheik. The only other white person there was the District Officer. Major Adair briefed me that we would be sitting on the floor around a carpet on which would be placed a great quantity of good food. I was to pick up food only in my LEFT hand and try ALL the food on offer; this included sheeps' eyes. The thought alone made me want to heave! Throughout the meal the Company Commander never stopped watching me. It was like a trial. Eventually, I had no option but to pick up and eat a couple of the so-and-so sheeps' eyes. Swallowing them whole, I could imagine them having a good look around my stomach. Afterwards, when we

The author at Dhala in the Radfan Mountains, 1965.

were on our own, Major Adair congratulated me AND roared with laughter (as he reminded me many times in later years).

Another constant source of amusement was *The Golly Gazette*. This was a Company weekly newspaper that I started for issue when the Company was up country. Anyone could enter articles for publication and some remarkable talent appeared. As I was the editor, and the Company Clerk (the excellent Lance Corporal Russell) was the typist, we were able to ensure that everything was quite lighthearted. The seniors in the Company, including Major Adair and myself, took constant 'knocks' and insults. Fortunately, the Company Commander had the same wicked sense of humour as I did.

Corporal Russell and some of his chums had started what they called 'The Blue Club'. Membership was by invitation only and rather surprisingly, the Commanding Officer and I were made honorary members. Meetings were sporadic and occasional and the other members of the Company thought that really important subjects were being discussed. The truth is that we talked mainly about sport, especially cricket. If the England selectors had listened to us, our team would have won every series. One wonderful thing came out of this for me personally. Colonel Jardine and Lieutenant Heywood put me up for membership of the MCC on our return to the UK.

Wilf Pickles, CQMS of Number 4 Company, and I had decided to take our 'local' leave back in England. We were the only two members of the Battalion to do so and this was very much against the wishes of the Commanding Officer. In fact he saw us separately to try to talk us out of it. However, he could not stop us as we were paying our own fare. This came at the right time as it was just after the deaths at Ad Dimnah. We had a great time to say the least. Years later Major Adair told me that I was on the list put forward for an operational award, probably the MBE, but Colonel Jardine would not endorse this and quoted the above as the reason. I HAVE NO REGRETS!

Serving abroad under operational conditions brings soldiers very close and by the end of the tour I was very fond, and proud of, 'The Fighting Three,' as we had become known. So I was dismayed on returning from disembarkation leave to be told that I was to be promoted to Drill Sergeant. This was completely out of the blue, as I had only been Company Sergeant Major for about 16 months and was one of the junior Warrant Officers in the Battalion. My promotion coincided with the publication of the operational honours list and in view of what Major Adair has since told me, I wonder if the two things were connected. Only Colonel Jardine knows but unfortunately he died many years ago. R.I.P. He was a great Commanding Officer and every man in the Battalion adored him.

The RSM was Don Willis, not an easy man to get on with but very good socially, and the other Drill Sergeant was Keith Badham. I was the Treasurer of the Sergeants Mess and with alternate weeks 'In Waiting', was kept very busy. The battalion was stationed at Pirbright, so on the days on which we were finding Queens Guard and/or Windsor Castle Guard a complete morning and part of the afternoon were lost.

In September I was unexpectedly posted to Mons Officer Cadet School as Drill Sergeant. Whereas the books in the 2nd Battalion Sergeants' Mess were in immaculate condition, the ones at Mons were in very bad order. I was disgusted, as both the RSM and Drill Sergeant were Coldstreamers. It took me several weeks to get them right. Also, I had to get rid of the civilian Bar Steward, as he was dishonest. Things improved dramatically when RSM Harrod, Irish Guards, took over and a former Black Watch Pipe Major, Jock Egan, became the Bar Steward.

There was a rapid turnover of Officer Cadets, as Commissioning Parades took place every eight weeks.

A tour at Mons was invigorating in every sense and this was due in large measure to the representatives from so many Regiments and Corps, both on the staff and at officer cadet level. In most cases the latter were there because they wanted to be and their enthusiasm knew no bounds. The course of 20 weeks was very tough, both mentally and physically, and it was not uncommon for some young men to fall by the wayside. All the four Brigadiers (Glennie, Heidenstam, Cunningham and Darell) who were Commandants during my two tours were quite ruthless with cadets who were not up to scratch.

The Sergeants' Mess consisted of about 50 members and there were representatives from 39 Regiments or Corps. Regular functions took place of excellent quality and this helped to create an outstanding team spirit. It also helped with such a high intensity course.

As the only Drill Sergeant, I was responsible for all aspects of drill and in particular the Sword Drill for the Under Officers. The exercises at Thetford and on Dartmoor carried out by the Cadets were tests of endurance in every way. During one period, while I was acting RSM, two overseas Cadets died of exposure whilst training on Dartmoor. Nobody was held to blame but it was a terribly sad time. The African boy was buried with full military honours in a cemetery in Aldershot.

In the middle of 1968 I was to be posted back to the 2nd Battalion as the Regimental Quartermaster Sergeant. Mary and I decided that it was time for us to buy a house locally to give Terry and Bob continuity of education. So we left our married quarter in Aldershot and moved into our new home in Farnborough. This is a decision that we have never regretted but we never dreamed that we would own that house for 27 years. It is worth mentioning that we were unable to sell our house at Pudsey for several months as we had sitting tenants. This attracted a big bill from the tax man that did not amuse us one bit. CASH WAS TIGHT!

The boys benefited enormously from this settled period at the Salesian College. Between them they passed 24 subjects in the General Certificate of Education, Terry went on to qualify as a chartered accountant and Bob as a solicitor. We are very proud of their success.

The next fifteen months were difficult to say the least. For example it was the first time that I had to spend long periods in an office. However, I got on well with the Quartermaster, Major Douglas Glisson, and I learned a lot from him and his excellent staff. The Regimental Sergeant Major was a personal friend and a great hero of mine, Peter Clifford, so I had much to be thankful for.

The Battalion was in Chelsea Barracks performing public duties on the Royal Palaces and the Tower of London. It was also preparing for a long tour in Germany. I commuted daily to and from Farnborough. The roads were much quieter than they are now!

The next fifteen months or so were quite frenetic, not least because the Battalion was preparing to hand over Chelsea Barracks and move to Munster in Germany. Long periods of training took place in addition to continuing public duties. Both the 1st and 2nd Battalions visited the town of Coldstream but I was left in charge of the rear party in London. This did not please me!

Six weeks before the Battalion was due to move, the Quartermaster disappeared on leave and then straight to Germany with the advance party. The Battalion had been in Chelsea for several years, so it was frightening to think of the complex handover. Nevertheless this gave me the opportunity to introduce certain systems that had always taken my fancy. Hopefully these still operate to this day.

I summoned the Company Quartermaster Sergeants and the heads of my various departments. I emphasised to the Quarter Blokes that they should declare ALL surpluses ('buckshees') of any type. This meant that any sub-unit showing a deficiency could be helped out and brought up to scale.

At the same time Lance Sergeant Sid Lockwood, who ran the accommodation stores, left Chelsea in a 3-ton truck (complete with a couple of bottles of whisky) to visit the Ordnance Stores, and returned with various items to make up any deficiencies.

Lance Sergeant Blakeway and I sweetened up a terrific friend of the Battalion, the Brigade Ordnance Warrant Officer (Rex Harrol), who 'wrote off' various items of full dress clothing that were in a poor condition or were non-existent!

I had terrific support from everyone involved. When the advance party of the 2nd Grenadiers arrived, I was to meet a man who had a great influence on my life and also became a wonderful friend. This was the Quartermaster, Alan Dobson. He was a giant in size and a giant as a man. Every quality you could want in a leader was to be found in him and he set an example in every way, especially in man management. In fact he was a copy, though a larger framed one, of Arthur Ramsden. He ruled by respect, not fear.

When Alan arrived, he asked me to take the lead in everyday matters and let the respective Company and Department representatives get on with their own handovers and takeovers. He and I, with the Battalion Pioneer Sergeants, did the handover of the living accommodation and other buildings. Where a damage was found to the 'bricks and mortar', Alan simply asked if the Pioneer Sergeants could fix it, and they did!

Remarkably, the Battalion left Chelsea Barracks without a bill of any description. This reflected credit on every member of the handover/takeover team. However, I have always thought that it was the attitude and example set by Alan Dobson which made the move such a happy one. So much for the talked-of ill feeling towards the First or Grenadier Regiment of Foot Guards. Certainly in my case I have many friends in that part of the Household Division.

CHAPTER 8

Repeat Tours in BAOR
and Mons Officer Cadet School

S O IT WAS THAT THE Second Battalion, Coldstream Guards started another tour in Germany, but this time in a different mode, as an armoured battalion in 4th Guards Brigade. There was a lot to be learnt by every man in the Battalion, and not least by a very naive RQMS. About my only knowledge of vehicles was mending a puncture in a bicycle inner tube or cleaning the spark plugs of a car. Fortunately a number of senior ranks had been on pre-tour courses, learning about armoured personnel carriers.

Having rid myself of full dress clothing, I then took over a large amount of camp-like stores appropriate to the British Army of the Rhine. Numerous exercises were carried out at both sub-unit and battalion level to get us fit to fight. The first parade each weekday was maintenance on the 432 vehicles. Even the officers and non-commissioned officers wore coveralls – quite a change from being in tunics and bearskins.

On the personal front, I had been told by the Regimental Lieutenant Colonel (RLC) (Colonel Sir Ian Jardine) prior to leaving London, that I was to be posted back to Mons as the Regimental Sergeant Major in August 1969. As I had left Mary, Terry and Bob in Farnborough, the next few months could not pass quickly enough. It was a disappointment not to be taking over the 2nd Battalion from my friend Peter Clifford and I know that he was as disappointed as I was. The consolation was that the RLC had also told me that at the end of my tour at Mons I would return to the Regiment as a REGULAR Quartermaster. Rather cynically, I had not believed this at the time, as everyone I knew of had received short service commissions (SSC). TIME WOULD TELL!

A couple of weeks after arriving in Germany I was told to attend Commanding Officer's Orders the following day. Peter Clifford had no idea what this was for and it was unusual to say the least for an RSM not to know such facts. I was on tenterhooks as I was the last case to march in. When I did so, the Commanding Officer, Lt Colonel Windsor-Clive, produced a handwritten letter from Alan Dobson and read out the whole letter. It recommended me for the handover of Chelsea Barracks and went on to say that it was by far the best of many handovers that he had been involved in as Quartermaster. After reading the letter, the Commanding Officer stood up, shook my hand and added some complimentary remarks, finishing by repeating what the RLC had said, that I would return to the Regiment as a regular QM. Peter Clifford was absolutely delighted – this despite his only having been guaranteed a Short Service Commission at that time. HE DID GO ON TO BE A REGULAR MAJOR QUARTER-MASTER. Peter always got the best out of people in the nicest way and was a terrific soldier. I miss him deeply – R.I.P.

Leaving the Battalion was terribly sad as having joined 2 Coldstream Guards in 1946, it was the only Battalion I had served in. Thank goodness I was returning to the family and to a unit I knew, otherwise it would have been heartbreaking. The Sergeants' Mess gave me a terrific send-off and Peter Clifford made a most moving speech. He bet me that I'd be back. Little did I know that he would hand over to me as the Quartermaster of the 2nd Battalion and then the Guards Depot in 1975 and 1978 respectively. Truth is stranger than fiction, seeing that there are about a dozen Quartermasters in a Regiment to choose from and at least fifty in the Division.

I quickly settled at Mons and implemented several new ideas about drill, discipline and administration, but most of all how to treat Officer Cadets. Some of the things I saw as Drill Sergeant during my previous tour did not suit me at all. With regard to drill, I used just about everything taught by Academy Sergeant Major John Lord. He was the greatest, so why not? Of greatest benefit to the drill was the introduction of a weekly 'Instructors' Hour'. The Drill Sergeant, CSMs and Platoon Sergeants were the only ones in attendance and we went right through every period of drill to be taught the following week. This got rid of some of the sloppy and incorrect habits that had crept in. The standard leapt up. Interestingly, the one Line Regiment CSM on strength – who thought the Instructors' hours were unnecessary, always had the poorest drilled company.

The first Drill Sergeant during my tour was a rather useless one from the Scots Guards, who was not a 'team man' and expected to be told what and when to do things. He was also a clockwatcher. Fortunately a really great guy took over from him, Drill Sergeant Les Meade SG. He was outstandingly loyal to me and I could always rely on him. He was also a tremendous wit, full of fun and with a really lovely family. Indeed, his sense of humour could have had me sacked once or twice, as he would sometimes come out with a 'one-liner' at what should have been a serious time.

Most of the WOs and NCOs from the Guards Division were outstanding, and some of those who come to mind were CSM Glyn White, WG, Peter Goddard, Coldm, John France SG, and Sergeants Dean and Mather Coldm, Glennie SG, Kinane IG, and Corporal of Horse Slater. It is remarkable what I learnt from them rather than they from me! The other person I listened to was a black Colour Sergeant from the Royal Pioneer Corps – Joe Barrow.

The two Commandants during my three-year tour were both brilliant – but different. Brigadier (later to be Lt. General Sir Hugh) Cunningham was an ex-Sapper with an eye for detail and a very, very sharp mind. He had a 'short fuse' and it was best not to cross him, which I didn't! Brigadier Sir Jeffrey Darell was well known to me as he was the Second-in-Command of the 2nd Battalion when I was a young soldier. He was absolutely immaculate, a perfect gentleman with an unflappable nature.

They were supported by first-class deputies, Colonels Pike and Mackenzie, and two terrific Adjutants, Macfarlane and Wardle, who are both Coldstreamers. The two Quartermasters were very experienced, good guys and second to none, Colonel Harold King and Major Eric Ransley.

Three RQMSs served at Mons during my three years. They were all different in style and manner but outstandingly efficient and gave me wonderful support – Braine Gren, Ayres WG and Haylett Coldm. There was hardly a weak link in the Sergeants' Mess so it is very easy to see why the place was such a success. We all worked hard and played hard.

Field Marshal the Lord Montgomery visited Mons three times during my time there, to present a prize to the outstanding cadet of an intake. Needless to say, this was a book written by 'Monty' himself. On each occasion, on seeing my Coldstream star and white hatband, he related the following story. Several years ago a Peer in the House of Lords stood up and made the statement that the Highland Division was the 'cream of the British Army'. Monty said he took great pleasure in standing up and saying 'The Highland Division may be the cream, but the Guards are the elite of the British Army,' and went on to say what marvellously disciplined fighting soldiers they were. Brigadier Darell and I both grew about three inches during the tributes. Deputy Commandants from Line Regiments, present at the time, squirmed a little!

Because there was a Commissioning Parade every eight weeks, it was necessary for the Commandant to invite very senior officers or VIPs as inspecting officers well in advance. During my time we had Field Marshal Montgomery, numerous full Generals, and the Secretary of State for Defence, the Lord Carrington.

*The Lord Carrington inspects officer cadets at Mons Officer Cadet School,
May 1972.*

Without exception, they gave wonderful speeches. After the parade attended by Lord Carrington, the local paper published a picture of him inspecting the Cadets being commissioned, but criticising him for having long hair. Later in life, when I joined the House of Lords staff, I gave Lord Carrington this photograph of the occasion, but, needless to say, did not mention the newspaper comment.

Nicholas Soames, later to be Minister to the Army, was a very poor Officer Cadet and after a few weeks at Mons almost got sacked by the Commandant. It took a visit from his grandmother, Lady Churchill, to save him. His Company Commander was most displeased to say the least. Perhaps this scare made him a better M.P. and Minister!

Talking of inspecting officers reminds me of one of the Commissioning Parades during my previous tour as Drill Sergeant. The evening before the parade was due to take place, the Adjutant sent for me with a request from the Commandant. Would Mrs Horsfall host Princess Margaret, the inspecting officer, at the Reception after the parade? At the last moment Mrs Harrod had said she could not attend. Naturally, Mary was very nervous about this when I told her, so she recruited a couple of her friends to stay with her.

Before the parade I briefed Colour Sergeant Joe Barrow that he was to keep a watching brief so as to ensure that HRH was provided with pink gins and Turkish cigarettes. I never gave a thought to what he should give Mary and her women friends. By the time I arrived at the Reception about half and hour after it had started, this select group was in great form. I understand from Mary that Princess Margaret was very easy to talk to, especially about children, education and Army married quarters. Anyhow, HRH went off with the Commandant to have lunch in the Officers' Mess. We moved to the Sergeants Mess to continue the celebrations. Not long after we arrived in the Mess, someone told me that Mary was tipsy – and she WAS! I had no option but to take her home, where she went straight to sleep. Goodness knows what Joe Barrow fed the girls with, but it was my fault for not reminding him that Mary is virtually teetotal.

Many hilarious, odd, unusual and nonsensical things happened during my two tours at Mons but space only allows for a few to be told. I had my first taste of dealing with women soldiers there. There were about eight members of the Women's Royal Army Corps (WRAC) in various administrative posts. One day Sergeant Beauzovel WRAC came to see me and wanted to put Private Harris WRAC on a charge (I cannot remember the alleged offence). We had never charged a woman before, so naturally I was cautious and suggested that the offender should be brought in front of me.

This is where things went slightly askew! Some time later there was a loud knock on the door. Sergeant Beauzovel appeared in quick time and within seconds Private Harris was in front of my desk standing to attention. Then, as quickly as Sgt Beauzovel had appeared, she disappeared, closing the door behind her. Imagine the scene, a young lady of possibly 19, standing in front of this fearsome-looking Guards RSM, with a short haircut and waxed moustache – not a pretty sight – (I refer to the RSM, not the girl!) I was just about to start questioning her when Harris burst into uncontrollable tears. I told her to sit down on a chair at the end of the office. She could not stop sobbing. So, being a coward, I went for a walk around barracks for about 15 minutes. When I returned, I told Harris to 'fall out'. Nothing was said about the matter but I often wonder what the outcome would be if something similar happened in the present 'politically correct' times. Needless to say, I told Sergeant Beauzovel that she was to remain with any future offender at ALL times.

With the help of Company Quartermaster Sergeant (CQMS) Banks, a

'Teenagers' Club' was formed for the 'children' of our soldiers and a few civilians. The eldest son of the Quartermaster, Peter King, who was about 18, helped to supervise the discos. Brigadier Cunningham's fifteen-year-old daughter was a member and attended some of the discos. One morning after a disco the Commandant appeared unannounced in my office, more than a little distressed, and related the following: the daughter had come down to breakfast that morning wearing a silk scarf. Mrs Cunningham had smelt a rat and made her remove it. Both Brigadier and Mrs Cunningham were horrified and asked me to investigate how their lovely daughter came to have love bites on her neck?

The investigation took about five minutes! When questioning CQMS Banks, he told me that the only teenagers he caught in 'close embrace' were Peter King and the Commandant's daughter. Blimey! this was Court Martial stuff. Anyhow Banks had banned Peter from the weekly discos for some time. I reported back to the Brigadier that the offending male was 'unknown' but was probably a guest. Regrettably, the Commandant's daughter never attended another disco. Mind you, she was an attractive girl so it was just as well.

The Wives' Club, with Mary at the helm, went from strength to strength. Most functions were held in the Sergeants' Mess but in an effort to get the wives of junior soldiers to attend, they also tried meeting in the NAAFI. This did not have the desired result and it was mainly the spouses of Sergeants' Mess members who attended regularly. When Brigadier Darell arrived, he wanted to know how his wife could get to know the wives. Mary and I suggested a Wives' Club cheese and wine party. On the evening concerned, I met Lady Darell, spent a few minutes introducing her to some wives, then absconded to the Sergeants' Mess bar. Returning about ninety minutes later, I found nearly all the wives, including Lady Darell, somewhat 'tiddly' and very noisy. Fortunately a staff car was taking the VIP guest home. The next morning Brigadier Darell told me that his wife Bridget had had a wonderful evening.

When Colonel Pike was leaving on completion of his tour as Deputy Commandant, we dined him out in the Sergeants' Mess. I asked him to confirm to Mary what I had told her but she did not believe. This was the terrific long write-up he had given HER on MY annual confidential report. Not only did he confirm it but he rattled it off about word for word. What is it that is said about 'behind every successful man is a good woman'?

The Librarian at Mons was an ex-professional Irish soldier called Victor Gray. He was a wonderful guy, always helpful, very polite, immaculately turned out and a real asset to the School and in particular the cadets. Unfortunately he had a drink problem and was occasionally ill. When he was about 70, I heard that he was ill and was refusing to eat. I took one look at him and ordered him into the Cambridge Military Hospital. Almost every evening for about three weeks I visited him on my way home. I was really worried to see this usually immaculate man neglecting himself, with his hair not groomed, unshaven, untidy pyjamas and dressing gown. Then an extraordinary thing happened. I arrived at the ward at about 6.15pm and Victor was sitting up in bed looking really bright and very well groomed (he had cut himself several times shaving). We had a proper conversation and I left him at about 6.50 pm. Arriving home about 15 minutes later, I was just telling Mary how pleased I was with Victor when the telephone rang. It was a nurse telling me that Victor had died a few minutes after I had left him. Some soldiers say that the RSM is God. Could it be that old soldier Victor wanted to look his best for his God on earth before meeting his God in the great parade ground in the sky?

An infantry regiment provided a Demonstration Platoon for Mons Officer Cadet School which was invariably good. At the time of the handover of Brigadier Cunningham to Brigadier Darell, it was the Royal Anglian Tiger company. I warned the Platoon that I would be bringing the new Commandant to meet them and at the specified time and date they lined up in all their finery. As the Brigadier arrived in front of each NCO, I made what I thought was a good introductory remark. As we approached one particular barrel-chested but chubby NCO, I said 'This is Corporal Parnell, sir; I've ordered him to lose some weight.' 'Good' said the Brigadier, 'and how are you going to do that, Corporal?' Without blinking, and looking the Commandant straight in the eyes, Corporal Parnell replied, 'Chop an arm off, sir'. No other comment was necessary but I imagine that the Platoon Sergeant had more to say later. Secretly I enjoyed the joke, especially as Parnell was an excellent NCO, and I suspect that the Brigadier did too.

One morning Academy Sergeant Major Ray Huggins telephoned me from Sandhurst to ask what he should do with our sentry box. The Sergeant of the Guard had not even noticed it was stolen, at about 2 a.m. that morning, from its site about forty yards from the guardroom. He was absolutely staggered when I sent for him and told him to go and get it back. I WAS JUST GRATEFUL THAT THERE WAS NO SENTRY IN THE BOX WHEN IT WAS TAKEN!

During my two tours at Mons Officer Cadet School, my moustache had caused much comment, some favourable and some critical. Mary hated it, Terry despised it and Bob was simply amused at it. I soon discovered that my nickname was 'Catweazle', after an ugly character on a Sunday evening children's television programme. One thing is certain, it fitted the image of a Guards Sergeant Major, making the wearer look fierce and strict. This suited me as I remember 'Jan' Freeman, when a Superintending Sergeant at the Guards Depot, making faces at himself in the mirror as he said the recruits took no notice of him. He had a round 'moon' face which made him look very pleasant. My 'catweazle' moustache seemed to put the fear of God into my subordinates, EXCEPT FOR MY TWO SONS!

The Salesian College relaxed their rules on the length of hair for the students in about 1971. Terry was 16 at the time. Hair could be worn long if it did not touch the collar. He took this rule literally and had lovely curly hair which just cleared his collar. I got fed up with this and tried my hardest to get him to have a haircut. He said that he would when I 'shaved off the stupid moustache'. Naturally this did not suit me so in desperation I stopped his weekly pocket money. Nothing was said or done for about six or seven weeks, so I restored his allowance. The very next day he went out and had a haircut and he has never worn it long since. Oh for the trials of parenthood!

I heard later that the officers and cadets were amused that I had two moustaches, a waxed one when on the barrack square or when in mess dress, and a droopy one when on tactics in the field. The offending hair was shaved off on the 1st September 1972, the day I was commissioned. The two sons noticed immediately but Mary did not do so until about a week later. Terry and Bob were very amused at this, but it does pose the question: how often do married couples look at each other properly?

To digress a bit. Whilst a Sergeant at Sandhurst, I had shaved my moustache off during the long summer leave – I was working as a navvy on the building site at Pirbright and did not think this fitted the image. Academy Sergeant Major Lord took one look at me on Old Building Square and ordered me to attend Adjutant's Orders. Major Philip Ward, Welsh Guards, made it very obvious that he expected me to re-grow the moustache, which I did. Several years later I met Sir Philip when he was a Major General and recounted this story. He roared with laughter and said he thought that his advice had been correct.

Unfortunately there were some very sad times too, including several deaths. These included a cot death and the lovely young wife of QMSI Taylor. There was even a suicide, Trooper Richards, who was only 19. We almost lost our outstanding Armourer, Sergeant Jock Taylor, when he had a

massive loss of blood after what should have been a routine operation. Happily he survived to tell the tale, living in Australia, with regular jogging and golf of a very high quality.

1972 was a wonderfully happy time for our family. Mary was doing well at work, both boys were passing all sorts of exams, we celebrated our 20th Anniversary, I was awarded the MBE in the Birthday Honours and I was given a Regular Quartermaster Commission in the Regiment.

As a cost-cutting, but controversial exercise, Mons Officer Cadet School was due to close down at Aldershot and be relocated at Sandhurst with the Academy. I therefore arranged a Sergeants' Mess dinner with all past Commandants and Regimental Sergeant Majors in attendance. We had a band and trumpeters and all the trimmings. I made the main speech and General Sir Basil Eugster replied. This was a spectacular and wonderful occasion and one to be remembered by all involved.

As we were not going to Camberley, the Sergeants' Mess gave Mary and me a marvellous farewell dinner. Although I was to be commissioned, it was a sad time in many ways. Without question this was the best three years of my service and the family had hardly had a night apart. Most of all, it was such a satisfying posting, being with first-class officers and soldiers and turning out excellent young men to be the leaders of the future in the

Army. Many of these went on to be very senior in rank and/or very successful businessmen.

In August 1972 the Mons Barracks gradually emptied and on the last day of that month I was literally the last soldier to leave it.

Since the Officer Cadet School at Aldershot closed down, I have met officers and men who served there, in whatever capacity, all around the world. Everyone agrees that it was a mistake to concentrate all cadet training at Sandhurst. Even to this day there is a place for a unit to train short-service officers; particularly the more mature young man who has 'seen life' and probably been literally round the world. This is not intended as a criticism of the Academy at Camberley, as I think that this does a superb job for the leaders in the modern-day army. The two separate systems used to complement one another.

CHAPTER 9

A Thing of Dreams – A Commission

WHEN IT WAS CONFIRMED in May that I was to be promoted in
September, the RLC told me that I would be posted to the 1st
Battalion in Berlin as the Families Officer. When I pointed out to Colonel
Smyth Osborne that I had never served in any other Battalion but the 2nd,
he simply said, with a twinkle, 'It's about time for a change then'.

So I was not particularly upset when just a few weeks before my
commissioning, the posting was changed to the Guards Depot at Pirbright. I
was to be the Catering Officer in place of a Grenadier Quartermaster who
was to be court martialled, along with many members of his staff and some
from the Ordnance Depot, for stealing rations.

Because I was so busy at Mons, the full implications of this did not sink
in. I only started to suspect that all was not as it seemed after meeting some
Army Catering Corps Officer Cadets at a party, who told Mary and me
something about a course I was destined to attend. This was a six-months
course at the ACC Depot for potential Catering Officers. They also added
that I would be expected to wear cook's whites, complete with a chef's hat.
Mary and I did not believe this.

I have to explain that the ACC Depot in St Omer Barracks was literally
alongside Mons Barracks, and the two were linked by a tiny wicket gate.
The reader can imagine how I felt at leaving one side of the fence, where I
was the so-called God, and finding myself on the other side of the fence just
a few days later as a very junior officer. YES – DRESSED IN COOK'S
WHITES AND CHEF'S HAT. My ex-Cadets who were commissioned
themselves by this time, simply loved this.

The next six months were frenetic in every way. For three months this
was the practical side of all aspects of catering and cooking. I had never
realized before how physically demanding it was for cooks to be on duty in
a hot kitchen for days at a time. There were five of us on the course and I
was twelve years older than the next eldest. We were made to spend about
two weeks in every department: butchery, pastry, sweets, delicatessen, sauces
included. For about six weeks each of us had to produce a meal for five
soldiers and these were taken to the men's dining room each day. More

about this later. The hardest two weeks were spent in the kitchen of the ACC Officers' Mess.

The second half of the course was in the classroom, learning about menu planning and every aspect of administration for foodstuffs and allied subjects. The Malayan student officer and I struggled like mad on the French cooking terminology, as we had no previous experience of the language, whereas the other three had.

The two main instructors were Major Eric Capp in the classroom and Warrant Officer I. Toyne in the kitchen. They were both brilliant and gave us every possible help. Eric taught us a wonderful saying that has stood me in good stead ever since: 'Half the meal is in the eye appeal!' Without question, it is a truism that the presentation and layout of a meal really sets the old taste buds going.

Space does not permit much detail about this high-grade course, but it is worth recounting the following. Each of the five officers had his own gas cooker and every item needed to prepare and cook a meal for five. Each morning we were given the menu and necessary ingredients. He had about ninety minutes to prepare four courses. Usually I was able to assist the officers on either side of my cooking area. The Malayan officer needed lots of help for obvious reasons. Early one morning I literally cut the the end off the middle finger of my left hand when preparing the meat for the meal. Mr Toyne tried to give me first aid but could not stop the flow of blood. I asked my two chums to keep an eye on my pots and pans on the stove while I went to the Medical Centre for treatment. When I got back, things did not look too good.

The officer who assessed our meal each day was Major Walter Anderson. A really nice guy but a rather dour Scotsman. When it was my turn to be called forward, he was marking me down on each item of food that I had prepared. I must have looked really crestfallen and forlorn. Mr Toyne and my fellow students looked just as sad. On completing his assessment, Walter suddenly put his hand on my shoulder and said in his lovely Scottish brogue: 'Let's face it, Peter, you've had a bloody awful day'. With that everyone roared with laughter and it seemed to take the pressure off us all. I even found out afterwards that I had been given a good mark for the meal.

At the end of the course, each Officer Student had to see the Commandant of the ACC, a Brigadier Wilson. He suggested that I transfer to the Army Catering Corps as I would have a good future. As politely as I could, I told him that I did not fancy having a job where I was always working when other people were playing. He accepted this in the right manner and said that he had never thought of catering in that way. I was given a B plus grading for all aspects of the course, which seemed to please everyone.

There was one final 'kick in the teeth', so to speak. At the end-of-the-course party Walter Anderson told us all our (excellently prepared!!) meals had gone straight into the swill bin on arrival at the men's dining room. The reason we were not told at the time of cooking was because the instructors did not want to destroy our confidence. WHAT CONFIDENCE? Even to this day the only French term I know is Bain Marie. For many years I thought that a micro chip was a miniature chip (edible one). But that's another story for another day!

I was given one day off during the course in order to go to Buckingham Palace to be invested with the MBE. Mary, Terry and Bob came with me and we had a great day. The Queen said what a pity Mons Officer Cadet School had closed down as it was such good training for officers. Garrison Sergeant Major Tom Taylor laid on a 'pick buffet' for our friends in the London District Sergeants' Mess. It was at no cost – typical of Tom! By a quirk of fate, Douglas Glisson had been at the Palace with us and he treated us all to lunch in a restaurant in Whitehall.

Throughout the course I had worked at the Guards Depot each Saturday morning. By doing this I was able gradually to pick up the reins of the job and get to know the staff. Colonel John Ghika, Irish Guards, was the Commandant in September 1972 but by the time I had finished the course, Colonel Iain Ferguson, Scots Guards, was in the chair. He was a super boss and allowed me to get on with my demanding job. The feeding strength was over 2,000, there were seven kitchens, and I had over fifty cooks.

The Master Cook, another Grenadier, had been sacked along with the previous Messing Officer and was awaiting court martial. This worked in my favour as I had a really first-class Master Cook, Warrant Officer I Dennis Brown, Scots Guards. He was a big man who called a spade a spade and led by example. His integrity was beyond reproach and I knew there would be no 'losses' whilst he was about. We still had three Sergeants, Farmer, Muir and Walker, who were allegedly involved in the massive fiddles that had gone on over many years. Ironically, they were never charged and could not be sacked, because each of them refused to give a statement to the Special Investigation Branch (SIB).

For several months after I arrived, the SIB were constantly visiting my area on various pretexts. Eventually Dennis Brown and I got fed up with this so I went to see the Commandant to complain. Colonel Ferguson had never known of these visits and had them stopped. Having done so, he ordered me to round up every member of the Catering Department, including civilians, for him to speak to. This I did and he spoke to them for about three minutes along the following lines:

'There are certain ones amongst you today who should have been court martialled. So be it! I have stopped the SIB visits with immediate effect, so you can count yourself lucky. But, let me tell you now: should any of you take so much as half a pound of butter away from your place of employment, if you're a soldier you'll be court martialled and if a civilian, you'll be sacked. That's all!' With that he walked out. During my two and a half year tour we did not have a single incident of theft.

Quite honestly it is beyond belief that those in authority at the Depot had not guessed that this monumental amount of thieving was going on. The Company and Depot minutes books recording weekly and monthly Mess Meetings were full of complaints, not just about the poor meals but also about the SHORTAGE OF RATIONS. With all sorts of supplements to be claimed, such as arduous duty, night duty, under 18 allowance etc. etc., it was almost impossible to be short. Within months of Dennis and me taking over, these same books were full of different comments: COMPLIMENTARY ONES! This was noted by the Commandant and his Second-in-Command.

About two-thirds of the cooks were from the five Foot Guards regiments. Some were excellent, some were awful. With the Commandant's blessing, I set out to transfer the Guards Cooks into the Army Catering Corps. Within about eighteen months only a couple of Guardsmen remained.

This meant that with support from HQ London District, we could get the cooks on appropriate craft and administration courses to fit them for promotion. Some of them whizzed up through the ranks and the morale was sky high. At the same time as this was happening, the Guards Depot and the resident Battalion in Elizabeth Barracks became part of what was called Group Catering, Aldershot. I was the Group Officer and Dennis was the Group Warrant Officer.

The idea of Group Catering is that many items can be prepared centrally and then delivered daily by specially made closed-in vehicles. This included butchery, pastry and delicatessen items, and is a major boon to chefs everywhere. In the early 1970s this was new but it is now common practice.

The Quartermaster was Ted Rose, a really great Coldstreamer. He looked after me and introduced me into the ways of the Officers' Mess. Ted liked a glass of port – or two – and I used to watch when I got involved with him at the bar. The biggest shock to the system when commissioned from the ranks is how friendly all the senior officers are. From being 'Sarn't Major and Mrs Horsfall' you're suddenly 'Peter and Mary'. It took me some time to realize that the person introducing himself on the phone by saying 'Iain here, Peter' was in fact the governor himself – Colonel Ferguson. I was expected to call him Sir in return but I'm sure I never did.

The first Ladies Night Dinner Mary and I attended at the Depot was memorable in many ways. For example, as we entered the foyer, the Commanding Officer and his wife (whom I did not know) greeted us with: 'Mary – I'm Iain, I'm looking after you' and whisked her away. 'And I'm Margaret – hello Peter' said his wife, and took me into the reception area. They stayed with us virtually all night. What a way to gain respect! We saw them do a similar thing several months later when Norman and Jo Alred joined the officers' mess.

Major Peter Johnson, Scots Guards, let Mary down one evening at the end of dinner. Because Peter was talking so animatedly, she failed to notice that all the other ladies had left the dining room for the drawing room to allow the men to have their port. She had to make a hurried, embarrassing exit, with all eyes trained on her.

The other officer who was inclined to treat us like royalty was Major Tom Wills – an ex-recruit of mine. He commanded the Coldstream Company, which was enormous and needed two Company Sergeant Majors, one of whom was the marvellous Jack Wragg BEM. Tom used to embarrass me because whenever I entered his office, he remained standing until I left. He seemed not to accept the fact that he was now my senior. As a Major, he no longer needed the six stars worn on the shoulders of a Captain, so he gave them to me. This was an honour indeed as they were the stars worn by his father, who had been killed in action in the '39-45 War, in a Coldstream battalion.

Colonel Ferguson 'suggested' that the Guards Depot should have an Open Day with a funfair, sideshows, stalls, a band etc. etc. etc. I was tasked with most of this, being the junior Quartermaster at the Depot, and being able to supply the food! Competitions were held where garden produce, hobbies, home-made wines etc. could be entered. To encourage other wives to enter, Mary decided to enter the home-made wine class. The two judges appointed were Major Fred Adams and Ted Rose, who had been Regimental Sergeant Majors and who were very knowledgeable about all types of booze! Unfortunately nobody thought to tell them that the idea was to 'taste and spit out'.

After tasting several *good* wines, they were rather tipsy and enjoying themselves. They saw Bobby Joyce, another Major/ex RSM, in the area, so recruited him as a judge. They had no idea whose wine belonged to whom so it was not their fault that they happened to select several of the wines entered by Mary to win prizes in various categories.

Of course when the announcements were made on the loud speaker system that Mrs Horsfall had won this, was second in that, first in this, there were many calls of 'fiddle'. Colonel Ferguson was gushing in his praise and kept saying, 'well done, well done, Mary'. Neither of us could pluck up the courage to tell anyone that most of the winning wines belonged to our neighbours in Farnborough. The prizes were £1 vouchers to spend in the NAAFI, so our way of life was not about to change. Mary would still go to work on a moped!

The two years absolutely flew by – not least because during the last few months the cooks had improved so much that they were winning all sorts of competitions, including those against civilian cooks at Earls Court, Hotel Olympia. There is no doubt that it was a really satisfying job, which prepared me for the biggest challenge of my life. This was to be THE Quartermaster of THE best Battalion in the British Army – 2 Coldstream Guards.

Unless it happens to you, there is no way of knowing the feeling one gets as a former ranker in the Battalion one had joined while still a young kid, when told that one is to take the top job. At first it is unbelievable and it takes a while to sink in. It only comes home when the Commanding

Officer continually seeks advice on a whole range of subjects, including assessing the merits of very senior officers and warrant officers.

March 1975 saw me taking over from my great chum Peter Clifford, who was leaving to be Camp Commandant in London District.

So much happened in the next three and a half years that it merits a separate chapter. Included in this chapter will be my second tour as a Quartermaster at the Guards Depot and my move to the House of Lords, which in many ways was stranger than fiction.

CHAPTER 10

Returning Home to the Battalion

❧

S O IT WAS THAT I RETURNED 'home' to the Battalion that started my education and to which I owe so much. The Sergeants' Mess laid on a dinner to welcome Mary and me back and I made this the theme of my speech. One young wife, whose name I cannot remember, told me afterwards that she was very moved by what I said and almost cried. I suspect that being an infantry regiment makes everyone feel as though they are in an extended family. Members of Corps are unfortunate as they move as individuals rather than as a complete unit.

As anticipated, the handover between Peter and me was a smooth one. There was an excellent staff in place and very few changes were needed. The RQMS was a nice guy, though weak, but not long after I took over, Gordon Garret took up this appointment and he was first class. The Technical Quartermaster/Mechanical Transport Officer (TQM/MTO) was Wilf Pickles and the Families Officer was Derek Cessford, both wonderful Coldstreamers and outstandingly efficient. What was particularly pleasing was that their wives, Rita and Maureen respectively, were great friends of Mary.

The Battalion was constantly busy, not just with public duties but also in taking part in lots of exercises and carrying out security duties at London's Heathrow Airport. This latter duty was most demanding, as there was always fear of a hijacking or some major incident.

The cooks were a mixed bunch, some outstanding and others weak. The Master Cook was a really first-class soldier, as well as a cook of a very high standard. As soon as Peter had left, the Master Cook asked me if we could get the cooks on long overdue courses. With my connections with the ACC at Aldershot, this was not a problem. Most of them achieved excellent results and in some cases quick promotion. This had an interesting knock-on effect that I only half anticipated.

When the details of the London District Cookery Competition were published, I asked for volunteers to enter. NOT A SINGLE SOLDIER VOLUNTEERED. I sent for the Master Cook and ordered him to enter someone for every category in the competition. He was not too chuffed as we were very busy at the time. However, he changed his tune when the competition ended and the results were published. Our cooks had won about 24 of the 30 events that took place. Not long after, the Master Cook left us on accelerated promotion to Warrant Officer Class I. I met him about two years later – as a Captain!

The Battalion was stationed in Victoria Barracks, Windsor. Although a very busy posting for a Guards battalion, it is a super place to be, not least because the locals liked us. There were few acts of indiscipline outside the barracks, which helped to enhance our reputation.

The Commanding Officer was Lieutenant Colonel (later to be Brigadier) Christopher Willoughby, the Adjutant was Captain Martin Somervell and the Regimental Sergeant Major was Brian Smith. They were a first-class team Lieutenant Colonel (later to be Colonel) Malcolm Havergal took command for Northern Ireland.

It was at this time that I met Major (later to be Lieutenant General Sir William) Willie Rous and his charming wife Judy. He was the Second-in-Command and we got on extremely well and became very great friends. His work rate was phenomenal and he simply lived for the Regiment. We did several recces together and apart from these being very hard work, they were great fun – due entirely to Willie's attitude to life in general.

Willie took pride in knowing the name of every man in the Battalion and frequently got me to test him out on this. HE WAS NEVER WRONG! During a recce to Cyprus that we did together, he seemed to know every serviceman on the island. These were not Coldstreamers and several of them were Royal Air Force.

The monthly Messing Meetings were different with Willie as the 2IC. Instead of simply being an opportunity to discuss food and associated subjects, Willie and I used these opportunities to get feed-back (no pun intended!) on other aspects of life for the soldiers. If the Mess Meeting books still exist, they will show the subjects covered; these included many on the A side as well as Q. This was a great lesson for me and helped enormously when preparing for, and serving in, Northern Ireland.

Later in this chapter I will relate the story about the sutlers' contract and I was always grateful that Willie kept a close watch on how things developed. He was highly amused on seeing a sutler and his associate turn up in the Officers' Mess married quarters looking for the Quartermaster – not realizing that I lived in Farnborough. Willie said he was tempted to pass himself off as me just to see what happened. Just as well he didn't, or he might have got a 'made-to-measure' suit and Judy a hair drier. There will be much more about this 'blue-red-blue' Coldstreamer later in the book.

As we had so many friends in the Battalion, the social life was excellent. The family continued living in our own house at Farnborough and I commuted by car daily to Windsor. Later, in 1975, the Battalion was warned that they would commence an eighteen-month tour in Londonderry in August 1976. This put a great deal of pressure on all members of the Battalion, as there were numerous Northern Ireland-type courses taking place whilst we were continuing to play a full part in guarding the Royal Palaces, the Tower of London and Heathrow Airport.

Both Battalions of the Regiment were due to receive new Colours in April 1976. Traditionally the Coldstream have such parades in the grounds of Windsor Castle. Being the resident Battalion in Victoria Barracks, this meant that the major administrative workload would fall on our Orderly Room and my staff. The parade went well and I was as proud as punch as this was my third Presentation of Colours, one as a Lance Corporal, one as a Colour Sergeant and this one as Quartermaster. According to RHQ, this had never been done by an individual before.

Unfortunately Field Marshal the Lord Montgomery died at almost exactly the same time as we received our Colours. As he was an officer of the Order of the Garter, this meant that the funeral would take place at Windsor. The workload on my staff was enormous – particularly for the Officers' and Sergeants' Messes and all the cooks. For two days the feeding strength in barracks was about 2000. On the night before the funeral, the Field Marshal's coffin was in the gymnasium under guard. Late that night I visited the gymnasium and paid my last respects to this great man. As far as I know, nobody did this after me.

Everything went well on the day, due to Garrison Sergeant Major Tom Taylor and the bearer party from our Battalion under the command of Company Sergeant Major Charlie Pratt. The only hiccup was that an officer's undisciplined dog peed on a gun carriage wheel with the television camera trained on him. I was spectating with Martin Somervell at the time, and I thought he was going to have an epileptic fit!

Prior to the 2nd Battalion's tour in Northern Ireland, the Queen attended a superb garden party in Victoria Barracks and met about 200 families. The visit 'overran' in time and this was due in part to her staying to have a portion of a cake celebrating Second Lieutenant Bertie Gore-Brown's birthday. During tea the Commanding Officer was telling the Queen how busy I and my staff had been. The Queen turned to me and said, 'Yes, Monty did pick a very bad time to die!' She then gave a hearty laugh.

The Queen has an infectious sense of humour and when she laughs,

Mary being presented to the Queen at Victoria Barracks, Windsor, 1976.
In the background are Judy and Willie Rous. On the right is Sir George Burns,
26th Colonel Coldstream Guards.

everyone does. Even the business of Bertie's cake caused some fun. I whispered to the Commanding Officer to remind him that when the Queen had gone, we had a cake for Bertie's birthday. Without a pause Colonel Christopher turned to the Queen and told her about the cake and about the celebration and asked if she would like a piece. She replied 'I'll be most upset if I don't'. This caused laughter all round and she DID have a piece of cake with her cuppa.

Service battalions always have a stock of rum for issue, in small measure, during poor weather operations or exercises. It is very rare that this happens, but it did so once during my tour as Quartermaster. On the Saturday of the final rehearsal for the Trooping the Colour, I was in my office at about 12.30 pm when Colour Sergeant Cook came in and told me that because the soldiers had got very wet on Horse Guards Parade, the Duke of Edinburgh had ordered all troops taking part in the parade to be issued with rum. I thought this was a legpull so rang the Duty Officer in Headquarters London District. He confirmed that HRH had in fact given the instruction passed on by Colour Sergeant Cook. Who was I to argue? The soldiers were delighted to be soaked inside as well as out!

As the time for our tour in Northern Ireland approached, there were many personal problems to sort out. The major one was renting our house, which meant finding accommodation for Terry. Bob was at Manchester University reading Law, so he was accommodated there. I was away a great deal as we were carrying out pre-Ireland training at Hythe and then Thetford.

We had one drama, which strangely enough revolved around the cooks. Egon Ronay gives awards for cleanliness of kitchens and high standards of hygiene. 2 Coldstream Guards cooks won one of these and the appropriate plate was issued for display in the main dining room. We were all extremely 'chuffed' with ourselves. HOW THE MIGHTY FALL! Just a few days after the awards ceremony, the Battalion went off to Lydd in Kent firing their weapons. The Master Cook and his staff had prepared a buffet lunch to eat in the field and this included turkeys. About two thirds of the Battalion got a mild attack of salmonella. It took a long time for the 'mickey taking' of the cooks to stop. I was one of the lucky ones, as I did not visit the range that day.

The summer of 1976 was scorching hot and seventeen weeks went by without a drop of rain. Mary and I travelled to Northern Ireland on the 26th August. The Adjutant keeps a battalion diary and it is recorded that it rained every day for the first six months we were in Londonderry. No wonder Ireland is known as the Emerald Isle! So much has been written about the Army in Northern Ireland that at this point it is only worth recording any out-of-the-ordinary events.

Without question one of the things that exacerbates the problems on the streets in Northern Ireland is the attention of the television cameras in potential trouble spots. It has been known for youths and children to be paid by TV crews to throw missiles, including petrol bombs, so that these events could be caught on camera. Lt Colonel Malcolm Havergal had taken over command of the Battalion just before we started our tour in Londonderry. On arrival there, he called all the officers and warrant officers together and told them, if any media people approached us, we were politely to tell them that there was no trouble in our area and that we were not expecting any. This seemed to work, as after a few weeks they stopped visiting us. The Battalion had a trouble-free tour of eighteen months, with only one minor casualty.

The junior NCOs and Guardsmen were terrific, always firm with the locals but extremely polite and well mannered. This was not the case with some units and the brusque manner of certain soldiers sometimes caused an overreaction from those pulled up for questioning or for a vehicle check.

Mary and I were in a married quarter in a place called Campsie. This was surrounded by barbed wire and brick-built 'sangers'. The sanger at the entrance was manned by two fully armed Guardsmen. At about 2 am one morning Mary, Terry, Bob and I were returning to our quarter by car, having been to the Sergeants' Mess. It was absolutely teeming with rain. As we approached the sanger, one of the Guardsmen came out, shone his torch into the car, recognised me and saluted. He then asked if we'd had a good evening, which I answered in the affirmative. After another exchange of pleasantries, I drove on, and as I did so, Bob said: 'Your soldiers are quite special, Dad'. I can think of no higher compliment about a Guardsman; especially when spoken by one young man about another.

At times during our tour we had members of the Battalion in thirty-seven different locations, and I tried to visit them regularly. Some were 'under cover' so I was not allowed to visit them. I always went in civilian clothes, unescorted and without a weapon. If stopped by anyone, I intended bluffing my way by saying that I was on holiday from the UK. As I was 46/47 and grey-haired, I thought I could get away with this. Young Guardsmen looked like young Guardsmen no matter how they dressed – and I suspect that they would have overreacted if pulled up by suspicious-looking types. Anyhow, I got away with it and all the sub-units seemed to appreciate my visits.

Sutlers, commonly known as 'Chah Wallahs', are invaluable in Northern Ireland. NAAFI had refused to provide a service in what they considered to be dangerous areas. Sutlers had no such misgivings and provided a wonderful service. Whilst still at Windsor, I had been approached by a number of sutlers with a view to them having our contract for the eighteen-month tour in N.I. They offered huge amounts of cash, which would be credited to battalion funds and could be spent on 'goodies' for the troops. Some of them offered bribes, including a car each for the Commanding Officer and me. As cowards and being of impeccable virtue, Colonel Willoughby and I turned these down. THANK GOODNESS WE DID!

By the time we arrived in Londonderry, I had built up a really thick file with every item of correspondence between sutlers and me. Nobody else in the Battalion was involved. I believe the one selected by the CO and me was Baghi Shah, who paid battalion funds £30,000 for the privilege. He had impeccable credentials for his families service to the British Army – abroad as well as in N.I.

Not long after arriving in Ebrington Barracks in Londonderry, the new CO telephoned me and said that he had two SIB non-commissioned officers with him investigating sutlers' contracts and could I spare some time to talk to them. Knowing that the Battalion had nothing to hide, I readily agreed to this. Colonel Havergal brought them into my office himself and after introducing us, left them with me. I asked for the letters file and started to go through it with them. After what seemed an eternity, I got rather testy with them and suggested that they took the file into a quiet corner where they could go through it in peace. This they did, and after a couple of hours they asked my permission to photocopy some of the letters on file. I told them that they could go one better than that and take the file away, on condition that it was returned in due course.

A couple of months later the file was returned to me and the two NCOs told the CO and me that they had learned more from the correspondence on file than from any other source. I often wondered at the outcome, as included in one letter were the names of a CO and a QM of one particular infantry battalion who allegedly HAD accepted cars from a sutler as appreciation for being given a contract. One sutler named another and said he had murdered his cousin. There were many other accusations. After all this, I unashamedly accepted a bribe – a suit which Baghi Shah said was 'made to measure'. If this was the case, he must have used an odd-shaped model for measurements. Mary also got a hair drier – which still works twenty-two years afterwards.

Our family, along with many others, had a lucky escape on New Year's Eve, 1976. The married quarter 'patch' in Nelson Drive had a Community Centre where families could meet for various activities and festivities. Some locals had been welcomed as 'associate members' and everyone got on well together. We intended to see the New Year in at this Centre. As we pulled up in our car, a young Guardsman who was on roving patrol came up to me and said that Guardsman Russell, his colleague, had spotted a black holdall under the building and so they had cleared the building and sent for the Bomb Disposal Squad. We quickly moved on to the Sergeants' Mess and celebrated in true style. During the evening we were informed that the holdall had contained enough explosives to blow the building sky high and probably some of the nearest married quarters with it. Interestingly, it was proved later that the IRA had planted the bomb and even more interestingly, not a single member of the local population had entered the club that night, either before or after the holdall was discovered. One can draw one's own conclusions from this. We returned to the Centre in the early hours of New Year's Day, where a really good party was in full swing. Guardsman Russell was awarded a Commendation for this alertness and quick reaction to the problem. His chum was Guardsman Armstrong. IT IS WORTH NOTING THAT THE BOMB WAS SET TO GO OFF AT MIDNIGHT!

The visit of the Regimental Band proved a success, volatile and in the end mystifying. Lt. Colonel Dick Ridings was the Director of Music and volunteered the band for every type of duty and function. They performed brilliantly, to say the least. However, the musicians had a shock when the CO made them march around Strabane in full dress clothing. The locals loved it despite this being an IRA stronghold, and the most troublesome area on the north/south border. Dick made me walk alongside the front rank throughout the display, working on the theme that if he was to go sky high, he would have a Quartermaster with him. I was never quite sure whether he expected to go to heaven or hell if the worst happened.

The Band gave a concert in the gymnasium, and without any warning he called me on to the stage, issued me with a side-drum and sticks, and struck up with the march Radetsky – not an easy part. Anyhow, the Guardsmen seemed to enjoy it. The volatile and mystifying part of the band's visit was at the end. On the way to the airport on the return journey, the truck carrying the band's equipment caught fire and numerous instruments and some full dress clothing were completely destroyed. Nobody claimed responsibility for this, so it was always assumed that the fire was an accident. Nevertheless, it remains a mystery to this day as to whether this was the case or whether it was sabotage or an act of terrorism.

The cost of living in N.I. for both soldiers and their families is extremely high. To offset this in part, there was an additional allowance of fifty pence per day per person. Fairly early in our tour there, the excellent Secretary of State for Northern Ireland, Roy Mason MP, with his charming wife, visited the Battalion. The CO and Mrs Fiona Havergal put on a really first-class dinner, to which Mary and I were invited. Throughout dinner Fiona kept bringing up the subject of prices of foodstuffs and heating-type fuels. Both Mr and Mrs Mason were most interested and sympathetic and asked me to fill in any gaps left by Fiona. Without question it was not a coincidence that within a few weeks of them returning to London, the N.I. allowance was doubled to £1 per day. Once again, the power behind the throne...!

Gordon Garret had left the Battalion at Windsor to become the RSM in the other Battalion. George White came for a short while and then left for civilian life. Tommy Cook stood in very well for a little while and then 2 Coldstream Guards backed a winner. RQMS John Savelle was an outstanding soldier and went on to become the senior Quartermaster in the Household Division. Not only is he excellent at administration, but he is also a wit and very amusing. There is never a dull moment when John is about and although life was very busy, we had lots of fun.

The highlight of the Battalion tour in N.I. was the visit by the Queen to Coleraine. The Commanding Officer had under his command Grenadier and Scots Guards, the Black Watch, the Royal Hants, the WFRs, the UDR and detachments from the Royal Engineers, Royal signals, RAOC, RPC and RMP. On several days in August 1977 the feeding strength was over 1000 and on the 18th it reached 1800. Meals were needed around the clock and the workload for the cooks was nothing short of incredible. The two butchers prepared almost 9,000 portions of meat in three days.

One of my ex-Officer Cadets at Mons was the Battalion Liaison Officer, Bill Stewart. He and I visited various farms to seek permission for units to set up camp on their land. Without exception, permission was given. One poor man left us speechless (not easy in Bill's case as he was an incredible chatterbox and great at getting people 'on side'). We had asked if a Company of 118 Scots Guardsmen could set up their tents near his farmhouse. The farmer said yes, by all means, but would we mind if his wife fed the soldiers a 'few at a time' as the range was not very big. Bill had a job explaining that the troops would cook for themselves. After the royal visit was over, we visited each farm and gave the occupants a Regimental Plaque. Ironically, with the troubles in Ireland, it is unlikely that the plaques have ever been displayed.

During the Queen's visit to Coleraine, there was a knock-on story to the garden party at Victoria Barracks fourteen months earlier. There was a garden party in Coleraine to which a party of Coldstreamers and their wives were invited. In the party was Sergeant Cavnor, and when he was presented to the Queen, she recalled without prompting a conversation she had had with him at Windsor the previous year. He was amazed and so were those listening in. Prince Philip played a full and active part in this visit.

All aspects of the social life of the soldiers and their families had to come from within the Battalion. Fiona Havergal, Lynn Smith and several other wives gave an enormous amount of help to the families. Each of the married quarter 'patches' had a Community Centre and the soldiers had the Lillywhites' Club in barracks. All of these were very successful and kept the morale high. The Wives' Club was also very active. Captain Albert Smith gave the clubs terrific support.

John Savelle prided himself on being able to obtain any type of store from official sources. On one occasion he got his 'come-uppance' and could have got me the sack. Prior to the Queen's visit, we put in requisitions for a huge amount of camp-type equipment, including wash-hand-type bowls. When we received the stores from the Ordnance Depot, in place of the latter were Bowls, Horse/Mule Feeding. He immediately put in another requisition for Donkey Irish (Bray not Neigh) for use in Paddock No. 1. I had signed the requisition, not dreaming that he would send it off to the Ordnance Depot. Unbeknown to me, he DID.

About two weeks later Colonel Havergal sent for me in his office. On entering he stood up and gravely said: 'Yours, I believe, Peter'. He insisted that I open the box, of which he had obviously seen the contents, in front of him and the Adjutant. There, beautifully packed in straw, was a 6-inch high donkey made of rope. Also, in the box was the fuel to keep the donkey warm. Fortunately everyone saw the funny side of this story, but it took months for us to live it down. The Northern Ireland military newspaper filled many columns with news of our donkey, asking after its health etc. I used to have it in my office but it is now hidden in a box in a top cupboard at home. Thank goodness for light relief in an operational station, even if on this occasion it was I who was the loser!

We had no cricket pitch for the Battalion, so Paddy Coyle, the civilian District Works Officer, managed to produce one in a field alongside the Officers' Married Quarters. One Monday morning my telephone rang and

The mule issued by the Royal Army Ordnance Corps.

it was the CO in a temper, ordering me to sack the groundsman at Cloony Park as the pitch was dangerous and in bad order. There was no point in telling him that there was no such person. John Savelle, who was very amused – especially as he had heard that the Commanding Officer had been out for a duck on Sunday, asked me what I was going to do about it. I said 'nothing', but by the Tuesday evening I had decided on my action: write a letter to the OIC cricket, who happened to be Captain Bill Stewart. This was a very long 'tongue in cheek' letter, which contained all my credentials for giving the merits and de-merits of a cricket pitch. I finished the letter by saying that I could not sack the groundsman as there was no such person. This letter was copied to Lt. Colonel Havergal and various other interested parties. Bill Stewart contacted me and was mortified at what the CO's reaction might be. He had no need to worry as the Commanding Officer rang me on the Wednesday morning simply saying, 'Touché, Peter', and roared with laughter. This was the end of the matter and I think the two most bemused people on the subject were Bill Stewart and John Savelle.

The relationship between Colonel Malcolm and me was volatile at times. He had a very short fuse and was inclined to tear a strip off someone who he thought had done wrong. I had known him since he was a teenager, and was the only man in the Battalion older than he. He was a brilliant CO, especially for a N.I. tour, but he did occasionally get things wrong, not on the operational side but on the man management/administration side. I think that I was the only person who was willing to tell him this. Once or twice I thought that he would sack me for my insolence but instead he respected my opinion and forthrightness. He put this fact in writing when he put me up for a 'Mention in Despatches' at the end of the N.I. tour. He did not get me an Oak Leaf, but he did get me a Commander-in-Chief's Commendation.

An event occurred in N.I. that was to shape my life after leaving the Army. Naturally I did not know this at the time. The Commander-in-Chief for Northern Ireland during most of our tour was Lieutenant General Sir David House. He made no secret of the fact that he held the 2nd Coldstream in very high regard, as his staff officers told us so. When he was due to leave Ireland, he came to say farewell to the members of the Battalion. The CO arranged a small luncheon party in the Officers' Mess, to which I was invited. During lunch he told us that he was retiring from the Army and going to the House of Lords in the appointment of Black Rod. This meant nothing to me at the time and went in at one ear and out of the other. Little did I think that this throwaway remark would affect about fifteen years of the life of Mary, the boys and me. Truth is stranger than fiction.

In researching material for this chapter, I have re-read copies of the Battalion magazine, *The Star*, which was published about every two months throughout the eighteen-month tour in Londonderry. Any Coldstreamer, or soldier for that matter, should read this excellent publication as it gives first-class information on what an accompanied unit gets up to on an operational tour. It is well written and edited, with lots of excellent photographs. This chapter has simply 'skimmed the surface' of the subject.

I have left until last details of our personal life, including what was the greatest setback in our time together. In theory we were not allowed to visit Eire/Southern Ireland, but in practice we visited Mary's family several times. Acting on advice from an Irish Guards Liaison Officer, Bill Mathews, we crossed the border at Aucnacloy and did not stop for a break fifty miles on either side of the border. Twice I was caught out by soldiers checking our car and documents on the border. The first time I showed my AA membership card as identification, not realizing that my army rank of captain was shown. The second time was even more stupid, as I had an army torch in the boot of the car. On each occasion I was given a friendly reprimand and told to be more careful in future. Eventually Colonel Malcolm got to know of our trips south and told me off for not seeking his permission; which he admitted would not have been given.

The setback was a medical one that could have cost Mary her eyesight. For several months, early in 1977, Mary was getting headaches and minor problems with her eyes. For example on one occasion, when giving Lynn Smith a lift in our car, Lynn pointed out that she had gone through a traffic light when at red. Opticians simply said that this was an eye problem. Eventually Mary told a civilian doctor, Dr. Brown, about the problem and he immediately diagnosed this as a medical problem and sent her to hospital. A specialist at Altnagelvin Hospital soon told Mary that she had a tumour on her pituitary gland and referred her to the Royal Victoria Hospital (RVH) in Belfast. She had permanent tunnel vision.

In hindsight, we were very foolish. We went to Gibraltar on holiday for ten days, which delayed her hospital appointment. We also insisted on celebrating our Silver Wedding anniversary on the 7th June before Mary was admitted to the RVH on the 8th June. So it was that we had the most worrying few weeks of our lives (apart from the time when Bob had meningitis as a baby). I believe that the RVH is probably the best hospital in the world for dealing with head injuries or illnesses. Thanks to the brilliant surgeon, Mr Gordon, and the wonderful staff at the RVH, Mary was successfully operated on. She had had her head shaved prior to the operation and her hair had just regrown when she lost large portions of it as a result of radiotherapy. As Mary has said many times since, this was a small price to pay for saving her sight. Sadly Doctor Brown died in a traffic accident without knowing that his diagnosis had paid such dividends. He must be in heaven, that's for sure.

I cannot leave the Northern Ireland section of this book without relating the daftest thing I did during the tour. Mary and I had a 'Smith's' alarm clock which was still covered by the warranty. It broke down, so I packed it carefully, addressed it to the Smith's factory in Scotland, and posted it. A couple of days later my telephone rang and a voice said 'Captain Horsfall?' 'Yes', I replied. 'Stay where you are, Sir, I'm coming to see you'. When he arrived in my office, he gave me the biggest rollicking of my life. He was the Sapper Corporal in charge of the Postal Depot and told me that our clock had started ticking and caused a huge bomb scare. It had closed their whole

Department whilst the Bomb Disposal Squad checked the 'suspect device'. It goes without saying that I have never felt so stupid in my life. I felt a 'right berk'. A story of the biter bitten!

The last few months of our tour simply whizzed by and shortly after Christmas 1977 Wilf Pickles and the RQMS went off to Caterham to start taking over the barracks there. Mary also moved there, which was just as well, as I had to work around the clock after I lost Wilf and John. The handover to the Greenjackets went without a hitch and I was the last Coldstreamer to leave Ebrington Barracks in March 1978. Before doing so, I went to see the Brigade Commander, Brigadier Webster, and he was absolutely gushing in his praise of 2 Coldstream Guards. It was fairly obvious that Colonel Malcolm would receive an award, so it was no surprise when he was made an Officer of the British Empire (OBE) some time after we arrived in Surrey.

Arriving in Caterham, I did not realize that my days were numbered in the Battalion I loved. Regrettably, Wilf decided to leave the Regiment. I was particularly saddened by this as, apart from him being a great pal, I saw him as my successor as the Quartermaster. Without doubt he would have been great in this post. A couple of months after we returned to the UK, Colonel Mitchell, the RLC, sent for me and asked me to remain as the QM of 2 CG for an extra two years. As Wilf had left by then, I was very pleased to agree. Then a very unusual thing happened in early September. A Scots Guardsman had been earmarked to take over the Guards Depot from Peter Clifford THAT MONTH. At the very last moment, he had decided to leave the Army. As a result of this I was ordered to go to. the Depot within a couple of weeks in his place. To say that I had mixed feelings is an understatement. I just loved the Battalion, but it is generally acknowledged that the job at the Depot is the top one for a Quartermaster in the Household Division. Also, we would be able to leave our awful married quarter at Caterham and move back into our own house at Farnborough. How ironical that the Regiment did not know about the above moves in advance, as Wilf would have been in his rightful place as the Quartermaster of the Battalion.

Mary and I were given a great send-off, so it was with heavy hearts that we left 2 CG for the last time.

The Commandant of the Guards Depot was Lt. Colonel David Lewis, a really great guy, and we remain friends of him and his lovely wife Sue to this day. Although we enjoyed the Depot and had some good times there, it was nothing like being in the Battalion. One of the off-putting things was that there were a couple of 'old and bold' Quartermasters in various posts who were very lazy and let the side down. The two exceptions were Major Lou Drouet, Grenadiers, and Major Fred Adams, Scots Guards, who were the Range Officer and Housing Commandant respectively, and they gave me terrific support. My staff was marvellous and RQMS George Winsome and Colour Sergeant Paddy Bambrick deserve a special mention. We sailed through all the inspections by officers from outside. Paddy Bambrick received the British Empire Medal for his efficiency in the clothing stores over many years.

I had always said that I would leave the Regiment at 50 as I considered that any infantry Quartermaster over that age would not be 'fit to fight' in the event of a war. Nevertheless when I put my notice in in November 1979, it caused shockwaves throughout the Division. All sorts of carrots were dangled to get me to change my mind. The Chief of Staff, London District, a Coldstream Brigadier, Peter Tower, guaranteed that I would be a Lt. Colonel within a year. As I was not due to be a Major until January 1980, it is doubtful if he could have fulfilled this promise. Anyhow the decision was made and I stuck to it.

Within a couple of weeks I had got a job, all signed and sealed, with a smallish Computer Company at Camberley. Life takes strange twists and there was about to be a big one. I was sitting in my office one day when the telephone rang and it was a friend called Bill Kirke, an ex-RQMS in the Regiment and a pal of mine. He was the Principal Doorkeeper in the House of Lords and he was speaking on behalf of Black Rod, whose name

Brigadier Peter Tower presents G.O.C. Northern Ireland Commendation,
September 1978.

he did not give. He asked if I knew of any Guards Quartermasters who
were due to leave the Army in the next few months, as Black Rod wanted
one as the Staff Superintendent. I was able to give him about six names of
really good guys. As a bit of fun at the end, I said that there was me as well.
Bill was enthusiastic but I squashed this enthusiasm by telling him that I had
got a job arranged, and anyhow would not be leaving the Army until June
1980.

Imagine my surprise when within ten minutes Black Rod rang me in an
attempt to 'chat me up' to apply for the post in the Lords. After some good
natured banter, he finished by saying he'd send me the job description. This
he did and it arrived in the post the next day. I had no intention of applying,
and it took a lot of persuasion by Mary to get me to do so. Space does not
permit me to tell the effort I put in to avoid applying. The end result is that
I was interviewed on the 28th December, 1979, along with three other

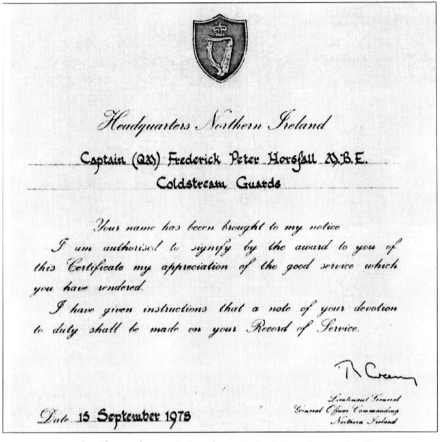

Certificate of appreciation, from G. O. C. Northern Ireland.

applicants. The remainder of the applicants were seen on the second Monday in January – a day when the Guards Depot received a lot of recruits/junior guardsmen. My duty was there and whilst I was busy, I received a message via Angela (my secretary) asking me to telephone Black Rod. By this time, of course, I had met the man who had left Northern Ireland to join the House of Lords – General House. It was lunchtime when I telephoned his PA and she put me through to Black Rod in his flat in the Lords. He told me immediately that I had got the job and congratulated me. I reacted by telling him that I could not report for duty until late April, after I had handed over the Depot to Frank Laurie. Black Rod said that this was his problem – not mine.

By the next morning, when I saw the new Commandant, Colonel Willie

With Peter Wright V.C. the day the author was dined out at the Guards Depot,
23 April 1980.

Mahon, Irish Guards, it was all cut and dried. From the 13th February until
the 24th April I would have two jobs: Staff Superintendent in the Lords on a
week-end, and Quartermaster of the Depot during the week. The Major
General commanding the Household Division had approved all this, so
there was to be no argument.

I will write about my takeover in the Lords in the next chapter, but I
have never kidded myself. Having General House as the C. in C. Northern
Ireland at the time of the 2nd Battalion tour there was a major contributory
factor to me being selected to join the Peers in the Lords.

Suffice to say, the Guards Depot gave me a fantastic send-off. The
Sergeants' Mess laid on a dinner for Mary and me and gave us a fabulous
present. All the Coldstream Officers, and many others, arranged a luncheon
party to dine me out on St. George's Day. I was honoured with the presence
of my friend Peter Wright V.C. What a way to leave the Regiment!

CHAPTER 11

Our New Home – Not a Bad Little Place!

TRYING TO DESCRIBE THE Palace of Westminster (POW) in print is like painting the Forth Bridge with a one-inch brush. However, it would be remiss of me not to give a rough outline. I am not exaggerating in the slightest when I say that the Great Palace is magnificent and beautiful both inside and out.

The present Houses of Parliament occupy the site of the old Royal Palace of Westminster, first built about 1050. From 1050 until 1066 it was the main residence of Edward the Confessor, and Henry VIII lived there from 1507 to 1509.

Nearly all the Palace, where most Parliaments had sat since the 13th century, was destroyed by fire in 1834. Interestingly, 500 Coldstream Guardsmen came from Wellington Barracks and assisted in fighting this fire. One book I read quoted a member of the Commons at that time, saying: 'It's great to get rid of the damp, wet, rat-infested, miserable building'!

The new Palace took from 1840 until 1860 to build and was designed by Charles Barry, assisted by Augustus Pugin. Together with the original Westminster Hall, the Palace contains Royal Reception Rooms, a chapel, the House of Lords, the House of Commons and extensive offices. It occupies eight acres and contains 11 courtyards.

The POW can be likened to a small town consisting of several boroughs. In addition to the two Houses, the building contains the Lord Chancellor's Department, the Inter-Parliamentary Association and the Commonwealth Parliamentary Association. The House of Lords is the highest court in the land.

I suspect that nobody knows exactly how many people work in the Palace, but I would hazard a guess at 2000. Worth noting is the fact that early in the '39-45 War the Commons was destroyed by fire caused by enemy aircraft incendiary devices. This resulted in the Commons sitting in the Lords' Chamber and the Peers using the Queen's Robing Room.

So it was that on Saturday 29th March 1980 I arrived at Chancellor's Gate to take over the Staff Superintendent's residence. It was located on the third floor, alongside the Royal Entrance at the foot of Victoria Tower. At

Lieutenant-General Sir David House K.C.V.O., G.C.B., M.C., the Gentleman Usher of the Black Rod, 1977-85.

that time the residence was rather 'scruffy' and neglected, and I will write about that later. Mary and I arrived in a car packed with personal items, and I was very concerned at the thought of carrying everything up to the third floor. My worry was without foundation as within minutes – yes minutes – the Porters descended on us and transported all our possessions upstairs. It is worth commenting at this stage that throughout our 15 years in the Lords this was the sort of service that the wonderful Porters gave us.

From 18th until 22nd February I had been attached to the Lords for the purpose of taking over from my predecessor (he was leaving on the 23rd to rejoin the Royal Navy). This handover was a mockery. The filing system was virtually non-existent and there was no system of accounting for stores or stationery. Lieutenant Commander Derek Brock spent the whole week talking and insisted on me meeting all sorts of people – some of whom had nothing to do with the Lords.

Fortunately his secretary/girl Friday, Mrs Margaret Curd, was absolutely superb. She was not just efficient but a very nice lady. From the 23rd February until I reported for duty on the 29th March, she telephoned me regularly at Pirbright for decisions and/or to keep me in the picture. Each Saturday I came to work in the Lords and took the opportunity to sign numerous letters, payrolls and other documents. Margaret even paid the Housemaids in cash each week.

One of the responsibilities of the Staff Superintendent was, and maybe still is, to cover for Black Rod during his absence. The 29th March–9th April was the Easter recess and quite rightly General House was on holiday. He and the Yeoman Usher worked very long hours and deserved every bit of leave they could get.

At the time I commenced work in the Lords, some parts of the Palace were open to the public most week-day mornings and all day on Saturday and bank holidays. These comprised what was called the Line of Route (LOR). Visitors were admitted at the Norman Porch and processed through the Royal Apartments, the Royal Gallery, Princes' Chamber, the Lords, Central Lobby, the Commons, St. Stephen's Hall and Westminster Hall. Guides were available at a very low cost but most people chose to make their own way through the building. On week-days the Palace had to be cleared of LOR visitors by 1 pm, to allow the staff to set up the House for the afternoon sittings.

During the week I was able to delegate responsibility for overseeing the LOR to the Ceremonial Advisor, Lt. Commander Bert Kemp. However, on Saturdays and bank holidays an officer of one of the Houses had to be on duty whilst the LOR was open. No officers from the Commons were on duty, so this duty fell on ME. This is why I was required during the Easter recess in 1980.

The full title of General Sir David House was Gentleman Usher of the Black Rod and his assistant in the HOL Chamber was the Yeoman Usher of the Black Rod, who was Brigadier David Stileman. David House likened the set-up to a military unit with himself as the Commanding Officer, the Yeoman Usher as the Adjutant and the Staff Superintendent as a combination of Quartermaster and Regimental Sergeant Major. This suited me as it was what I was used to.

Having performed Easter Duties, I returned to Pirbright until the 23rd April. A very amusing and interesting aspect of our private lives came up at this time. Son Bob had just qualified as a solicitor and had been given a position with Theodore Goddard in the city. He could not believe his luck at being able to live in the House of Lords from the date of his appointment, even in our absence. I was not too thrilled when I telephoned the residence from Farnborough, and instead of getting Bob, had my call answered by his friend John Stonard. He had not received permission to be in the POW. Parenthood remains an impossible/improbable task even in old age.

One thing was certain: I was not going to be lonely in the POW, as the following ex-members of the Household Division were in the Lords:-

Grenadiers – the Earl of Kimberley, the Marquess of Cholmondeley, Lord Carrington, Tom Taylor, Douglas Huxley. Scots: Lord Killearn, Lord Boyd-Carpenter, Sir Peter Henderson, Lord Lyell. Irish: The Earl of Shannon. Welsh: Lord Aberdare. Coldstream: Lord Digby, the Earl Ferrers, Lord Soames, Lord Suffield, Lord Fortescue, Lord Tollemache, Lord Somerleyton, Bill Kirke, Alan Barber. Household Cavalry: Lou Alder, Jim Hunter and Sam Keyworth. Without exception, they made me very welcome.

Being a member of the Marylebone Cricket Club (MCC), the only Lords I knew was the cricket ground at St John's Wood. Fortunately, having spent some time in the Palace of Westminster (POW) during February and March, it was not too much of a cultural shock when Mary and I started to live there.

In 1960 there were eleven residences in the POW. In the Lords they were those of the Lord Chancellor, Black Rod, Yeoman Usher, Staff Superintendent and Resident Engineer. In the Commons were the Speaker, Serjeant at Arms, Deputy Serjeant at Arms, Speaker's Secretary, the Head Office-Keeper and his Deputy. Now only the Lord Chancellor and the

Speaker reside. My residence was excellent but my successor's is awful – being the top floor, with sloping ceilings, in 7 Old Palace Yard, which is opposite the POW.

The decoration in our residence was very poor and the Works Department wanted to redecorate throughout. Having discussed this with Mary, we did not let them do this. For the first five years or so that we were in the Palace, we had one room decorated each year – usually when we were on holiday. This was a decision that we never regretted, because after that time the flat looked terrific.

In theory my boss was the Lord Great Chamberlain, the Marquess of Cholmondeley and my job description said 'attend on the Lord Great Chamberlain (LGC) on State Occasions'. I got along very well with him and it was a sad day for me when he died. Apart from state occasions, or meetings, the LGC rarely came into the Lords and therefore my day-to-day boss from 1980-85 was the Gentleman Usher of the Black Rod, General Sir David House.

The Lord Great Chamberlain changes on the death of a Sovereign and three families take it in turn to fill this post. Black Rod's post rotates through the three services, Army, Royal Air Force and Royal Navy, and is for a retired officer of General or equal rank from the other services. I will write more about these later. Black Rod has an assistant who helps with his duties in and around the House of Lords (HOL) Chamber. His full title is Yeoman Usher of the Black Rod but he is usually referred to as the Yeoman Usher.

My own staff consisted of an Assistant Superintendent, the clerical Officer in my office, 11 Attendants, a Head and Deputy Head Housemaid and 40 Housemaids. On behalf of Black Rod, I kept a 'watching brief' on the 25 Doorkeepers. My full job description was incredible; I had a 'finger in virtually every pie.' A major part of my time was taken up with answering queries from Peers, senior and junior members of staff and liaising with every department.

In 1979 a Conservative MP, Airy Neeve, was blown up in his own car in the exit from the House of Commons car park, alongside the Clock Tower (commonly known as Big Ben). This resulted in the Custodians (Security Staff) being taken over by the Metropolitan Police with a Chief Superintendent in charge. In 1980, when I arrived, this was Ken Evans.

The following mind-boggling figures may be mentioned: in 1980 the total security staff was 168 and when I retired in 1995, it was 462. The latter figure was not a luxury, if one bears in mind that security was necessary

24 hours a day for 365 days a year. I am unsure of the breakdown of how many were police and how many security staff, but would guess at one third being police officers.

Generally speaking, the rooms occupied by the Peers and staff in the Lords were very clean. This was due in large measure to the excellent Head Housemaid, Flo Dunn, and her first-class Deputy, Jean Ryder. They were very strict and set very high standards. Most of the Housemaids were very good and were inclined to have their own 'patch', treating it with reverence. Unfortunately, the areas of responsibility were in a muddle. Until the 1970s the House was poorly attended and many offices were not in use. As they became occupied, Housemaids were allocated to these rooms on an ad hoc basis. This meant that each Housemaid's 'patch' was split into various areas, in some instances on more than one floor. It took about two years for me to get this put right, by literally measuring rooms and other areas.

The corridors, lavatories, washrooms and common user areas were very poor, bordering on filthy. This was because three different Companies/ Departments were responsible for their cleanliness. One Company cleaned the uncarpeted areas, another the carpeted, and a third the lavatories. This meant that at times four different cleaners – including the Housemaids – would be cleaning within a few feet of each other! Naturally this led to arguments and bad feeling between members of my staff and others.

After about a year I became fed up with the situation and threatened to resign. As a result of this, Black Rod set up a small working party with representatives from the Commons and the Works Department to come up with the solution. It took them two years to resolve and one Contractor became responsible for all the areas not covered by the Housemaids.

By tradition, the Attendants in the Lords were responsible for the cleanliness of the House of Lords Chamber. This was most satisfactory, and despite the Attendants' pleas to get rid of this task, I would not change it. The reason was that the Housemaids' hours were from 7 am – 10 am, whereas the Attendants were on duty all day. Obviously the Chamber needed cleaning constantly throughout the day.

Initially the cleanliness of the Chamber was not of a high enough standard but thanks to the supervision of the Assistant Superintendent (AS), this quickly became better and eventually it was immaculate. Ray Scott was the AS and was an ex-Warrant Officer in the Royal Marines, so he knew the standards I demanded and he expected. We were pretty unpopular at times! On Mondays to Fridays, starting at 7 am, Ray and I inspected half of the building each and cracked the whip when it was needed.

Ray had joined the Lords a few years before me and after a while I realised that he had had a raw deal. To put it bluntly, some of the Attendants were useless. My predecessor was very idle and spent as much time away from the Palace as in it. This put far too heavy a workload on Ray's shoulders and his morale was low when I arrived. I did not realise this for a while and was inclined to blame him for the scruffiness, slovenliness and inefficiency of some of the Attendants. Once I did realise, I started to read the riot act to individual Attendants. They quickly improved once we got rid of a couple. I was able to recruit six super guys – Bull, Honeywood, Jelley, Nash, Nevin and Young. Within 18 months the standard had improved dramatically. Two Attendants already in post turned out to be absolute winners, Watts and Warburton.

Something happened a few months after I arrived that almost caused me to resign. The Attendants, via Ray, were always complaining about their poor pay. I never took much notice of this argument, as I was inclined to look at their gross pay, which included a lot of overtime. Several of the Attendants, and Ray, were earning considerably more than me, BUT were working between 72 and 98 hours a week. Eventually, in frustration, Ray produced a letter dated about 18 months before, from Black Rod, promising the Attendants a rise of £200 a year. I went to see Black Rod about this and a row developed. General House upset me by saying, 'Peter, we're only talking about £200' (or words to that effect). At that time the Attendants were on about £4000 a year, so £200 meant a lot to them. With that I lost my cool, told Black Rod to look for a new Staff Superintendent, and left his office. I meant it!

Black Rod followed me to my office, put his hand on my shoulder and apologised profusely. Bearing in mind that this was a General talking to a lowly Major, this took some doing. My regard for him leapt up. Within a month the Attendants had their £200, with a promise of more to come.

Another aspect in which the Attendants were treated badly was their awful changing accommodation and rest room. Also, the issues of replacement uniforms were always late. Ray and I set all these things right and the morale improved accordingly. Indeed, we all became a happy bunch and a great team. The Peers in particular appreciated both the Attendants and the Housemaids. General House became very fond of them and said so quite often.

At my suggestion, we started to have Christmas drinks for the House-maids. I believe this still continues. General House and his successors always made a speech and made the Housemaids feel ten feet tall. They, in return, made complimentary remarks about Black Rod's 'nice legs', he being in breeches and stockings! Ray Scott organized an annual Christmas Party for the Attendants and guests, and this was great fun.

This part of my story cannot be completed without the following very nice anecdote. When a vacancy for an Attendant occurred, I carried out interviews with applicants. James Nash applied for a post for which there were several excellent candidates. He had been in printing all his life, but in his late forties had been made redundant. I remember him saying that he was 'ashamed' as he had been unemployed for nearly a year. He was selected and when he had been in the Lords about two weeks, I asked him how he was managing for cash (being paid in arrears). He said, 'Do I get paid as well?' When I asked him what he meant, he said that he was enjoying being back in a job so much that he would do it for nothing. Those of us who have never been unemployed probably find this hard to understand. What a great guy!

The layout of the Palace is roughly as follows:- The Clock Tower is in the north, the side facing the Thames is on the east, Victoria Tower is in the south and the side facing Westminster Abbey is on the west. In general terms, the Peers' offices are on the west side, the Records Department is in the south-west (including Victoria Tower); the Lord Chancellor's Residence and Department are in the south-east, the Library, Catering Department, Committee Rooms and some offices for Peers are in the east. The south was initially a bit of a 'hotch potch', but is now occupied by the Accountant and some Peers.

Down the centre of the building are the more interesting and beautiful areas, the Queen's Robing Room, Royal Gallery, Princes' Chamber, HOL Chamber, Peers' Lobby, Central Lobby and HOC Chamber. The Upper House is in red upholstery and furnishings and the Lower House is in green.

I was determined to discover what every nook and cranny was for, especially as I maintained the Accommodation Plot for the House of Lords. Every Saturday morning, once the Line of Route was open to the public, I toured the building with my clip board. The building is a 'rabbit warren' and I visited everywhere, noting who occupied each room or area. This included the loft/attic area and the basement/cellars. Some people, including the Works Department staff, were mortified to see me where no other officer or Peer had ever been. Within six months I knew my area in detail and had this in a proper register in my office. The register was really meant for Black Rod and me but by the time I retired, about 20 different Departments had asked to be included on the distribution list. It was updated by me every few months and the Telecommunications Manager in particular found this very useful.

The junior staff in the Works Department were willing horses and always tried to be helpful. Unfortunately they were poorly led at the top and middle management level, and no one supervisor followed up whether or not tasks were completed. It therefore fell on Ray Scott and me to do organised and sporadic 'spot checks'. The exceptions to this were the Resident Engineer, Roy McNeil, and the Depot Superintendent, Eddie Norton. What a sad day it was for me when after a few years Roy retired through ill health and Eddie moved to Windsor Castle to oversee the works there! No satisfactory replacements were appointed during the remainder of my time in the Lords.

The Parliamentary Works Officer (PWO) was Wynne Lewis, a great guy but one who 'looked for glory' rather than dealing with the routine or mundane tasks. His main failing was that he would say 'yes' to virtually every major job requested by Black Rod and/or Senior Officials or Peers. As a result his huge Department was continually overstretched and in a muddle. Recesses were horrendous and the last few days were chaotic as we struggled to get the House and associated areas ready for the new session to start. At the end of the recesses, my life was a nightmare. I spent almost all my time in chasing people to get jobs done. I must emphasise that in most cases this was not due to the workmen or contractors; it was just that too much work had been planned – or unplanned!

After Wynne Lewis came Brian Sewell, a very nice bloke but one who left too much to his subordinates. The then Black Rod had no time for him and this did not help my cause in the least. It meant that both Black Rod and I were inclined to bypass him and deal direct with his various Departments. Fortunately the boss of the Furnishing Group was excellent and helped me enormously.

Things improved dramatically when Henry Webber took over as the PWO and Barry Hall became the Principal Planning Officer for new major and minor projects. Henry was seen during recesses and Barry and I had regular tours of the Lords and we had monthly meetings. These latter were initiated by me with the support of General House. He was absolutely fed up with not getting feed-back on how works were progressing and he was delighted when these meetings got off the ground. They provided an ideal time for me to put over Black Rod's policies and thoughts.

The Clerk of Parliaments in 1980 was Sir Peter Henderson, who was a really great guy. He was ex-Scots Guards and had been badly wounded during the War. I had a terrific rapport with him and the Lord Chairman of Committees, Lord Aberdare. I always felt comfortable with them and tried my damndest whenever they asked me to do anything. They were both natural leaders and led by respect rather than fear – perfect gentlemen but real bosses, a great combination.

If I were to write a job description for Black Rod, I suppose one all-encompassing word would be 'Housekeeping'. However, this would only tell about one tenth of the story. Apart from his duties in the Lords, he is also an Officer of the Order of the Garter, with occasional duties for the Royal Household, including some at Windsor. In fact his tasks could not be listed as they are so varied. He is a very, very busy guy. He also has a major ceremonial roll and until recent years spent a lot of time in the Chamber when the House was in session.

I soon made my mind up that my aim in life was to make life easier for him, and to a lesser extent for the Yeoman Usher. To do this, I made it obvious to everyone that all routine and 'nitty gritty' work would be carried out by me. For example, I was very proud of the fact that the Unions never once saw Black Rod during my 15 years at the Palace. According to General House this was not the case prior to my arrival, and he was always being involved with their reps. During recesses I never contacted him at home and made all decisions in his absence. He, and the two who followed him, never told me I had got it wrong, but I am sure that I did at times.

The Lord Chancellor's Department was a thorn in my side at times. Really those involved were 'squatters', as most of their work could have been done elsewhere. In 1980 over 90 occupied offices in the Lords. Really only the Lord Chancellor's 'personal' staff of say, a dozen needed to be in the Palace. It took until the late '80s to get some of these people moved out and to reclaim the offices for the Peers and our staff.

The 25 Doorkeepers in the Lords were ex-Warrant Officers from the Army or of equivalent rank from the Royal Navy and Royal Air Force. A few of them were real 'prima donnas' and/or childish. They did not like being told to do things or that they had got something wrong. What a stroke of luck for me that in the early days the Principal Doorkeeper was Bill Kirke – ex RQMS in my Regiment, who knew me well. I think that he must have told his men that I was not to be messed about with. The one Redcoat, who greets everyone at Peers' Entrance, was my very dear friend and outstanding ex-Garrison Sergeant Major, Tom Taylor MVO, MBE. He gave me the most wonderful support and advice.

To summarise some of my duties: overseeing the Lords' bookstall and the account appertaining to it, as well as emergency stores such as bedding, robes and hats for introductions and state occasions, first-aid equipment, and spare clothing for the Attendants and Housemaids. I had to liaise with the Garter King at Arms, provide guides for Peers' visitors to the L of R and Refreshment Department functions, and exercise control over the Counsel Robing Room.

In addition to my early inspections with the Assistant Superintendent, I did a walkabout each morning. This enabled me to report items for repair or replacement promptly to Engineer Control, who generally gave excellent service. I was also able to 'chat up' anyone who had a grievance and sort out problems on the spot. The Crypt Chapel is in the Commons territory but Black Rod expected me to keep an eye on it, as his office controlled the bookings for its use by Peers and MPs. Due to General House's initiative, the Chapel is now used by various denominations.

One task I hated was having to tell Housemaids over the age of 65 that they had to retire. Some of them were 70 or more and were doing an excellent job. I was on the management side of the Whitley Council meetings. Nevertheless, I did not always side with the 'powers that be'. For example, when the Establishment Office tried to make the whole of the Lords a non-smoking area, I sided with the staff and they won the day.

I sympathised with them as it was not unusual for some of them to work a 13 or 14 hour day.

To make the team in Black Rod's Department complete, there were two absolutely top-class secretaries. Although these changed several times during my tour, they were always 'Jewels in the Crown' and a wonderful asset to all three Black Rods. They constantly supported and helped me, particularly during recesses.

CHAPTER 12

The State Opening of Parliament

M Y FIRST STATE OPENING of Parliament was in November 1980. It is necessary to give some background to the ceremony before going into the details of the event itself. The SOP takes place annually and is the start of what is known as the parliamentary year. HM The Queen has attended virtually every year since 1953. Other members of the Royal Family accompany the Queen as do all the other Officers of State. To say that the SOP is a major operation is a gross understatement.

Prior to the SOP, Black Rod makes the appropriate arrangements in conjunction with the Works Department, police and other interested parties. He is also responsible for liaising with the Buckingham Palace authorities. No changes are made to the ceremonial without prior permission from the Queen, so the liaison has to be beyond reproach. In theory, the Earl Marshal (the Duke of Norfolk) and Lord Great Chamberlain (the Marquess of Cholmondeley) should take the lead in organising the SOP, but in practice they do not appear until late afternoon of the day prior to the event.

Now back to 1980. I had a shock when I looked at the SOP file in August. Expecting to find a detailed 'brief', all I found was one and a half pages of close type and the programme for the 1979 ceremonial!

Included in the brief was 'check that your morning dress and medals are OK'. This was the least of my problems. Both Black Rod and the Yeoman Usher took off for the whole of the summer recess, so I had no guidance.

I had already studied the video tape of the 1979 SOP in detail – with General House in attendance, so I knew exactly what to do on the day. Black Rod also made it clear that I was to be responsible for all the timings on the day. What I was not expecting was the questions raised by the Works Department, Security Force, Police, and the Furnishing Group. In the case of both the Works Department and Furnishing Group, there was no one person nominated as team leader. Therefore it was a case of 'the blind leading the blind'!

The idea was that the work would be carried out over the two weekends prior to the day of the Opening of Parliament. As mentioned previously, the Line of Route (LOR) was open to the public from 10 am to

117

4.30 pm on Saturdays. However, on these two weekends the Palace was closed to the public. BIG DEAL! The spectator stands in the Royal Gallery consisted of old railway sleepers and metal frames, which had to be man-handled up the long royal staircase. There will be more about that later.

Anyhow, over the two weeks prior to the event, everything somehow came together. This was in the main due to how well the members of the Works Department mucked in. They responded magnificently to my instructions, cajoling, chatting, tips, bullying; but most of all to my praise. I was amazed that not a single 'boss' from the Works Department appeared during the week-ends concerned.

In 1980 I recorded every aspect of the lead up for the SOP and every year afterwards added or subtracted items as appropriate. I would like to think that by the time I retired in 1995, there was an excellent typed brief for my successor.

One aspect of the occasion which I did not need to worry about was the part played by the Housemaids. The Head Housemaid, Flo Dunn, and her Deputy, Jean Ryder, were superb. They were responsible for the cleaning and layout of the Queen's Robing Room, including the royal lavatory, where Her Majesty would robe and disrobe. There were no properly laid down tasks for the Attendants, so the Assistant Superintendent, Ray Scott, and I set about allocating their duties correctly.

The greatest disappointment was the lack of co-ordination in the Security Force. This was unforgivable because after Airy Neave had been killed by a bomb planted by the IRA in 1979, the Metropolitan Police took over the administration of everything to do with security in the Palace of Westminster.

I should have smelled a rat and realized that things would be as chaotic as described above. Prior to the summer recess, Black Rod had told me 'to get involved in anything and everything to do with the SOP'. In the event, he was delighted with the way things went both before and after the event. Praise indeed, as General House had a short fuse and had no time for inefficiency.

The early morning rehearsal for the SOP was the cause of a few headaches for me in the early 80s. This was caused by no one person in the Works Department being responsible for all aspects of the arrangements. Everything had to be ready for 6.30 am, which in itself caused problems. The funniest incident was connected with a Coldstreamer, Alec Dumon, who had taken over from Tom Taylor as the Messenger Sergeant Major of the Queen's Bodyguard. He asked me a question to which I did not know

With Messenger Sergeant-Major Tom Taylor M.V.O., M.B.E., May 1986.

the answer: Should the small iron gates at the side of the Sovereign's Entrance be open to allow the 'footman', on dismounting from the Queen's coach, to walk through ready to assist in stopping the coach? When I asked the Works staff, they could not find the key to the padlock. A hacksaw had to be produced to cut through the chain. I have never forgotten the wink Alec surreptitiously gave, as if to say 'GOTCHA'!

To summarise some of the tasks I either supervised or checked on:- the pool of robes ready for issue, installation of televisions in the Royal Gallery and Queen's Robing Room, the royal 'loo' cleaned and appropriate items placed in there, the purchase of perfume for the Queen, brandy for the medical tray, shelf for clock in Norman Porch, Annexe to Queen's Robing Room prepared for use by Gentlemen at Arms, 'Cherry Picker' for use by window cleaners, removal of railings in Old Palace Yard for the rehearsal and actual day, dates for erecting and dismantling canopy outside Chancellor's Gate, removal of security scanners at foot of Royal Staircase, safe keeping of hamper for use by the Queen's party, stands for umbrellas, signs cleaned and placed in position, the ordering and paying for flowers for the Queen, the arrival of the second Throne from Houghton Hall and wheelchairs for the

disabled. Quite honestly, the list was endless. Fortunately I had two tremendous allies in the Furnishing Group in David Kempton and Tony Frost. The workers themselves were terrific; it was the leadership that was poor.

The worst example of 'neglect' was the poor treatment the magnificent cover for the table for the Crown received. This would arrive in my office on the morning of the SOP in a cloth bag and in an almost 'screwed up' condition. Sylvia Heathfield, one of the Housemaids, who was an expert with a needle, invariably had to do a quick repair of damaged areas. It took me ten years to get permission to keep the cover in my store with an appropriate purpose-made wooden case to give it protection.

On the day of the SOP I had Attendants and Housemaids at strategic positions in the Lords to give assistance to the Peers and guests as required. This included robing, needlework and numerous other minor tasks. Ede and Ravenscroft gave massive and efficient support in providing robes and dressing Peers. The Doorkeepers gave exemplary advice to anyone and everyone. The three Comptrollers of the Royal Household during my tour, Sir Eric Penn, Sir Johnny Johnston and Sir Malcolm Ross, were always gushing in their praise for all arrangements made connected with their duties.

As I had known Malcolm Ross, late Scots Guards, since he was a young officer, I was able to introduce him to Black Rod. Without question this made liaison with Buckingham Palace better and resulted in some adjustments and fine tuning of the SOP, for the good of all concerned.

The afternoon prior to the SOP is, to say the least, chaotic, but unfortunately in 1980 nobody bothered to tell me! The only instructions Black Rod gave me were to have the door to the Norman Porch unlocked and manned by a Security Officer (SO) or a Police officer. What he did not tell me was that at various times Officers of State, the Heralds, Gentlemen at Arms, The Queen's Bodyguard of the Yeomen of the Guard, the staircase party from the Household Cavalry, television crews, media commentators and senior officials from the Royal Household would arrive, not only at the Norman Porch but at other entrances to the Palace of Westminster.

Added to the above were Peers and officials from both Houses, who battered me with questions on the ceremony and administration appertaining to the SOP. By 5pm I was punch drunk. The Lord Great Chamberlain (the late Marquess of Cholmondeley – a super man to say the least) arrived mid-afternoon and wanted various answers, some of which I knew and some I had to find out! This was the first time I met the Earl Marshal (the Duke of Norfolk), who as well as being a smashing guy, loved to stand and gossip. Being very busy, I did not always appreciate this. The one point that both the Lord Great Chamberlain (LGC) and Earl Marshal (EM) made to me was that I was responsible for all timings to be strictly adhered to.

At exactly 5 pm, the Duke of Norfolk, in a booming word-of-command-type voice, said: 'Gentlemen, it's 5 o'clock so we'll get started'. For the next 50 minutes or so he ran the rehearsal of the internal aspects of the SOP like an early morning drill parade controlled by a VERY STRICT Regimental Sergeant Major. It was a joy to behold as he got a grip on everyone, including the young lady acting as the Queen and (his words) the 'pack of cards including the joker' (the nickname for the Heralds, who were past masters at MARCHING OUT OF STEP with each other – no easy task!)

Several questions took me by surprise and I had no warning whatsoever: e.g.: 'Where do the Yeomen store their Partisans (huge axes) overnight?'; 'Where is the Standard for the Gentlemen kept?'; 'Has the route used by the Yeomen been recced and cleared?'; 'Where is the hamper for the Queen to be kept and is it secure?' To be frank, the afternoon was a shambles and my cuff got longer and longer. One very unusual aspect that afternoon and evening was that it seemed that every second person in the royal procession, Royal Gallery and Princes' Chamber knew me and acknowledged me. General David House, an ex-Royal Green Jacket, commented on this fact and said that I knew more people than he did. Obviously this was due to

State Opening of Parliament, 1989.

my tours at Sandhurst, Mons Officer Cadet School and as the Quarter-master of the 2nd Battalion Coldstream and Guards Depot.

At about 10 pm I had my last walkabout and visited all the inside areas to be used at the SOP. I expected to meet just a few Security Officers during my tour but had a surprise. Black Rod and his two secretaries were still laying out the name cards in the Chamber of the House of Lords.

Part of my job description read 'Attend on the Lord Great Chamberlain on State Occasions in the Palace of Westminster'. Regrettably I don't think that the LGC knew that my day started at 6.45 am. From then until the Chamber is ready for the afternoon sitting – more about that later – the Staff Superintendent does not have a minute to himself. He is expected to be a fountain of knowledge on EVERY aspect of the SOP. In many ways 1980 was a nightmare, but thanks to the excellent rapport I had with everyone, all seemed to go well.

The best description of the ceremonial aspects of the SOP is written in a novel by (Lord) Bertie Denham. Although the book is fictional, Lord Denham is able to give the factual events – because he was the Government Chief Whip in the Lords for about 14 years. He writes here in his (fictional) position as the Deputy Chief Whip, which carried the appointment of Captain of the Yeomen of the Guard. He has given me permission to use the following text in my book:-

'The procession was moving in slow time up the Royal Gallery, through banks of seasoned spectators. In front of them, lining the route on either side, were spaced members of The Queen's Body Guard of the Yeomen of the Guard, of whom I was the Captain. Known as 'The Oldest Guard', it was made up of retired warrant officers and sergeants wearing Tudor hats, doublets, breeches and stockings, and armed with partisans, the infantry weapon of the period, all virtually unchanged since the time of the first Elizabeth.

'My own uniform consisted of a double-breasted, tailed scarlet tunic, with a stand collar and gold epaulettes, aiguillettes, embroidery and sash, known as a coatee, skin-tight overalls of dark-blue cloth. With a wide gold oakleaf striped over the side-arms and long-spurred wellington boots; my sword was slung on the left and I carried a black silk cocked hat with its plume of swan feathers in one white-gloved hand and my stick of office, ebony mounted and tasselled in gold, in the other. To my right marched the Captain of Her Majesty's Body Guard of the Honourable Corps of Gentlemen-at-Arms, 'The Nearest Guard', composed of retired field officers, was more or less similarly dressed, his being the cavalry, mine the infantry, version of army full dress circa 1836. But he, poor chap, had to carry a bulky cavalry sword with its steel scabbard on his left hand, leaving his right to cope with his heavy brass helmet, surmounted by its high plume of longer white swan's feathers, as well as his gold stick.

'The Royal Gallery, one hundred and ten feet long, forty-five feet wide and forty-five high, decorated and gilded from floor to ceiling throughout its entire length, is in reality only a passage. Its sole purpose in life is to enable the Sovereign, crowned, robed and accompanied by her great Officers of State in full dress, to walk the procession from the Robing Room at one end, through the Princes' Chamber at the other, and thence into the Chamber of the House of Lords, there to meet the Lords Spiritual and Temporal and the Commons, in Parliament assembled, at the State Opening of Parliament. These four rooms, the most magnificent in the entire Palace of Westminster, were conceived by Barry the architect and Pugin his designer with this one annual occasion in mind.

'There was an air of almost tangible drama and solemnity as the procession moved slowly forward. The point of the stick in my right hand tapped the thick blue carpet noiselessly, in time with each pace of my left foot. When we had shambled through the un-dress rehearsals the night before under the patient guidance of the Earl Marshal, it had been hard to believe that anything remotely approaching the impressive could come out of it, but with the metamorphosis from workaday clothes into the butterfly colours of the pageantry, so had our very movements transformed themselves into an entity of military precision.

'To my immediate front was the Lord-in-Waiting on duty, wearing his scarlet or ermine parliamentary robe and keeping pace with the navy-blue-and-gold figures of the Vice-Admiral of the United Kingdom. Some way ahead, I was dimly conscious of The Queen herself on the arm of the Duke of Edinburgh, the bejewelled Imperial Crown shimmering on her head, with her train held by four scarlet-frocked Pages of Honour, preceded by an Admiral of the Fleet and a Cabinet Minister bearing the Sword of Honour and the Cap of Maintenance respectively. Beyond them again were the scarlet-uniformed Lord Great Chamberlain and the Earl Marshal of England in faded ducal robe, carrying wand and baton of office respectively, they alone of the whole procession walking backwards so as to be able to face their Sovereign all along the way.

'We turned into the Princes' Chamber, the rooms here being lined by the Gentlemen. They wore their white-plumed brass helmets and held tall seventeenth-century ceremonial battle-axes, and it was at this point that the procession split, entering the Chamber of the House of Lords by each of the two doors.

'We spaced ourselves in our allotted places to the right of the Throne while The Queen and the Duke mounted the steps and turned to face the assembled Peers in scarlet and ermine, Peeresses in long evening dress, long white gloves and glistening tiaras, Judges of the High Court in their scarlet robes and Members of the Corps Diplomatique, accredited to the Court of St James, each in national or ceremonial dress, all of whom had risen at her entry.

'The Pages of Honour arranged the long velvet train of her robe so that it lay displayed down the steps to her right.

'She bowed to the House as a whole. "My Lords, pray be seated."

'I stood there with the other members of the procession on our side of the Throne as everybody else resumed their seats.

'The Gentleman Usher of the Black Rod, in full court dress of black velvet and lace and holding, sloped on his shoulder from one black-gloved hand, the ebony rod from which he takes his name, came to the Bar of the House at the far end. He bowed to The Queen, turned about and left the Chamber to summon "the faithful Commons" to the Bar.

'We could hear the cries of "Hats off, strangers" fading progressively down the corridor as he passed along the way.

'A low murmur of conversation arose around the Chamber. I couldn't help glancing across to the bench on the far side where the Viscountesses sat.

'After a long pause the cries of 'Hats off, strangers' could be heard approaching again. This time they were accompanied by the shrill chatter of a hundred voices. I could never help wondering whether the Commons were genuinely unaware of just how much noise they were making or whether perhaps they did it on purpose.

'The doors were flung open and Black Rod reappeared, ushering in the Serjeant at Arms, Madam Speaker in gold-bedecked gown, the Clerk of the House, the Speaker's Chaplain and her Secretary. Together, these five bowed three times to the throne as they approached the bar. Then the rest of the Commons arranged themselves behind and around them.

'The Prime Minister and The Leader of the Opposition were in the forefront. Behind them stood the Foreign and Commonwealth Secretary.

As soon as they were all in, the Lord Chancellor in his ceremonial wig and robes and carrying his Purse, left his place to my front right and mounted the steps to the Throne. There he knelt to Her Majesty, took out the official copy of the "Gracious Speech" and presented it to her. Then he rose to his feet and took the three more precarious paces backwards down again.

'"My Lords and Members of the House of Commons..."

There was complete silence in every part of the Chamber and Galleries, as in a clear, level voice, The Queen began to read.

'In common with the other front-bench members of all the Parties, I had already heard the contents the night before, behind closed doors and under conditions of the strictest secrecy. Both Houses would hear it again that afternoon, repeated by the Speaker and the Lord Chancellor, before they began to debate the motion that 'An humble address be presented to Her Majesty thanking Her for Her Most Gracious Speech".'

So ended the wonderful description by Lord Denham.

After the Queen has entered the Queen's Robing Room (QRR) to disrobe and remove her Crown, a very moving and intimate 'ceremony' takes place. Her Majesty in person gives the four page boys a glass of squash and has a little chat with them prior to them leaving the room. Regrettably, this never gets reported on or seen.

When the Queen leaves the QRR, she pauses for a little while to speak to the Lord Chancellor (Lord Hailsham 1980-87) and the Duke of Norfolk and thanks them and congratulates them. This is a most friendly chat and humorous, the Queen being in a chatty and relaxed mood. No cameras are allowed at this time.

As soon as the Queen and other members of the Royal Family have left the Palace of Westminster, there is absolute mayhem. My task was to clear the Royal Gallery, Princes' Chamber and the top of the Norman Porch Royal Staircase. This meant signalling the Gentlemen at Arms, the Queen's Bodyguard of the Yeomen of the Guard and State Trumpeters to leave their respective areas. This allowed the Lord Chancellor to return to his quarters via the hidden door in the Queen's Robing Room, and for the spectators in the Royal Gallery to leave the building and/or meet their hosts.

At the same time the Works Department, assisted by the Attendants, prepare the Chamber for the afternoon sitting of the House. In the early 1980s the House sat at 3pm but nowadays it is at 3.30 pm. This is a major operation as it has taken about ten days to prepare the Chamber and everything has to be returned to normal within two hours. Quite honestly, those involved were, and probably still are, brilliant. By the time the Peers enter the Chamber for Prayers, not a thing is out of place and it is hard to believe that major ceremonial has taken place a few hours before.

Whilst the above is happening, various parties and festivities are taking place throughout the House of Lords. Some are in the offices of Peers and senior Clerks, but most are in the Peers' Dining Room and Bars. These are joyous occasions. Mary and I invariably had a luncheon party in our flat. The nine Housemaids who had been on duty during the SOP held their own party in my office. This meant that from about 12.15pm until 2.30 pm I had divided loyalties: to my guests in the flat, supervising and encouraging the workers in the Chamber, and (most importantly!) having a drink with the superb Head Housemaid (Flo Dunn BEM) and her lovely ladies. My marvellously efficient secretary, Margaret Curd, 'held fort' in my office with the latter. They enjoyed themselves enormously!

Two aspects of the day worried me greatly on each of the first three SOPs I took part in. Firstly, the Bar of the House was moved several feet towards the rear of the Chamber the week-end prior to the SOP, a massive task to say the least, as the timbers supporting the Bar recess into the floor by about five feet. When returning the Chamber to 'normal' for the afternoon sitting, there were several minor accidents due to the speed at which work was carried out. When I drew the attention of this to Black Rod, he agreed that in future this part of the operation would be postponed until the following day.

Secondly, and more important, was the lack of seating in the Royal Gallery (RG) for most of the guests. Never a year went by without several invited guests fainting or feeling queasy and having to leave the RG before the Queen processed through on her way to the Chamber. There was no fresh air in this enormous hall and the atmosphere was overpowering after about one hour. In those days there were three small sections of seating. They were allocated to guests of HRH Prince Philip; the Earl Marshal and the Lord Great Chamberlain, and totalled about 75, whereas 900 guests were standing!

The final 'straw that broke the camel's back' was a personal one. My two dear friends Don and Janet Hazzard had to leave the RG because Janet was overcome by the heat. They missed virtually every aspect of the ceremony, including the Royal Procession. After the 1983 SOP I asked the then Black Rod, Sir David House, if I could arrange for all the guests to be seated. Although he agreed with my views, he refused because an all-seated gallery would only hold a maximum of 650.

There were more faintings in 1984 so I once again raised the question with Sir David. This time he refused because he was due to retire a few

The Lord Great Chamberlain, The Marquess of Cholmondeley.

David Cholmondeley who succeeded his father as The Lord Great Chamberlain.

weeks later, at Christmas, but suggested that I raise the issue with the new Black Rod, Air Chief Marshal Sir John Gingell. I did so both before and after the 1986 SOP and again before the 1987 SOP. He would not even consider my proposal because of the loss of numbers it entailed for spectators.

A remarkable thing then happened. Fairly early in 1988 Black Rod told me that he had approached the Lord Chairman of Committees (the wonderful Lord Aberdare) and that he had readily agreed to my proposal. Incorporated in the works would be the erection of new purpose-made steel stands for the chairs in the RG to stand on. This was great news as a couple of years earlier a member of the Works Department had literally dropped dead when carrying one of the 'railway sleepers' (used for the old-fashioned wooden stands) up the royal staircase.

The result of the works referred to above was perfect, and I was immensely proud of the fact that the initial idea was mine. Ironically Sir John took all the credit for the works on himself even to the extent that when a new Yeoman Usher arrived, he briefed him thus when showing him the layout of the Royal Gallery: 'The guests used to stand but I have had seating installed'. In recent years I have heard many other 'officials' take the credit. Fortunately, many other people – including the seniors in the Parliamentary Works Department – knew the truth, as I had raised the issue many times in meetings from 1983 onwards.

Some funny and unusual things happened during several SOPs. On one occasion a Security Officer appeared at my office door and asked where the Duke and Duchess of Gloucester should be at that time. I was just about to give him a rocket for bothering me when I realised that the royal couple were with him (in all their splendid regalia). The Duke, rather bashfully, told me that their driver had dropped them at Peers' Entrance instead of at the Norman Porch. I had to rush them to the correct place, via a back staircase, where a very worried Yeoman Usher, Brigadier David Stileman, heaved a huge sigh of relief and escorted them to the Queen's Robing Room.

I completely 'bogged it' one year and unwittingly let down the late Lord Great Chamberlain. As mentioned earlier, I was responsible for all the timings. His Lordship was inclined to panic at times and one year I was answering a question raised by the Comptroller Royal Household when the LGC approached me and said that he thought it was time to move the Crown from the Royal Gallery into the Queen's Robing Room. Not being sure, I turned my back on him to check my written brief. Turning to face him with the answer, I was horrified to see him entering the RG to carry out his important task. With the television cameras on him it was impossible for me to call him back. HE WAS FIVE MINUTES EARLY! Remarkably, nobody but the members of his own family had noticed the cock-up. Afterwards I apologised to the Marquess of Cholmondeley and he was very nice about it. Interestingly, as far as I know, he never told General House. Also, each year he wrote me a charming 'thank you' note and the wrongdoing was never mentioned. This did not lessen my guilt.

The most scary moment was in the late 1980s, but I am unsure of the year. I entered the Queen's Robing Room to give the Lord Great Chamberlain the signal that it was precisely 11.26 am and time to invite the Queen to leave the Robing Room and process into the Chamber. As I performed the court bow, the Equerry to the Queen called out, 'What position does the Prince of Wales take up in the procession, Major Horsfall?' With the Queen, Prince Charles, Princess Diana, the Ladies in Waiting and a camera crew looking on, I told him. A whispered conversation took place between the Equerry and Prince Charles. 'And where does the Princess of Wales process?' Once again I answered. Another whispered conversation! 'When they arrive in the House of Lords, where do they sit?' said the Equerry. By this time I was getting worried as I could see that the Queen was getting exasperated. Nevertheless, I gave the answer from memory. In a booming voice the Equerry said, 'Thank you, Major'. I gave the appropriate court bow and left the Robing Room greatly relieved.

At the first opportunity, I checked my written brief and also the photographs in Black Rod's office to confirm that the answers I had given were correct – WHICH THEY WERE. Later I told Black Rod, John Gingell, expecting some sympathy, but he simply roared with laughter. That afternoon the Equerry telephoned me to thank me and said if I had not answered in a positive manner, Prince Charles would not have moved. Seemingly he had arrived back from Washington the previous evening and had not read his brief or told the Princess of Wales her position at various times in the ceremonial. The Equerry was most discreet but what he really meant was that HRH was in a foul mood!

Without question the State Opening is the highlight of the parliamentary year, particularly for Black Rod's Department. It was demanding, very hard work and tiring, but most enjoyable and a treat to take part in. Fortunately, by the end of my 15-year tour, I was an expert on every aspect of both the administration and the ceremonial. This was just as well, as the Marquess of Cholmondeley died after we had done 10 SOPs together and my last Black Rod, Sir Richard Thomas, had a massive stroke in 1993. My services were required in large measure to advise their replacements, David Cholmondeley and Alan Curry.

To finish this chapter on a light note. Due to the televising of the SOP, the part played by Black Rod when he acts as the Queen's Messenger on entering the House of Commons is well known nowadays. Black Rod is dressed all in black from top to toe, except for his white ruffle collar and chain of office. One year Sir John Gingell proceeded into the Commons, arrived at the Clerks Table, and as he was performing his first court bow, Dennis Skinner MP (from right alongside Black Rod) said in a stage whisper, 'I bet he drinks Carling Black Label.' The House was in uproar whilst Sir John, remaining poker-faced – no mean feat – said, 'The Queen commands that this honourable House attends on Her Majesty immediately in the House of Peers'.

No words can follow that!

CHAPTER 13

Hereditary or Life – It Matters Not to Me

THROUGHOUT MY TIME in the Lords, I aimed to maintain a neutral view with regard to politics. So whenever requested to assist a Peer, I totally ignored his or her politics. Indeed, in most cases (apart from the front benchers where it was obvious) I never knew what Party they belonged to. Similarly, it never entered my head to ask whether a Peer was hereditary or life. I did know that the Lords of Appeal and the Bishops were Life Peers, but that was about all.

If I had written this book a few years ago, the section about Peers would have been relatively short. Because of the ongoing discussions about 'Reform of the Lords', it is now necessary to write a full chapter on the subject. In doing this, I intend to write about approximately 90 Peers. For the sake of brevity, I will use the term (LP 19??) to indicate a Life Peer and leave hereditary Peers blank. Also, I will describe a Woman Peer as BNS rather than Baroness in full. Whilst talking about the women, it is worth noting that the wife of a Peer is known as a Peeress (NOT a Woman Peer).

Having a military background myself, I will start with those Peers who are from the armed forces. Without question Peers such as Admirals of the Fleet – the Lord Hill-Norton (LP 1979) and the Lord Lewin (LP 1987), Field Marshals the Lord Bramall (LP 1987), Lord Carver (LP 1977) and Lord Vincent (LP 1977) make a massive contribution to the Upper House. Lord Bramall has many outside interests and until recently was the Lord Lieutenant for Greater London. Lord Carver is a first-class author with a special interest in defence, science and technology. Both the Admirals have too many interests and hobbies to list here. However, one would question the hereditary peerages given to such past military leaders as the Earl Alexander of Tunis or the Viscount Montgomery of Alamein. This is not to criticise the present Peers with those names, but it does seem odd.

During my time there were three outstanding Lords Chairmen of Committees, a most important post to say the least. Lord Aberdare 1976-1991, Lord Ampthill 1991-1994 and Lord Boston of Faversham (LP 1976) 1994 onwards. Each of these brought their own style and charm to this

The Rt Hon Lord Hailsham of St Marylebone K.G., C.H., F.R.S.,
The Lord High Chancellor, 1970-74 and 1979-87.

demanding appointment. The Leaders in the House were also a mixture and it is interesting to see how they fared. BNS Young (LP 1971) 81-83 was outstanding. Viscount Whitelaw 1983-88 was highly respected and popular and good, Lord Belstead 1988-98 was outstanding, Lord Waddington (LP 1992) 1992-94 was very good, Lord Wakeham (LP 1992) was poor, and The Viscount Cranborne 1994-98 was outstanding.

The Lord Hailsham of Saint Marylebone was the Lord High Chancellor from 1979-87. I have no idea how good he was at law, but what I do know is that he had a great presence and dignity. He had a bit of a reputation for a quick temper but I never found this. If I ever did anything for him there was always a charming 'thank you' note or telephone call. His eyes always had a twinkle in them and I think he had a wonderful sense of fun. In the mid-80s he almost tripped on his robe when walking backwards, having given the Queen her speech during the SOP. I was present afterwards when the Queen told him that in future he must turn round and walk down the steps normally (he was almost 80 years old). He politely refused! Several days later we received a 'royal command': the Lord Chancellor would turn his back on the Queen in future.

After the 1987 General Election Lord Havers took over as the Lord High Chancellor in controversial circumstances. He was very ill at the time. Due to his illness he lasted about three months. During these three months a massive programme of refurbishing his residence had taken place. I have forgotten the exact amount, but I think about £60,000 was spent on decorating and furnishings. This is worth noting because when Lord Irvine of Lairg became the Lord Chancellor in 1997, an enormous amount of money was spent on refurbishing the residence.

The Lord Mackay of Clashfern was completely different to Lord Hailsham. A quietly spoken man with a Scottish accent, he had great dignity and a likeable nature. Both he and his charming wife were highly respected and got along well with everyone, Peers and staff alike. When they took over their residence in the Lords, the only expense was a different sort of bath! I was surprised when Lord Irvine made uncomplimentary remarks about the 'poor state of the residence' in 1997. Lord and Lady Mackay were most undemanding and very easy to please. It was plain to see why they were so popular.

I have no first-hand information about Lord Irvine as he took over as Lord Chancellor after I retired, but I have heard a lot about him, mostly unfavourable, I'm sorry to say. On one occasion recently I asked a member of staff who knows him well what he was like. He replied that he was not popular and was hard to work for. A sad indictment for a man in such an important and prestigious post.

Many interesting points come to light in the Lords. For example, two ex-Prime Ministers, in opposition for many years in 'the other place', got along well in the Upper House. One of the most moving things I saw was Lord Wilson of Rievaulx (Labour LP 1983) shuffling out of the Chamber in old age and Lord Home of Hirsell (Conservative LP 1974) waiting for him at Brass Gates and asking him how he was, before handing him over to Lady Wilson. Lord Callaghan of Cardiff (LP 1987) was a bit of a loner, with impeccable manners. When created a Peer, he was given a pokey little office in 1 The Abbey Garden. I had the job of showing him this and expected 'fireworks'. In fact he was most gracious and thanked me profusely.

When BNS Thatcher was introduced into the Lords, it caused much excitement, to me as well as to the Peers. I had been instructed to prepare an office on the riverside for Lady Thatcher, and we had a weekend only to do this. The room was tiny and we only had time to give it 'a lick of paint' and fit a new carpet. A few days later I received a message from Black Rod's secretary at 2.13pm asking me to meet Lady Thatcher at Peers' Entrance at 2.15pm. I got there at the same time as she arrived by car. She was quite gushing and greeted me like an old friend. Lady Thatcher had just arrived back from America, and throughout our walk through the building she was chatting away telling me about her super trip. Occasionally she stopped to speak to a policeman or Peer, animatedly, to say the least. She even kissed a couple of Peers.

On arriving at her new small office, instead of being upset as I anticipated, she expressed delight and congratulated me and my staff. Lady Thatcher told her secretary and woman detective that this would 'do fine'. Then came a classic moment as she said to me, 'Major Horsfall, if I bring a couple of pictures in, would I be allowed to bang a few nails in the wall?' I replied, 'No, my lady. If you bring in some pictures, WE will bang a few nails in the wall'. With that she grinned and said, 'Well, you know what I mean. Thank you'.

After that Lady Thatcher asked me to take her to the Refreshment Department Gift Shop, where she proceeded to spend about £100 on presents for a number of friends. The Head Housemaid, Rita Bird at that time, was the salesperson and did a wonderful job advertising her wares. For most of the ten minutes they were together, they were talking at the same time. Those who christened her 'The Iron Lady' would not have believed this hilarious scene. Within four days of the above happening, I received a lovely 'thank you' letter from this amazing baroness and lady.

Another interesting point about those given life peerages is: Should those from the arts or show business be selected? These included Lords Olivier, Miles, Grade, Attenborough, Lloyd Webber, Menuhin and Rix. One would raise the question despite the high calibre of these great men: Are they truly in touch with what goes on in the real world? Should they represent the public in the Upper House? The exception may be Lord Rix, as he got his peerage for his work for MENCAP.

Nobody can argue the merits of such figures as an ex-Commissioner of Police, Lord Imbert (LP 1999), former Speakers of the Commons, Viscount Tonypandy and Lord Wetherill (LP 1992), a General Secretary of the TUC, Lord Murray of Epping Forest (LP 1985), the founder of, and creator of, the Sue Ryder Foundation, The BNS Ryder of Warsaw (LP 1978). Anyone who has not read the latter's book, *Child of My Love*, is advised to do so.

On one occasion Lady Ryder came into my office, described herself as 'the biggest scrounger in the world', and proceeded to ask if I had any old office machinery. Needless to say, I gave her some. This continued during the rest of my tour in the Lords.

During my tour, controversy was caused by the selection of some undeserving life Peers. The best example of this was in 1992, when included in the same honours list as distinguished men like Jack Ashley, Denis Healey, Geoffrey Howe, Merlyn Rees, David Owen, Norman Tebbit and Bernard Wetherill, was one who had done charity work. There still seemed to be no reason for him to be created a Peer. This raises the question: why not a Knighthood or a 'gong' for such work?

The three most difficult Peers from the point of view of the staff and the Works Department were Lords Cocks of Hartcliffe (LP 1987), Kennet and Molloy (LP 1981). Recently I have been told that Lords Kennet and Molloy have mellowed – thank goodness! Despite the above comments about Lord Cocks, I must say that I agreed with many of his criticisms about the waste of public money on projects in the Palace of Westminster.

BNS Llewelyn-Davies of Hastoe (LP 1967) was very popular with everyone and the Housemaids loved her. She had carried out many senior appointments in the Lords and was very proud of the fact that she was the Captain of the Corps of Gentlemen at Arms 1974-79 (a special 'uniform' had to be designed for her!). General House was smitten with her and whenever he telephoned to say Lady L-D had requested so-and-so, it was like a royal command. Without question, Pat Llewelyn-Davies was the nicest lady I have ever met and I was terribly sad to hear of her death. R.I.P.

One of the mistakes Margaret Thatcher made as Prime Minister was sacking Francis Pym (LP 1987) from the Cabinet. He was an excellent MP and he is just as good in the Lords. Lords Richard (LP 1990) and Scarman, law men both, contribute to the workings of the Lords as do two ex-heads of Churches/Synagogues, Lord Jakobovits (LP 1988) and Lord Runcie (LP 1991). Lord Pitt of Hampstead (LP 1975) must be a very special guy as one of the first black men to be made a Peer. My staff liked him enormously. The Lord of Appeal whom I came to know best was Lord Keith of Kinkell (LOA 1976) as his office was next to my residence. It was not unusual for me to find a Lord of Appeal in his office early in the morning, late at night, at week-ends and even during recesses. This does not seem to be well known, which is a pity.

An extra special woman Peer was BNS Hylton-Foster (LP 1965). For most of my time in the Lords she was the Convenor of the Cross Bench Peers. Her enthusiasm, and that of the Earl of Shannon, have helped to see the numbers of Cross Benchers rise from about 70 to over 300. Her kindly attitude to those all around her is entirely the opposite to the present Leader of the House, BNS Jay (LP 1992).

I made a fool of myself with a Doorkeeper in the early 80s. I saw James

Prior MP sitting on the steps in front of the Queen's throne whilst a debate was in progress. I asked the Doorkeeper on duty why he had allowed this and he didn't reply. With a whimsical smile he pointed to a sign in Princes' Chamber which said Privy Counsellors COULD sit on the steps. A lesson learnt!

General House's last appointment prior to leaving the Army in 1978 was Commander-in-Chief, Northern Ireland. He told me that Roy Mason (LP 1987) was a wonderful Secretary of State for the Province and never shirked making a decision, no matter how difficult. BNS Falkender got a bad press and in the media, but she was very popular in the House. Three highly regarded women Peers were BNS Seear (LP 1971), BNS Stedman (LP 1974) and BNS Warnock (LP 1985).

Two Peers who were not popular with many of the staff were Lord Jenkins of Hillhead (LP 1987) and Lord St John of Fawsley (LP 1987). Lord Hunt (LP 1966) of Everest fame was highly popular, to say the least – great humility and a lovely personality. Ray Scott became very friendly with him and they did some trekking and climbing together. Nobody was surprised when Sir Peter Henderson was honoured with a life peerage on his retirement as the Clerk of Parliament in 1984.

Lord Boyd-Carpenter (LP 1972) caused constant problems for the Assistant Superintendent and the Attendant who looked after the Committee Rooms. Nothing seemed to please him and I was mystified by the whole thing. Most Peers were gushing in their praise for the service they received. Two stalwarts of the Labour opposition were Lord Cledwyn of Penrhos (LP 1979) and Lord Graham of Edmonton (LP 1983).

Two Peers in the House were in a squad of potential officers for the Household Division I trained in 1959: Viscount Massereene and Ferrard and Lord Tollemache. I was the Platoon Sergeant to Lord Somerleyton when he was a Lieutenant in the Coldstream Guards in 1953. Lord St Oswald served as a civilian in the Malayan Police with the 2nd Battalion Coldstream in 1948. Lord Monteagle was the Senior Instructor on the NCOs' Cadre I attended as a student in 1953. I became friendly with Lord Middleton MC who, as well as being a Coldstreamer, had a brother Christopher, who commanded the 2nd Coldstream when I was the Quartermaster. The Earl of Lucan, who went 'absent without leave' in 1974, was also in the Regiment, but I never served with him. Three of my favourite Peers were Scots Guardsmen: Lords Lyell, Westbury MC and Killearn. Lord Westbury's son was an officer cadet at Mons when I was the RSM; he went on to be a highly successful officer in the Scots Guards and the SAS.

I can relate a terrific story about another famous Scots Guardsman, Major General the Earl Cathcart, CB, DSO, MC. By tradition, in the Lords a military Peer is asked to reply to the Queen's Speech on the afternoon of the State Opening of Parliament (SOP). In the mid-1980s Lord Cathcart was invited to perform this task, which he did extremely well. On the evening prior to the SOP the Prime Minister holds a dinner in Downing Street. In attendance are all the members of the Cabinet and the Peer who is to give the reply to the Queen's speech. A few days after the SOP, Mary and I were at a private birthday luncheon party hosted by Lord Westbury. Towards the end of the lunch, where wine and port had flowed freely, Lord Westbury asked Lord Cathcart how the pre-SOP dinner had gone. At that His Lordship began to laugh and laugh. Eventually he said that he was the only person at the table to enjoy his meal. He went on to say that it was like a Spanish Inquisition, with Margaret Thatcher asking each Minister in turn to comment on the contents of the Queen's speech. He forecast that three of the Cabinet would be sacked – and shortly afterwards they were!

Ray Scott became a specialist in telling when a reshuffle of the Government would take place. When he found out that the Prime Minister was in the Leader's Room, with nobody but the Leader in attendance, he told me to expect a reshuffle. He was invariably correct. Incidentally, reshuffles were particularly unkind to those leaving a post and not taking up another one. One day they would be in a rather splendid office and the next they did not even have a desk or telephone. Two sackings nobody could understand were those of Lords Glenarthur and Lyell, who were both outstanding Ministers of State for Northern Ireland. When Lord Sandys lost his job as Assistant Government Chief Whip in 1992, he was more upset at ceasing to be Captain of the Yeomen of the Guard than losing his position as a Whip.

Another Coldstreamer, the Earl Ferrers, wore so many hats at one time that he could have set up his own shop. This was in addition to being an exemplary Deputy Leader of the Lords in 1979-83, and again 1988-95. A Grenadier in the House held a very unusual record which I heard him boasting about: the Earl of Kimberley has been married six times! Obviously he is a charming man with great charisma. An 'early bird', whom I saw sometimes at 7 am with his baby son, was Lord Avebury. I never liked to ask him why so early – and why the baby?

Other Coldstreamers I served with in the Regiment were Lord Alvingham, Clifford of Chudleigh, Digby, Dilhorne and Suffield MC. I never served with the Viscount Ridley KG, GCVO, TD, who has a fantastic track record, including holding the post of Lord Steward of Her Majesty's Household. Having met him socially, I can tell why he is so popular and respected. The Earl of Shannon is ex-Irish Guards and has many interests and hobbies, and is one of the senior Freemasons in the United Kingdom. His hospitality is of the highest order. Another senior Freemason is Lord Swansea, who is also a brilliant Olympic rifle shot.

I have tried in this chapter to be even-handed in giving an all-round view of both hereditary and life Peers. Many of them have very special qualities and tremendous experience in several fields. Some Peers I have left out of this part of the book, as I wish to mention them elsewhere.

One of the subjects that attracts a bad 'press' for the hereditary Peers is the fact that several of them are from 'down under' and from other countries, including Canada. I don't give an opinion; I just mention this in passing!

How to finish a chapter on Peers proves to be difficult. Living 'above the shop' did give me the opportunity to see who were the most industrious and hardworking. I cannot say how good each Peer was, but without question I got a 'feel' for what made the House 'tick'. Many hereditary and life Peers make a massive contribution and many serve no purpose – more about that later.

CHAPTER 14

Ceremonial and State Occasions

IN A PREVIOUS CHAPTER I referred to attending on the Lord Great Chamberlain on State Occasions. This included events other than the State Opening of Parliament such as visits by foreign Heads of State and other dignitaries.

The visit of the President of the United States, Ronald Reagan, on the 8th June 1982, caused quite a stir. We were half expecting this to be either cancelled or postponed, as the Falklands War was on at the time. The Royal Gallery in the Lords was chosen for the President's speech. Although no official announcement had been made, the original venue was to be Westminster Hall. Three people have an equal say in when the Great Hall can be used for such ceremonials. These are the Lord Great Chamberlain (LGC), The Lord Chancellor and the Speaker of the House of Commons. Unfortunately the White House in Washington 'leaked' this announcement before the Commons had been asked or told. Quite rightly, the MPs objected so the LGC had no option but to switch to the Royal Gallery. The Americans were upset but they had created the problem.

About two or three weeks prior to the visit, the Chief of Staff to the President, Mr Deaver, had a meeting with the LGC, Black Rod and me. Most of this was held at the foot of the Royal Staircase, underneath Victoria Tower. Some interesting points were raised and in particular the question of where Mr Reagan would enter the building. General House explained that only the Queen used the huge double doors which are described as the Sovereign's Entrance. The President would use the tiny entrance door in the Norman Porch. Mr Deaver got quite annoyed and tried to insist that the Sovereign's Entrance should be used. General House got very hot under the collar and disputed this. After a while The Marquess of Cholmondeley, a wise and tactful man, simply said, 'I'll ask the Queen, Black Rod'. Mr Deaver had no option but to shut up. A couple of days later the LGC gave us the answer from Her Majesty: the President would use the small entrance door into the Norman Porch.

General House reminded Mr Deaver that no arms and ammunition were allowed into the POW. I was told by Mr Deaver that no liquid refreshment would be needed for Mr Reagan, as the Americans would bring their own bottled mineral water, but I was asked if I would supply some ice (I used a Coldstream Guards ice bucket!). The final question I asked Mr Deaver was how many vehicles would be in the President's party. After a few seconds' pause, he said 'about five'. When he had left, Black Rod suggested that I double that number. On the actual day there were twenty – ALL LIMOUSINES!

On the 7th June two Lieutenant Colonels from the Signals branch of the American army appeared with an enormous piece of equipment. They asked if they could set this up in the Queen's Robing Room, which is immediately behind the dais where the President was to make his speech (hidden behind double doors and curtains). It turned out to be a teleprompter, which I immediately and irreverently nicknamed 'idiot's guide'. Whilst I was talking to these two officers, they told me that they were amazed and amused how everyone in and around the Royal Household was known by his appointment rather than by name. They gave numerous examples such as Earl Marshal, Lord Great Chamberlain, Master of the Household, Gold Stick, Woman of the Bedchamber, Comptroller, Master of the Horse, Mistress of the Robes, Black Rod, Garter King at Arms, Crown Equerry and many more. They were quite relieved when I told them to call me Peter!

Prior to the big day, Black Rod had told me that I was to look after Prime Minister Margaret Thatcher. I seem to remember that we laid out about 500 chairs and, despite the threats from the left wing MPS that they would not attend, every one was used. The State Trumpeters were in the Royal Gallery and the Queen's Body Guard of the Yeomen of the Guard lined the Royal Staircase, while five of them stood behind the President on the dais. The LGC had ordered me to ensure that NOBODY came up the staircase ahead of him and the President.

When the Prime Minister arrived about 30 minutes ahead of the President, she asked me to confirm the part she had to play in the proceedings, as she had missed the rehearsal the previous evening. After a few minutes, I excused myself as I had other duties to perform; she was standing at the top of the staircase where she was to greet the President. Several minutes later she called me over and asked if anyone would 'object if I sat down'? I told her that would be all right, so she did so. A few minutes later she called me over again and said (quote): 'I'm rather annoyed, Major Horsfall,' (silent thoughts – what have I done wrong? – Tower of London here I come!). I asked her why. Mrs Thatcher then said, 'If I'd known that I would have such a long wait, I would have brought some work with me.' IT WAS OBVIOUS THAT SHE MEANT IT TOO.

Within seconds of the President's car arriving, two great big guys leapt out and before anyone could stop them, raced up the Royal Staircase two at a time. The look on The Marquess of Cholmondeley's face was beyond description. What was even more annoying was that it was obvious that they were bodyguards and their jackets bulged.

Fortunately the whole morning went well and everyone seemed pleased. The President spoke brilliantly for about 38 minutes and his speech was rapturously received. The Lord Chancellor, The Lord Hailsham of Saint Marylebone, made a wonderful welcoming speech and the Speaker of the Commons, George Thomas, made a speech of thanks in his own inimitable Welsh style. Only those nearest to the dais realised that the President was using a teleprompter and most of those present thought that Mr Reagan had spoken without notes of any kind.

Mrs Thatcher is most feminine and charms the socks off everyone – me included! The 'Iron Lady' image built up by the media is not in the least fitting when she is not 'on the stage', so to speak. I looked after her on several occasions and she never ceased to thank me most graciously. Other people who have done her small favours or tasks tell me that she is the same with them.

On the day following the President's visit, there was a marvellous cartoon in the *Evening Standard*. This shows the two heavies rushing up the Royal Staircase, hands on left breast, with one saying to the other, 'Watch these guys in skirts – they look suspicious to me!' Needless to say, the Messenger Sergeant Major of the Yeomen of the Guard was not best pleased.

To digress, following upon my mention of the Yeomen of the Guard. In 1980, before my first SOP, I invited the Messenger Sergeant Major (MSM) of the Bodyguard to visit me so that we could do a recce of the 'Search' route and other aspects of the ceremonial. As much as everything else, this was a lesson for me to ensure that I knew the form. I had already carried out a walk of the route with Charlie Curd, the Assistant to Lt. Comdr. Kemp. On completion of our recce, MSM Cyril Philips and I went up to my flat for a drink. Whilst having this, I gave Cyril the printed programme for the SOP. He immediately 'blew a gasket'. The Queen's Bodyguard was described in the programme as 'Beefeaters'. This is the title of the officers who perform duties at the Tower of London and they are considerably junior to the Queen's Bodyguard. After Cyril had left, I went to see General House. He instructed his staff to destroy all the 1000 new programmes and ordered a new lot with the correct description of the Bodyguard. Black Rod also wrote a letter of apology to the Comptroller of the Household, which I copied to Cyril. All ended happily.

On the 24th October 1984 President Mitterand of France visited the POW and similar arrangements to those above were made. One thing stands out in my mind regarding this visit: I was asked to provide 'vittel' water for the President. Rumour had it that this ceremony would not take place in the Royal Gallery. This was to avoid any chance of the French guests seeing the huge fresco painted by Daniel Maclise of Wellington's victory over Napoleon at the battle of Waterloo in 1815. In the event, the Royal Gallery was used and so one wonders what the French thought of this. The arrangements for President Mitterand were similar to those for President Reagan but one got the feeling that the welcome was not so passionate or friendly.

Two thousand members of the American Bar Association held their centenary celebrations in Westminster Hall on the 15th July, 1985. The Queen attended with HRH The Duke of Edinburgh. A similar ceremony to that held for visiting Presidents took place, with speeches by the Queen, Lord Chancellor and Speaker. The Great Hall looked magnificent, with a huge bank of flowers, while State Trumpeters, a Guards Band, the Gentlemen at Arms and Queen's Bodyguard of the Yeomen of the Guard were all on duty. A super affair in every way.

After the ceremony in Westminster Hall, about 200 of the Americans, as well as about 100 other guests, were invited to a reception in the Royal Gallery. This was when I saw the Queen and Prince Philip doing what can only be described as a Jekyll and Hyde act. In Westminster Hall they both looked very formal and serious – all televised of course! There were no cameras in the Royal Gallery, and the two royals were completely relaxed, laughing a lot and really enjoying themselves. They overran their time-schedule, as they spoke to everyone. Fascinating to see. The Queen has an infectious laugh and when she laughs, everyone else does so too.

One of the most interesting and successful visits to London was by the President Weizsäcker. The President and his wife came to the POW on the 2nd July 1986 and Herr Weizsäcker addressed both Houses and selected officials and staff in the Royal Gallery. Nobody was sure what kind of reception he would get, but in the event he got a great one. One of the sentences in the President's speech was enlightening: 'With their Parliament, the people of your country have provided the best example of how to make freedom, justice and reason a reality through the democratic process. Democracy in Germany too was greatly influenced by the 'Mother of

Parliaments'. (This begs the question, what happened in the Third Reich in the 1930s?). He went on to say: 'We have not forgotten the lessons of the past. We Germans had to face the bitter consequences of a destroyed parliamentary democracy when we lost first our freedom and then peace. On this occasion here today, I am moved by the memory of those who suffered, here and in our country, as a result of violence of war. Forty-five years ago, parts of this venerable building too were destroyed by bombs'. The speech was all-encompassing and he deserved all the applause he received.

The welcome by Lord Hailsham and the speech of appreciation by Speaker Bernard Wetherill were quite excellent and drew enormous applause. It is worth recording the Speaker's final words: 'It has been said that today your country, Sir, is Britain's best friend in Europe and it is in that spirit that we welcome you to Westminster — as President of one of the world's great democracies; as an ally; as a partner in the European Community of free nations; but above all as a friend.' One would have been interested to know the thoughts of those present who had lost family and friends in the Second World War!

Mikhail Gorbachev became a household name in the 80s and early 90s but at the time of his first visit to London as General Secretary of the USSR Communist Party, he was hardly known. This was from the 15th until 21st December and one morning was allocated to the House of Lords. The Marquess of Cholmondeley asked Black Rod to organise the tour. He in turn told me to proceed ahead of the distinguished guest and party and make sure all was well. All went well except that I managed to shake Mr Gorbachev's hand four times — unwittingly of course! Because I was standing near the next place to be visited, he welcomed me at four different venues. The interpreter obviously did not like to tell him that we had met already.

We arrived at the Lord Chancellor's office a few minutes late and a quarter of an hour had been allocated to this part of the tour. Lord Hailsham greeted Mr Gorbachev like an old friend — gushing in fact — and took him into his office, closing the door behind him. General House got a bit testy at this stage and after about 25 minutes said to me, 'You'd better get him out, Peter.' Reluctantly, I knocked on the door, went inside and respectfully told the Lord Chancellor that it was time to move on. He, Mr Gorbachev and the interpreter were sitting round a small table and were obviously getting along famously. Even then it took several minutes to get the party moving.

Mr Gorbachev made it plain that he thought it was marvellous that so many attractive women worked in the Lords. He added that he thought that the Kremlin could learn from this, as only men worked there. What a charmer! No wonder Margaret Thatcher said, 'This is a man I can do business with!' Talking about women, General House was smitten with Mrs Gorbachev and described her as 'very attractive'. I agreed! I also took to her husband, as he looked one smack in the eyes when talking and had a dazzling smile.

Unfortunately his visit to London was cut short as the President of the USSR was very ill and not expected to live. Little did we know that this man was to play such a major part in bringing the East and West together.

In November 1987 a State Visit ALMOST took place! I say almost because it was cancelled four days before it was due to take place. Signor Francesco Cossiga, The President of the Italian Republic, was due to visit the POW on Wednesday 18th November and address both Houses in the Royal Gallery. As was our custom, on the previous Saturday we had a huge workforce preparing the Royal Gallery and surrounding area. Almost as much preparation is required for these events as for the State Opening. This includes building stands for the television and stills cameras, erecting a dais, bringing in various soft furnishings, placing out over 1000 gilded chairs, and improving the lighting, carpeting the gallery and Royal Staircase, laying out the Queen's Robing Room for the President, printing programmes (I still have my copy, although the visit was cancelled) and various other tasks.

After dismissing the Works Department staff late on the Saturday afternoon, Mary and I set off in our car for Farnborough. I could not believe my ears: on the 6 o'clock news the announcer said that Buckingham Palace had issued a statement announcing that the state visit was off due to the Italian Government 'falling'. As soon as I arrived in Farnborough, I tried ringing Black Rod, Sir John Gingell, without success. So I took a chance and telephoned Rick Braddock, who was in charge of the DOE workforce, and ordered him to have everything stripped down on Sunday. He did not want to do this without authority from his boss, but I insisted. Fortunately, when I contacted Sir John on the Sunday morning, he agreed with what I had done. By Monday morning everything was back to normal and it was impossible to know that anything out of the ordinary had happened.

On the 20th July 1988 a magnificent ceremony took place in Westminster Hall. To give it its full title, it was a 'Presentation of Addresses by Both Houses of Parliament to Her Majesty Queen Elizabeth II on the Occasion of the Revolution 1688-89, The Bill of Rights and the claim of Right'. We are indeed fortunate nowadays that these great events can be seen on colour television, but even this cannot do justice to the setting, atmosphere and splendour. In attendance were eight State Trumpeters, the Gentlemen at Arms, the Queen's Body Guard of the Yeomen of the Guard and the Band of HM Royal Marines.

In addition to the Queen and Prince Philip, the following accompanied them: Princess Margaret, The Duke and Duchess of Gloucester, The Duke of Kent and HRH the Prince Orange. Delegates from the Netherlands and the United States represented their countries. The Lord Chancellor, Lord Mackay of Clashfern, and The Speaker, Bernard Wetherill, read the Addresses from the respective Houses. The Queen replied to the Addresses.

Those readers who have visited Westminster Hall will know how impressive it is when empty. Imagine what it is like when laid out in all its glory, the stairs banked with beautiful flowers and all the dignitaries and military in all their finery. The words 'stupendous' and 'magnificent' come to mind.

During my 15 years in the POW several other major ceremonial and VIP occasions took place, but I think those mentioned in this chapter were the extra-special ones.

The reason I chose the photograph of Margaret Thatcher for the front of the book is to give further proof of her femininity. Prior to the Reagan visit, she missed the rehearsal in the Lords (the Falklands War was taking place). On the morning of the ceremonial, when the Prime Minister arrived, she insisted on showing LGC and me what her representative at the rehearsal had written on her programme. She said 'How clever she is' (etcetera), writing such things as: *Stand up, Move forward five paces, Greet the President, Turn left and enter the Royal Gallery.'* Margaret Thatcher was most animated and this certainly belied her 'Iron Lady' image!

CHAPTER 15

Sporting Heroes and 'Showbiz' Friends

SOMETHING HAPPENED IN 1980 that was to change my whole way of life. It was meeting the Bedser twins of cricketing fame. They were working directors of the contract cleaners who were responsible for large areas of the POW and the outbuildings. Eric came to see me shortly after I arrived in the Lords, and a little while later he introduced Alec. They were both excellent ambassadors for their company and wonderful public relations men. Having been brought up in Woking, which is a military town, and being in the Royal Air Force throughout the War, they were interested in 'all things military'.

A close friendship quickly developed and they sponsored me for Surrey County Cricket Club. I in turn took them to the Trooping the Colour and other ceremonial events.

Alec had had a most distinguished playing career with England, and when I met him he was the Chairman of the Selectors for the English cricket team. He and Eric frequently took me to cricket, both international and county matches, and I was given the VIP treatment. For example, during Test Matches I would be invited to lunch and invited to sit with England selectors and ex-international cricketers. One occasion sticks out in my mind: in a group seated at a round table of 10, only Eric and I had not played cricket for England. I sat there enthralled, saying 'nowt', whilst such giants as Alec, Peter Parfitt, Brian Close, Fred Titmus, David Allen, Alan Moss, Bob Appleyard and Peter May came out with anecdote after anecdote.

During other matches I met numerous ex-players and famous people in international sports. The biggest treat was meeting my boyhood hero, Leonard Hutton. When I met him for the first time in the Surrey Committee room, I told him just that and he simply said, 'How kind of you to say so.' Two great journalists I met and had long conversations with were Jim Swanton and John Woodcock. Unbelievably, I sat for a complete afternoon with Gubby Allen, and as there was nobody else in the Middlesex Committee Room, I watched and talked cricket with him throughout. I remember him complaining bitterly about the poor quality and high cost of tea in the members' dining room. He ORDERED the secretary to do something about it. This was Joe Hardstaff and he did so!

Micky Stewart, John Poland, Sir Alec Bedser, the author, Eric Bedser, Edward Crofton, March 1999.

Space does not allow many names to be named here, but some will be mentioned elsewhere. Two non-cricketers I met were the golfer, Henry Cotton, and the footballer, Ted Drake. One wonderful memory concerns the world-class former champion, Henry. We were in the Surrey Committee Room when Eric mentioned to him that he was having trouble with his putting. Before we knew it, Henry was giving Eric a lesson on putting with an imaginary putter. A great sight! Ted Drake told me a lovely story: in one international match he had scored five goals and was convinced that he had scored a sixth, which the referee disallowed. When he next caught up with the referee, he told him politely just that. The referee replied, 'Bloody hell, Ted, you've got five – I could hardly give you a sixth!' Ted accepted this with good grace but one wonders what a modern centre forward would say.

When Mary and I went to Australia for the first time in 1981, Alec gave me a letter of introduction to Neil Harvey, who had been the youngest player in the great Bradman team of 1948. As will be seen later in this chapter, this has had a great 'knock-on' effect on our lives. We have accumulated a vast number of friends, mostly through cricket and other

With Denis Compton, Keith Miller and Colin Ingleby-MacKenzie.

sports. Our first meeting with Neil resulted in a lunch lasting all afternoon – rather boozy at that! When we parted late in the day, Neil asked to exchange ties and I still have his and wear it occasionally with honour.

During this visit I met the fabulous Keith Miller, and Mary and I remain very close friends of him and his lovely wife Peggy. His best pal in England was Denis Compton; arch-enemies on the field but the best of buddies off it. It became an annual ritual for me to lay on a lunch in the Lords for these two great characters and their mates. When Denis died in 1997, I wrote the following article for the *Cricketer Magazine*.

'The friends of Denis Compton called him "Compo". I was more inclined to call him "M'lud", "Sir", "Your Reverence" or even "Your Royal Highness". This was because of the high regard I held him in for all the pleasure he had given me, particularly when playing for Middlesex in 1947. That was the season when he and Bill Edrich, aided and abetted by Jack Robertson and a superb team, broke numerous records, some of which still stand.

'When Alec Bedser introduced me to Denis in the early 1980s, I soon forgot about addressing him so royally. This was because he was the sort of guy who made friends easily. Indeed, once you met Denis, it was as if you had known him all your life. At the time of meeting him, I was the Staff

Superintendent in the House of Lords. I quickly learned of his reputation for poor punctuality. However, I had a shock one day. I had just arrived in my flat 'above the shop', so to speak, for lunch when the telephone rang and a Security Officer asked if a friend of mine could speak to me, a Denis Compton! Denis came on the 'phone and said 'I am terribly sorry, old boy, but I have arrived for a Reception in the Commons *2 hours early* and am looking for somewhere to wait'. I had great delight in inviting Denis up to the flat and spent almost two hours talking about cricket and listening to his wonderful anecdotes. I took the opportunity to get him to sign my copy of *The Lords Taverners Fifty Greatest*.

Most summers during my time in the Palace of Westminster I hosted a lunch for some of the greatest names in cricket. These included Keith Miller, Alec and Eric Bedser, Neil Harvey, Arthur Morris, Alan Davidson, Colin Ingleby-Mackenzie and the one and only D.C.S. Compton.

Mary and I met Don Sharpe, an Australian who directed the film '39 Steps' at Colin Welland's house. He told us an extraordinary story about his experience when he first came to England as a young actor many years ago. Whenever he auditioned for an acting part, he was turned down because of his Aussie accent. He therefore took elocution lessons. Having developed a perfect English accent, he never acted again, being, by then, a director of some repute. I felt for him as I have lost count of the times someone has said to me, usually when I was on the telephone, that they did not expect to hear a Yorkshire accent in the Lords.

Carl Giles, the brilliant cartoonist, was a member of the Coldstream Guards Association, having been a war correspondent with the Regiment during the last war. I sat next to him at a dinner in Ipswich and he held me spellbound with his repartee, at the same time sketching on a pad throughout the meal. These sketches were then auctioned for charity.

Arthur English introduced us to Tommy Steele in his dressing room at the Prince of Wales Theatre after his one-man show. The performance was great, as was Tommy's hospitality. Another well known figure who entertained Mary and me in her dressing room was Pauline Collins. This was not long after she had been to Hollywood to collect an Oscar for her acting in *Shirley Valentine*. She was very modest about this.

One of the most amusing incidents I have ever seen involved my Aussie rugby league friend, Arthur Clues. Doug McClelland invited Arthur, Muriel, Mary and me to Australia House to meet the Australian Prime Minister, Bob Hawke. There were a lot of guests at the reception so Doug kept us until the last, by which time we had consumed large amounts of

With Arthur and Teresa English at the Sergeants Mess Summer Ball at the Guards Depot, 1982.

excellent wines and a few lagers. Eventually the Prime Minister arrived and within seconds Bob, Doug and Arthur were all talking at once. It seems that all three of them had had the same 'Sheila' (girlfriend) when they were in their teens, and they were arguing about who had her first! Muriel, Mary and I were in hysterics and enjoyed ourselves enormously, but we never did find out who 'dated' the 'Sheila' first.

Sometimes The Earl of Longford, a real cricket fan, joined us for lunch. On one occasion we were heading towards the front of the House of Lords after a really good, lengthy (!) lunch. The Earl of Longford was in front with Compo and I was following with Alec Bedser. His Lordship was heard to say this: 'Why aren't you a peer?' Before the great man had time to answer, Alec said in a stage whisper: 'It had to be a b. . . . y batsman, didn't it!'. Although a very amusing story, there is a twist to the ending. Only four months before Denis died, his close friend received a knighthood in the New Year's Honours.

Prime Minister John Major obviously recognised the last remark as he referred to *SIR* Denis Compton in the tribute to him in the *Daily Telegraph* after Denis died. Presumably if he had lived a little longer, Denis would have been a knight – or even a peer, as mentioned by Lord Longford! So much has been written and said about the 'Brylcreem/Golden Boy' that hardly anything remains to be said. Nevertheless the following points are worth recording:

In the mid-80s I attended a small luncheon party at Lords hosted by Denis. During lunch I got involved in a conversation with a fellow guest on coaching in general, team talks and what skippers said to batsmen prior to them going out to bat. The guest and I disagreed over most of these points so decided to ask for Denis's views. I firstly asked Denis what he thought about coaching, particularly with regards to teenagers. He said that many youngsters were *overcoached* (and he included soccer and rugby in this) and lost a lot of natural ability in their late teens. This view is shared by the Bedser twins (and me!).

I then asked what kind of 'team talks' captains had given to teams he had played for – including England and Middlesex. Denis said, 'I can't remember team talks being given. If there were any, they must have been very short.' Finally, I asked what skippers said to a batsman prior to him leaving the pavilion to bat. Denis replied, as only he could: 'Good luck, old boy.' What was noticeable at this event was that everyone was chattering away until the questions were asked and EVERYONE stopped talking to listen to Compo's answers. How true it is that modern-day cricketers don't play the game like the one and only D.C.S. Compton! What a privilege to have known him!

Before moving on from cricket, I must pay tribute to the marvellous hospitality in both the Middlesex and Surrey Committee Rooms. One always meets interesting people and is always made to feel welcome and at home.

One of the men I met through the Bedsers was Arthur Clues, an Australian Rugby League international player who married a Leeds girl and has lived here since 1949. Arthur was 'larger than life' in every way, a kindly man with a very generous nature and a wonderful sense of fun. His wife Muriel is a gem and we always enjoy her company. Arthur died in 1998 and the turnout at his funeral was huge. Colin Welland, of 'Chariots of Fire' fame, gave the eulogy.

On the 10th November 1982 Arthur telephoned me and asked if I could show the touring Australian Rugby League Team around the POW on Saturday as they were in London to play Fulham on Sunday. I was absolutely delighted to agree. Thinking that I knew the Aussies reputation for a 'a tube or two of lager', I asked Mary to empty the fridge and fill it with booze. This she did. After the tour of the Palace, I took them to our flat for 'refreshments'. Imagine my surprise when only one can of lager was consumed – all the rest had squash or a mineral water. The Doctor, Bill Monaghan, had a whisky. John Fleming, the Manager, told me that this was common practice during the tour. The team beat Fulham by over 60 points on the Sunday and were unbeaten throughout the tour. Included in the party that visited us was Rohan Hancock, Mal Meninga, Rod Morris and Wayne Pearce, all world-famous names.

As the Palace was empty on the Saturday morning, I allowed the usual photocall, including some of these huge rugby players sitting on the Queen's throne. To my knowledge, none of these photos has ever been published, so with luck I shall escape being imprisoned in the Tower. Similar things happened when some of the 1986 touring team visited the Palace. We also entertained the 'Aussie Rules Footie' people in October 1988 and the

Mollie Sugden and Bill Moore.

Rugby Union tourists about a month later. By this time Mary and I had visited Australia another couple of times, and I had started to be called 'our man in the House'. We did not mind this as they were wonderful hosts and friends. The phrase used by them, 'Pommy b . . . . . . s', is a form of endearment!

From about 1969 we had started to make 'showbiz' friends, due to Arthur English living quite near us at Farnborough. He was introduced to me when I was the Regimental Sergeant Major at Mons Officer Cadet School and he was using our Sergeants Mess. When I was commissioned in 1972, we kept in touch with each other and he introduced us to many stars of television and theatre. We met all the cast of *Are You Being Served?* and *In Sickness and in Health*. Three of our greatest friends to this day are Mollie Sugden, William (Bill) Moore, her husband, and Bill Pertwee of *Dad's Army* fame.

We have on occasions 'mixed and matched' our sports friends with our showbiz pals with great success. For example Keith Miller, Arthur Morris, Alan Davidson, Oz Cricketers all, get along famously with Mollie, William and Bill. One dinner party attended by Keith Miller, Mollie Sugden and William Moore were absolutely hysterical, to put it mildly.

Although not 'showbiz' the following is worth relating:

In 1995 my dear friend Ron Gerard invited Mary and me to a reception, dinner and ball at Brooklands to celebrate the end of the 1939-45 War fifty years before. 1995 was also the opening of the 'Fastest on Earth' exhibition at Brooklands.

For the younger readers, it is necessary to set the scene for the following two anecdotes. In 1925 the following took place at Brooklands:-

One of Brooklands' greatest duels took place, a match between Parry Thomas in his Leyland Thomas and Ernest Ridridge in 'Mephistopheles'. Thomas won. The Crown Prince of Japan visited Brooklands and the August bank holiday meeting saw the largest crowds of any meeting since World War One. A new and exciting course was instituted for the JGC 200-mile race on the 26th September.

Another of Brooklands greatest duels took place, this time between Archie Frazer-Nash in a Frazer-Nash and J.A. Joyce in the 'Amazing AC' for the Test Hill record. In May Frazer-Joyce took the record to an average speed of 29.83mph but Joyce achieved 30mph the following July. The next month Frazer-Nash snatched it back. On 12th October Joyce reclaimed it, but exactly one month later Frazer-Nash rounded off the year with a record 31.27mph.

Jim and Pat Mace on board the QE II, 1998.

This interesting fact is relevant to the first story:-

Malcolm Campbell took his first Blue Bird Land Speed Record car to Pendine Sands, where he achieved 150 miles an hour.

The Guest of Honour for the evening was HRH Prince Michael of Kent. Early in the Reception, Ron and Pat were presented to Prince Michael, whom they had met on a number of previous occasions. When we went in to dinner, there were tables of 10 but at our table there was one absentee, the lady on my left, who sent apologies for her absence due to ill health. After the first course, I asked the waiter to remove the place setting and chair on my left. I then 'closed ranks' with the man on my left.

As an opening remark to my new neighbour, I said to him: 'What is your connection with Brooklands?' He replied, 'I am the fastest man on earth and hold the land speed record'. Seeing the shocked look on my face and acute embarrassment, he then went on to say, 'I'm Richard Noble and at Black Rock Desert, Nevada, on the 4th October 1983, I went at 633.468 miles per hour'. This was hard to comprehend, so I asked him to repeat the figures several times and record this on my menu!

Richard Noble is a charming man and very good company. Ron and I were fascinated by his conversation. Not long after we met, he led the team that broke the sound barrier and created a new land speed record. What a guy!

During the same dinner I told Ron that the last time I had met Prince Michael was when he was an Officer Cadet at the Royal Military Academy, Sandhurst. I was a Sergeant Instructor there at the time. Officer Cadets performed one 'Barrack Guard' to give them a feel for what junior soldiers had to put up with. I happened to be the Sergeant on Guard when HRH performed this duty. I could tell by his attitude that Ron did not believe this fact.

At the end of the dinner, Ron insisted that we went and spoke to Prince Michael. Choosing his moment well, Ron looked down at him and said rather pompously, 'My friend, my very dear friend, Major Peter Horsfall, ex-Coldstream Guards, says that he was the Sergeant on Guard when you were on duty at Sandhurst as a Cadet'. Quick as a flash, the Prince shook my hand vigorously and said he remembered me well and was delighted to meet me again. He then became quite animated, telling the lady on his left how he, and other Cadets, had tried everything to avoid fierce Guards Sergeants such as me, etc. etc. We had to excuse ourselves after several minutes.

So, in the space of a couple of hours I was embarrassed by the 'King of Speed' and one of my best friends was embarrassed by a Royal Prince.

The author, Mary, Pat and Ron Gerard at the Garter Ceremony at Windsor.

As Arthur English took us to the Water Rats Ball in November for many years, we met quite a number of 'showbiz' people. Most of them are very nice and easy to get along with. The funniest speech we ever heard at the Ball was by Tommy Cooper. Matt Munro was the best singer by a street, and Frank Carson the most amusing comedian. Wendy Richard is a very attractive lady and not a bit like the dowdy Pauline in Eastenders. Mary and Wendy share an interest in house plants, and we have some of Wendy's to this day.

A very good friend of ours, Raphael Djanogly, introduced us to Ernie and Doreen Wise, and we have dined with them several times. They are really nice people and Ernie is the most modest of men. In January, 1995 they did me the honour of attending my retirement party at the Hyatt Carlton Tower Hotel. Another very special person was Charlie Chester. For many years he had advertised Coldstream Guards reunions for me on his 'Sunday Soapbox', programme, so in appreciation Mary and I invited him to dinner in the Peers' Dining Room with his charming wife 'Mouse' (Joan). He was over 80 at the time and his memory was remarkable; his anecdotes from the 30s and 40s were incredibly detailed and funny. After our dinner in

With Ernie and Doreen Wise, and Pat Gerard, February 1994.

the Lords, he sent me a number of poems he had written – but at the time had not been published. As I am approaching 'three score years and ten', my favourite is:

> Which is the road to contentment
> The question was asked an old man
> He paused for a while … and then offered a smile
> and the highway his eyes seemed to scan …
>
> Then softly his voice said … you haven't a choice
> The pathway through life has its rules
> There's only one way to proceed, step by step
> Walking backwards is only for fools
>
> You will find there are many diversions
> There are times when you must stand and wait
> There are twists and some turns … but a wise fellow learns
> That the best way to travel is straight …

And even when travelling cross country
You will find there is many a stile...
And each one that you can climb, an achievement
And you'll learn as you pass every mile...

There are cross roads of hate and resentment
There are pastures of joy and of love
And finding the road to contentment...
Is 'tween you and the good Lord above

There's a choice in the road to contentment
Let your brain and your heart guide your tread
For memories are cleft...to the pathway you left
And life's dreams...are the roadway ahead

And while you are making your journey
Think not of what you might have done
But think more about your destination
That's the road to contentment my son

A natural ending to this chapter is to write about one of the oldest members of the Lords and his connection with sport and young people. The Earl of Longford gets a bad time from the media due to his views on Myra Hindley, the moors murderer. I have seen him in entirely different situations. At my 'annual ritual' lunches in the Lords, he always more than held his own with famous sportsmen, talking about sports in general. On one occasion Colin Ingleby-Mackenzie invited his lordship and me to lunch in his house at St John's Wood. Several youngsters were present and Lord Longford got along so well with them, covering every possible subject. A similar thing happened when I took him into a box at the Oval during a Test match. When I meet him nowadays, he invariably wants to talk about rugby or cricket. Not a bad epitaph.

I was invited to join the All Party Rugby League Group in 1988. This most charismatic idea seems to have been the inspiration of David Hinchliffe, The MP for Wakefield. They meet monthly and have a huge input into what is happening in modern Rugby League. We are invited to international matches and the Challenge Cup final at Wembley. I have been able to get Arthur Clues, Colin Welland and the High Commissioner for Australia, The Hon Douglas McClelland, involved with the Group. I had a bit of fun with some of the MPs from the Group a few years ago. The Australian top-class coach, John Monie, who was managing Wigan at the time, arrived in my office with two huge cardboard boxes, one containing the RL Challenge Cup and the other containing the plinth. Without warning, we went to the Terrace Bar in the Commons with the cup and plinth. It was amusing to see the MPs rushing off to get their cameras to take pictures of John and the trophy.

Knowing that the readers of this book can keep a secret, I wish to share the following news with them:

I have bowled to two of the greatest cricketers ever to represent Australia, Alan Davidson and Neil Harvey. What I do NOT tell everyone is that with Alan this took place in his son's garden in Sydney, and in Neil's case in our garden in North London. Readers are asked not to mention the latter part of this story!

Enough of reminiscing. It's time to return to the Palace of Westminster and the serious business.

CHAPTER 16

All is Not as it Seems – or Is It?

In an earlier Chapter I glossed over some of the problems in the early years of my time in the Lords. The cleanliness and general maintenance were the major ones. There were no strictly laid down guidelines as to who was responsible for what, and this created many anomalies, and at times bad feeling, between different bodies. For example, State Officers' Court was nearly always like a rubbish tip. At midday a member of the Works Department would clean the whole area but by mid-afternoon it would be a tip again. Rubbish, including bottles, would appear from every corner of the Palace and be deposited there. In theory, the local council collected this refuse each morning but invariably the vehicle would be late. The place stank. Unbelievably it took six years of complaining to get the appropriate closed-in skips and containers. Although not officially part of my job, I got all the complaints!

The basement underneath both Houses was always a very bad area, with rubbish and every possible type of builders' material scattered about. I visited the basement almost daily and 'read the riot act' to various staff in their 'warrens'. The risk of fire was enormous and I asked the Fire Officer to write to the Heads of Departments. He was after a quiet life and refused to do so, but kept writing to me! At the monthly meetings with the Works Department 'Heads', I would read these out – to very little avail. Things did not improve sufficiently until the football stadium in Bradford burned down and it was proved that neglected rubbish caused the fire. I told the Departments, by letter, that this could have been US!

Black Rod was always pleased with the standard of cleanliness of all the rooms looked after by the Housemaids but was ashamed of the decorating in what he called the 'black spots'. Included in these were the ones in the South-East Tower and South Return. General House retired in January 1985 so did not see that by 1987 every area in the Lords was immaculate. The prestigious areas were restored to the state planned by Barry and Pugin in the 19th century and all other areas were beautifully decorated. The superb coats of arms were painted and restored by a Mr Vere Collings, belonging to the third generation of his family who had performed this task.

Flo Dunn and Jean Ryder, the Head Housemaid and her Deputy, led by example with a terrific work rate and very high standards. Several of the Housemaids had been in the Lords for many years and these included Lill Hall and Nell Rudd, who had both been there for over 20 years when I arrived. Flo, Lill and Nell all received the British Empire Medal when they neared retirement. Cleaning the books in the Library was a massive problem. until 1988 we had to employ outside contractors during the summer recess for this job, which they did badly. After a long battle, and support from the Librarian, we were allowed to take on two additional Housemaids, whose full-time duty was to keep the books and shelves clean. This was a definite 'painting the Forth Bridge' task, which they still do outstandingly well.

My working week was supposed to be Tuesday to Saturday inclusive, and I will enlarge on this later. The Housemaids' week consisted of Monday to Saturday inclusive from 7 am to 10 am. This added up to 18 hours, but for some extraordinary reason they were paid for 21 hours. One of my predecessors in his wisdom had said that only 50 per cent needed to come in on alternative Saturdays, but I soon discovered that they sat around doing virtually nothing on a Saturday. Nobody, including Flo, could explain why the Housemaids were needed on a Saturday, but my own theory is that it was an overhang from the days prior to 1965, when the heating was supplied by coal fires in nearly every room. The fireplaces would have required cleaning out and in some cases the fires would have had to be relit. Also, until about 1970, many stone floors had to be scrubbed. After several years of negotiating with the interested parties, I was able to stop the Housemaids' Saturday work at no loss of salary; work 15 hours, paid for 15.

Another crazy situation affecting Old Palace Yard existed. The pavements had to be cleaned by the Works Department and the parking areas (inside the railings) by the Local Council. The courtyards were cleaned by the Works Department – inconsistently, I might add. The Manager of the Refreshment Department in 1980 was a lady who paid no interest to what happened to the waste and refuse from the kitchens and dining rooms. Fortunately Alfie Bibbiani took over a few months after I arrived, and things improved immediately. Throughout my tour he and the Banqueting Manageress, Lorna McWilliam, gave me tremendous support in every way. To digress a bit: in 1988 Mark Thatcher took over as the Chef in the Lords (this was not the son of the Prime Minister!). I mentioned earlier the 'working parties' set up regarding the cleaning contractors. In 1983 General House did me another good turn. He wrote a very strong letter to the

Treasury in which he likened the POW to a Rolls Royce rather than a Mini. There was never enough cash allocated to the maintenance of the building and in the letter he said that if a Rolls Royce was neglected and not maintained properly, eventually the 'big end' would go. From then onwards we seemed to get the cash we needed, which helped the Works Department and me to raise standards in every way.

Both the Houses of Parliament Sports and Social Club and the Rifle Range, which served all those in the Palace, were in the Lords area, which meant me keeping a 'watching brief' on them on behalf of Black Rod. Indeed, I was the Treasurer of the Club for six and a half years, having been asked to take over for a 'few months' in 1989.

By tradition, Westminster School's rowing eight arrived annually from the Thames at the steps leading to Black Rod's garden on one afternoon in June. The first time I saw the steps, it was obvious that they had not been cleaned for years and years. They are now hosed down regularly. Thieving was rife, particularly in the summer recess. Vehicles of contractors and strangers were checked coming on to the site but not on the way out! In 1983 several Pugin clocks were stolen and a huge photocopier disappeared.

On a smaller scale, most of the washrooms in the Lords had lovely linen hand towels supplied, plain white with the letters HOL in the centre. We 'lost' about 100 of these per a week on average, and each one cost over £2.

The pegs for hanging clothes in the Peers' Cloakroom are made of good quality brass, with an exquisite 'acorn' on the end. These can be unscrewed, with difficulty, and regularly disappear. We were mystified where these items went to, but one could draw one's own conclusions!

Included in the stores I requisitioned from the supply depot at Liverpool were black and brown shoe polish, matches, shoe laces, combs and shoe horns for use by the Peers. A number of Peers complained when Black Rod ordered me to stop ordering matches and shoe laces to save cash. An unusual requisition was the paraffin required for the hurricane lamps used by the Yeomen of the Guard when carrying out the Search of the Cellars prior to the SOP. Talking about the Search reminds me of the Gunpowder Plot. In 1983 the *Daily Mail* held a competition for children about Guy Fawkes. The prize was a visit to the POW to see the site where the gunpowder was placed. After much research I found the exact spot underneath the Lords – but what an anti-climax! It was in a nicely painted passage complete with fluorescent lighting. There is not even a plaque to mark the spot. Anyhow, I showed the winning children the area and they appeared to be pleased.

Prior to the Woolwich Barrier being built on the Thames, there was an occasional danger of flooding throughout the whole Palace. Once a year Brigadier David Stileman and I would visit the Connaught Rooms in Great Queen Street and update our plans on what rooms the Lords would occupy if our building was flooded; it was quite a chore and we were glad when the Barrier was completed. The Commons had a contingency plan similar to ours.

Black Rod and I worried continuously about the fire risk and the lack of fire escapes in certain areas. For example, there was no escape from the Yeoman Usher's flat and inadequate escapes from the Hansard offices on the third floor on the west front. Black Rod ordered Fire Drill practices at about six-monthly intervals, but rather ironically these took place early AM before the Peers and Hansard staff arrived in the building.

Judgments took place in the Chamber at 2 pm each Thursday and the House sat at 3 pm on that day. This meant the staff setting the Chamber up as a Court of Law for the Judgments and a rush-around to revert to a normal layout for the parliamentary work. It was not easy because the layouts were completely different.

How history is made! In 1986 the Lord Chancellor complained that the Woolsack was sagging and rather grubby. Black Rod told me to have it refurbished during the summer recess, which I did. Every country in the Commonwealth contributes wool to fill the Woolsack. When the task was complete, David Kempton, Furnishing Group, a really good guy, came to see me and told me that those re-covering the Woolsack had some spare deep red material left and asked whether it would be all right to make four huge rosettes, one for each corner. Initially I said 'No' but then had a 'rush of blood to the head' and said OK, but if anyone complained they would have to be removed. EVERYONE LIKED THEM! Amusingly, I quite often heard Guides telling parties that Lord Hailsham had ordered the rosettes.

Really odd things occurred at times. For example, one of our three superb carpet fitters came to see me in 1981 and told me that all three of them were to be made redundant within a couple of weeks. This would have meant us going out to contract for even the most minute job. Goodness knows what the cost would have been. I saw Black Rod and he had the redundancy notices cancelled. On checking, we found out that the PWO had made this decision without reference to Black Rod or the Sergeant at Arms. This was typical of how decisions were made without thought for the 'customers'.

Traditionally the Attendants had always looked after the incoming mail for all sources. According to Ray Scott, when he arrived in 1977, the outside mail could be put in a 'shoe box'. This is probably an exaggeration of the truth, but I do believe that it was minimal. By the time I retired, about 20 huge sacks a day was the norm. During December this would be trebled at times. This included Saturdays. 1988 was the year that Black Rod agreed to something that, with hindsight, was wrong and made too much work for the Attendants. A messengerial system was instituted, which meant that an Attendant would deliver mail to selected offices in the Lords and the outbuildings. Initially this went well because there were only about 20 drop-off/collection points. In 1980 there were about 10 pigeon holes for Peers' mail in the Attendants' office and by 1995 there were 260.

Within two years EVERY Department had jumped on to the bandwagon. By the time I retired in 1995 there were over 50 of these points. This would have been all right if there had been an increase in staff. Unfortunately the Staff Adviser – I insisted on calling him Inspector (!) – convinced Black Rod that the present staff could cope. There was not a problem when all eleven Attendants were present but with one or two away, things became difficult. One tragic event aggravated this as Ray Scott was taken seriously ill in late 1987 and did not return prior to his death about a year later. R.I.P. The two Senior Attendants and I ran the show, but life was tough for everyone. Now, on looking back, I must have been daft to accept this and should have insisted on some outside help. The Staff 'Adviser' was of no help whatsoever and there will be more about him later.

One of my duties was to look after the wand used by the Lord Great Chamberlain on State occasions. This was a white ebony 'cane' about 5'6" in length. Hugh Cholmondeley was very casual and left it lying around at times and on more than one occasion, gave me a scare that it was lost. David Cholmondeley was more careful. Writing about his lordship reminds me of an embarrassing story about myself. When I had been in the Lords about a year, my secretary, Margaret, said to me: 'I hope you don't mind me telling you, Major, but it is not pronounced "CHOL MOND ELEY"; it's CHUMLEY'. I had been pronouncing the name wrong all that time.

The rod used by Black Rod was kept in a steel security locker, alongside my office, as it is a collector's item and priceless. The description of the present Rod dates from 1883, although some details have been altered since. It runs as follows:-

'It is three and a half feet long, and of ebony. At one end (the top) is a gold lion holding a shield, surmounted by a crown, and bearing the initials E vii R which stand for King Edward the Seventh. It is surrounded by the Garter bearing the motto 'Honi soit qui mal y pense'. At the centre of the Rod is a gold orb embossed with oak leaves. At the bottom is a gold knob surmounted by a 1904 gold sovereign; the side A visible is the reverse, which shows Saint George on horseback, slaying the dragon.'

During the early 80s the Staff Inspector in the Lords was Harry Bunkell, who was a hardworking, industrious and nice guy. He seemed to be making good progress, particularly with the junior staff. It came as a shock, therefore, when he was replaced by John Parker in October 1984. His tactics were completely the opposite to what was wanted. Within minutes of starting his review of the Attendants' duties, he said to the Assistant Superintendent: 'I've been around a lot and you can't bluff me!' Ray Scott was hopping mad and I had to stop him complaining to Black Rod. Much of his information came from over a drink at the bar!

General House had never allowed the Staff Inspector to get involved with the Housemaids, but soon after the Air Chief Marshal replaced him, he allowed a full review of their duties. Naturally this proved to be a disaster. John Parker said that he had talked to every one of the 42 Housemaids. In fact he had spoken to three only, including the Head and her Deputy. Unbelievably he recommended that the strength of the Housemaids should be reduced to 26. John Parker had promised me that he would show me the report in draft form so that I could make appropriate comments. The first time I saw the report was when Black Rod sent for me to show it to me. A copy had already gone to the Clerk of Parliaments. I was so furious that Black Rod knew that if this was implemented, he would need a new Staff Superintendent and Head Housemaid. We kept our 42, and later on got the extra two for book cleaning.

Until 1982 there was no relationship, other than strained, between the two Houses. In my early days Black Rod would ask me to find out what the Sergeant's office in the Commons was doing about a particular thing and report back to him. I once asked General House about this and he said simply that HE WOULD NOT BE WELCOME IN 'THE OTHER PLACE'. He gave me a couple of examples of this. Things changed for the better when Major Victor Le Fanu took over as the Sergeant at Arms in 1982. Victor was the Adjutant in the 2nd Coldstream when I was a young Drums Non-Commissioned Officer. We even share a birthday!

During the period 1982-89, whilst Victor was the boss, the 'barrier' between the Houses gradually disappeared. David House started this process and John Gingell continued it; I got along very well with all the four, later five, Sergeants and I think this helped Black Rod. The Yeoman Usher, Brigadier David Stileman, was a terribly nice guy and got along well with everyone. By the time I retired, there was a terrific relationship with the Commons and hopefully this is the case until this day.

I have mentioned the Clerks briefly, but it is necessary to enlarge on this subject. Most of the Clerks come to the Lords in their 20s, having obtained a really good degree at University. They gradually gain promotion, having moved around various Departments, and the best ones finish as a Clerk of the Table – a most prestigious and important post. Peers rely on them giving sound advice on many and varied subjects, and in particular on procedures in the House.

I got along outstandingly well with Sir Peter (now Lord) Henderson (1980-83), Sir John Sainty (1983-90) and Sir Michael Wheeler-Booth (1990-95). They were all different and I found them appreciative of anything done for them. In fact, after one particular summer recess, Sir Michael wrote me a two-page closely typed letter on behalf of the Clerks and all the staff for the work I had done for them whilst they were away. Sir John Gingell was absolutely amazed and pleasantly surprised, as he found the Clerks difficult to please at times. When I retired, Sir Richard Thomas implied that it was Sir Michael who had stopped me getting an honour. This is hard to believe for the reasons given above.

Although the public Line of Route (LOR) had caused me personally a lot of extra work on Saturdays and public holidays, I was terribly sad when it had to be closed for security reasons in May 1981. This was brought about by the death of the IRA hunger-striker, Bobby Sands. We had always been under threat and I had had to close the LOR at various times at short notice. Fortunately these always turned out to be hoaxes or false alarms, but the police had to clear the building and bring in the sniffer dogs. I always informed General House after these incidents and he said that the right action had been taken. However, after the death of Sands, the risk became too great and he had to recommend the closure of the LOR to the Security Committee. Every time there was talk of reopening the Route, another major bomb incident occurred in London.

The LOR remains open for the guests of members of either House or for parties sponsored by a Peer or MP. These are always accompanied by the member concerned or a Guide hired by him or her. Recently I have heard that the LOR may reopen to the public during recesses but on payment. This is a pity as until the closure in 1981, it was free. As mentioned elsewhere in the book, I became an expert on the LOR and regularly took friends, or 'friends of friends', through the Palace.

1981 also saw the commencement of the programme of stone cleaning of the whole of the exterior of the Palace. High pressure cold water jets were used and the time taken was about eight years. Mary and I suffered, as all our windows in the flat were sealed for over three months – in summer too! Without question, it was well worth it as the building now looks fantastic. The Works Department and contractors did a wonderful job.

By the mid-80s I was having to spend every Monday in the Palace. This became essential to try to keep up with the paperwork. As Treasurer of the Sports and Social Club, and as I was receiving cheques for the Staff Christmas Fund, I had a great deal of accounting to do. Also, annual confidential reports for each member of the staff were introduced. I tried to do such work in the flat, where I had some privacy and 'hush'. Whilst General House was there I didn't mind, because he was so appreciative, but later this was taken for granted by everyone. Richard Thomas was shocked when he arrived, and set about getting some help for me. He only achieved it in 1994 not long before he and I retired. There will be more about this later. I NEVER got days off in compensation for being on duty when officially off duty!

Despite all the trials and tribulations mentioned in this chapter, there was one overriding thing that made my job worthwhile – it was an absolute joy to serve the Peers themselves for reasons mentioned elsewhere. Proof of this can be seen when I say that in the early 80s I was offered two jobs away from the Lords which were better paid and much easier. These I turned down because by then I had become so fond of the Attendants and Housemaids. I have no regrets.

CHAPTER 17

Anecdotes and Tales Galore

M OST OF THOSE WHO WORK in the Palace of Westminster could probably tell dozens of true tales about events affecting them. I probably accumulated more than most due to living on site. This chapter is not in any particular order or sequence; some sections are serious and some amusing.

In September 1984 a close friend from the Regiment, Fred Dooley, asked me if I would show the 'Postmaster General' of Berlin and his wife the Line of Route. Both Houses were in recess so I was able to give them and Fred a really good and detailed tour. All went well until we arrived in the Commons Chamber, which had been rebuilt after the 1939-45 War. I mentioned the rebuilding briefly, intending to gloss over the events that led to this. Before I had a chance, my German guest asked me why this was. I had no option but to say: 'Your lot burnt the House down'. Fred nearly choked as he tried to suppress his laughter, and for years after I heard him telling people of my 'faux pas'. My words cannot have upset the German too much, as he sent me a superb set of Bundespost stamps in an album afterwards. These are with Mary's 'first day covers' until this day.

When the Baroness Trumpington was a Minister of State, she shared a rather smart office with two other Ministers. She is a smashing lady, full of good humour and bonhomie. The Attendants told me that she enjoyed a flutter on the 'gee gees'. One day she tackled me in the corridor and asked me if her office could be repainted – DEEP RED WALLS. I agreed to the redecoration but tried to talk her into having a pastel colour. Lady Trumpington refused point blank and insisted on deep red. I sought advice and help from General House, but he would not get involved.

Some time after the redecorating had taken place, I met Lord Lyell, who shared the room, in the corridor and asked him why deep red was chosen. He said that Lord Glenarthur and he were given very little say in the matter, as Lady Trumpington was a heavy smoker and red hid the stains. When her ladyship ceased to be a Minister and vacated the room, it took literally half a dozen coats of paint to cover the red. Indeed it still showed through several years later.

One evening Lord Fitt, an expert on the Northern Ireland situation, was speaking in the Chamber during a debate about the Province. He went on for quite a while and would not 'give way' to other Peers wishing to interrupt his speech. After a time Lady Trumpington was seen writing a note. This was passed along one side of the Chamber, across it, down the other side, and finished up in Lord Fitt's hand. Whilst in mid-sentence, his lordship opened the note, read it and sat down immediately. What grand political point had Lady Trumpington scored, one asked? Shortly afterwards Lord Fitt left the Chamber and proceeded to show all and sundry the note written by this senior Minister. It said, 'Gerry, your flies are undone'! Lord Fitt being the great character that he is, did not take offence and carried the note around for years.

By common assent the most brilliant speech in the Lords during my time was The Earl of Stockton's (Harold Macmillan), made on the 13th November 1984. He covered every possible subject and most aspects of politics, past and present. This speech was 60 years after his maiden speech in the 'other place'. Describing himself as a political Rip van Winkle, he went on to talk about some of the decisions he had been involved in, including the creation of Life Peers and the introduction of Premium Bonds. He recalled that the Archbishop of Canterbury said that he had 'debauched the people with the introduction of the Bonds, driving them to gambling'. Lord Stockton was gushing in his praise for what Reagan was doing for the economy in America by having broken the rules and upsetting the economists in that country.

What made the 33-minutes speech so remarkable was that it was so wide ranging. Space does not allow for everything to be mentioned, but suffice it to say that some subjects covered were young children working in factories and underground, the internal combustion engine, fuel oils, the motor car, aeroplanes, railways, steamships, computers, silicon chips, automation, scientists, interest rates and strikes. He finished with faith, hope and charity. When Hansard was published the next day, EVERY copy was snapped up within an hour. There had to be a complete reprint and they went just as quickly.

Whilst researching for this book, I learned something I had not realized at the time. The Lord Bishop of Lincoln followed the Earl of Stockton and paid the appropriate tribute to him including the following: 'I should also like to salute the noble Earl as a fellow Guardsman – although, I have to say that in that slightly cautious way in which a Coldstreamer approaches a Grenadier'. Authors note: these so-and-so Guardsmen get everywhere!

Mentioning a Grenadier reminds me of the Lord Carrington. Without question he was a first-class Foreign Secretary and everyone was shocked when he resigned over the start of the Falklands War. Nobody in the Lords thought he was to blame and it was obvious that he had resigned as a 'man of honour' and to save the Prime Minister and other politicians in the Commons. My staff adored him, as he always passed the time of day with them and never talked down to people. He never forgot that I was the Regimental Sergeant Major at Mons and we got along very well.

A great Coldstream chum of Lord Carrington's was Lord Soames, with whom I also got along well. Seen together, one would never believe they were from different regiments as they obviously enjoyed each other's company so much, with lots of good natured ribbing about 'seniority' etcetera. For example, one day the three of us were talking in the corridor when Lord Carrington put his hand on Lord Soames's shoulder and said, 'This guy, (pointing at me), 'only got this job because he's a bloody Coldstreamer'. With that Lord Soames said 'quite right too' and they both roared with laughter. Sadly I have to report that Lord Soames' son Nicholas was a poor Officer Cadet at Mons whilst I was a Warrant Officer there. His Regiment must have improved him as he became Minister for the Army in the Conservative Government.

Lord Shackleton was one of the most interesting Peers in the House. I first got to know him when we were both guests at Australia House. Being the son of the great explorer, Ernest Shackleton, it was obvious that he would become an expert on all things geographical and in particular Australia, the South Pole, Newfoundland and the Falklands. Studying his record in Dod's *Parliamentary Companion* is fascinating, to say the least.

During the 1980s and 90s I became very friendly with the High Commissioner for Australia and most of the Agents General for the six states in Australia, all based in London. On one occasion I invited David Fischer, the Agent General for Western Australia, to lunch in the Peers' Dining Room and my only other guest was Lord Shackleton. Without exaggerating, I can honestly say that David was spellbound listening to this great man talking about Australia and other areas down under. Lord Shackleton always talked in a matter-of-fact way and was not looking for kudos or praise. His conversation was always entertaining. Although he was a Knight of the Garter, he was absolutely delighted to be made an Honorary Companion of the Order of Australia in 1990.

The Rt. Hon. Douglas McClelland was the High Commissioner for Australia in the late 80s and early 90s, a period of well over four years. He and his wife Lorna were the most wonderful ambassadors for their country.

The Viscount Alanbrooke and John Todd.

They were outgoing, friendly and excellent at public relations. We have become very close friends. They have stayed with us in our home and we have visited them in Sydney. Their son Robert is a first-class MP in Australia and all the family are delightful. Doug and Lorna held magnificent dinner parties in the official residence at Stoke Lodge, Hyde Park and Mary and I have been invited on a number of occasions. Doug is keen on all sports, in particular rugby league, so we met several famous sportsmen through him. The person who introduced me to Doug was Warren Saunders, who used to open the batting for New South Wales in Australia.

Sometimes Doug would visit us in the Lords in his official car with the number plate AUS 1. The Peers were a bit mystified as to the purpose of the High Commissioner's visit. His driver, 'Jock', was sometimes asked where his boss was. The receptions held at Australia House during Doug's tour can only be described as fabulous. Australian wines are most potent and the glasses were always full. As for the buffets – yum yum! – the giant king prawns cannot be beaten anywhere. The official invitations said 6 pm - 8 pm but nobody wanted to go home. We have left as late as 9.30 pm and there have still been many guests remaining. The Australians can teach us a thing or two about hospitality.

I get fed up with the fact that the House of Lords is not given credit where it is due. For example 1981 was the 'year of the disabled' and the Lords took the lead in this. The Baroness Llewelyn-Davis played a large part in this initiative, but I am not sure where the main credit is due. Ramps for wheelchairs were installed in the Palace of Westminster before any other public building in Whitehall. Black Rod got the funding for this in the Lords, and not long after the Commons followed suit.

Similarly the Lords took the lead in the televising of debates in the Chamber and in some Committee Rooms. Credit for this is due to the BBC, who made that splendid series, 'The Great Palace' in the early 1980s. This was done so well that it won over the sceptics, including Black Rod and me. When the BBC made a formal request to the Peers, permission was given for 'a trial period'. The Commons refused permission. I am not sure whether General House planned this intentionally but televising did not start until about two weeks after he retired, in late January 1985.

As mentioned elsewhere, Christopher Jones, the BBC parliamentary correspondent, did the Lords a great service, as did Glyn Worsnip of 'That's Life' fame. Not only were they excellent commentators, but they were first-class at presenting their views. Television does strange things to people and in this respect Peers are no different. On the first day of televising, it was amusing to see the males grooming their hair and the females wearing selected dresses and two-piece suits. Also, during Question Time there was much 'jumping up and down' by Peers on all sides.

Interestingly, the standard of debate did rise after the introduction of television in the Chamber. The Peers would probably not admit this, but it is undeniably true. Prior to television, Peers were inclined to speak 'off the cuff' and/or without notes. Afterwards you would see them reading off a prompt card or, dare I say it, an 'idiot's guide'.

The Lord Griffiths became a Lord of Appeal in 1985 and we quickly struck up a good rapport. We had two things in common: we were both guardsmen and we had a great love of cricket. His office was near our flat and if we met in the corridor, we invariably talked cricket. During his tenure as the President of the MCC in 1991/92, he had me in his office a couple of times to pick my brains; especially as to my views on women becoming members of the MCC. Both of us were all for this, and are glad that this has now happened. He was a wonderful President and the two AGMs he chaired were first-class.

John Major is a real fan and supporter of Surrey County Cricket Club and attends regularly. In 1990 both he and I were guests in the Committee

Room at a county match. Alec Bedser introduced me to John Major whilst we were queuing for a very good cold buffet lunch. About mid-morning the following day my telephone rang and it was Alec to ask me if I had food poisoning. I asked him why and he told me that most of the people at lunch the day before were ill. Alec was delighted when I told him I was all right, which meant that the Chancellor of the Exchequer was probably so as well.

The Lord Kagan, of Gannex Raincoats and Harold Wilson's 'pink list' fame, became one of my mother's two 'toy boys' at the age of 77. After the death of Ray Scott, I had become very friendly with him and he discovered that Mother lived only a couple of miles away from him in Huddersfield. On several occasions he visited her, or had his 'Girl Friday' pop in, with a present of flowers, chocolates or other goodies. He even gave her two bottles of champagne on one of his visits. Mother was in her 90s by this time, so started to tell people that Lord Kagan was one of her 'toy boys'. When I told his lordship, he was absolutely thrilled but said to me, 'Oh dear, why did I have to wait until I was 77 before I became a 'toy boy'?' Her other 'toy boy', Arthur Clues, 60 plus, was not a bit jealous and was happy to share her!

During 1982 work started on a bust of the Lord Home of The Hirsel. The sculptor was a Mr Black. As far as I know, the only two people who saw the bust before it was unveiled were Margaret in my office and myself. Lord Home only had a couple of sittings. Margaret supplied lots of coffee and the work was carried out in the Annexe to the Queen's Robing Room, which was always locked, and when Mr. Black was not there, the bust was covered. When Prime Minister Margaret Thatcher unveiled it in the Royal Gallery in March 1983, Lord Home was rather bashful and kept asking, 'Is it all right?'. It is a superb likeness and has a really first-class site at the top of the Royal staircase.

I was sad to see the retirement of Sir Peter Henderson in 1983, not least because the staff respected him so much. Also, his wife is a first-class artist and painted some excellent pictures within the Lords. When tributes were paid to him in the House on his retirement, he would not sit in the body of the Chamber – he is a very modest man. Rumour has it that he hid in the tiny 'box' above the Queen's throne.

The *Daily Mail* and *Daily Express* found out in 1984 that Michael Heseltine had been one of my recruits in 1959. He was the Secretary of State for Defence at the time so the two reporters telephoned me and wanted to know what he was like when he was undergoing training. I said virtually the same to each reporter separately, but was annoyed when one of the reporters twisted my words with regard to his long hair. They each said that he was a first-class recruit but one newspaper said that he had been allowed to have long hair whilst undergoing training. Simply not true, but this suited Michael's image as he had become known as 'Tarzan' after his mace-swinging performance in the Commons.

1994 saw the saddest day in the Palace during my time. This was due to the death of John Smith. Apart from the fact that he was thought to be a great leader of the Labour party, the death was so sudden. I saw grown men – members of both Houses – literally crying unashamedly. When something like this happens, it puts everything else into perspective. Tributes were paid by all Parties in the Lords and business was suspended for the day. A complete hush descended on the building and it was really quite eerie. I never met John Smith but he must have been a really special guy. R.I.P.

Attendant Richard Jelley had been courting Millie the Supervisor of the contract cleaners for some time and announced his engagement in 1987. Mary and I were invited to their wedding in the city on the 17th April, 1988 during the Easter recess. The Viscount Tonypandy was invited and drove all the way from Cardiff to attend. He parked his car in Old Palace Yard and travelled to the wedding in my car with Mary and me. Not only did he go to the church, but he stayed at the wedding breakfast for a long time. Everyone was enthralled with his company because he was a man of such charm and friendship. Richard told me later that Lord Tonypandy had given them a sizeable cheque as a wedding present. There will never be his like again.

There is a special place in my memories for the Lord Shinwell. Each Christmas he gave me a dozen bottles of Glenfiddich whisky for distribution to the staff. For a relatively small man, he had a great presence. To celebrate his 100th birthday, a one-hour programme was recorded in the Palace, to be shown on television later.

Normally I would ask one of the Attendants to accompany the television crew so as to ensure that they complied with the rules. On this occasion Black Rod suggested that I stayed with Lord Shinwell and 'looked after him'. This I did with pleasure and enjoyed every minute. The filming took about four hours and the conversations he had with literally dozens of people were enlightening, fascinating and at times very amusing.

A plaque had been produced recording Lord Shinwell's 100th birthday. On the day of the unveiling in 1987, a huge crowd of members of both Houses assembled in the Royal Gallery. The Viscount Whitelaw, as Leader of the House, made a short speech, referring to his notes. 'Manny', as he was well known by all, spoke in great style for about 15 minutes – without

The Viscount Tonypandy with Mary and bridegroom Richard Jelley, April 1988.

notes. An amazing performance for a young man, let alone one of 100. When asked where he would like the plaque to go, he suggested the Main Library. There it is to this day. A tremendous tribute to a wonderful parliamentarian, regardless of one's politics.

Not long before his death, Lord Shinwell stopped me in the main corridor in the Lords and asked me if I could do him a favour, to which I replied in the affirmative. With that he asked me if I could 'get him a pair of new legs – PLEASE?' Off he went on his two walking sticks, chuckling like mad. He died three weeks later. I understand that he had just had a glass of his favourite tipple, whisky. Not a bad way to go. R.I.P.

The clock, commonly known by the name of the bell, Big Ben, stopped several times during my tour of duty. This was usually due to weather conditions or to a mechanical fault. On one occasion I was in Australia on holiday when the clock stopped, and on my return John Gingell threatened to stop my leave in future if I couldn't guarantee to keep the clock going. He had a smile on his face, so I think he was joking. The most amusing

The Poll Tax Protest March, 31st March 1990.

stoppage was caused by a workman who was assisting in decorating the inside of the Clock Tower. He leaned a ladder on the main spindle of the clock and whilst a man was on the ladder, the mechanism stopped – for about two hours. Amazingly, hardly anyone realized even though the clock stopped from 8 am until 10 am. True, it was a very foggy morning.

In 1998 I met the famous 'spoon bender', Yuri Geller. When he heard where I had worked, he immediately claimed the credit for stopping the clock on two occasions, one of them when he was out of the country. Initially I thought he was joking, but soon realized that he meant it.

At the start of the book I mentioned Lord Ted Willis of 'Dixon of Dock Green' fame. We met at the Guildhall when Lorna McClelland was made a Freeman of the City of London and we became close friends. What a gifted writer he was! He told me that he could write a book, in pencil in longhand, in 24 hours by literally working around the clock. We had several 'one-on-one' conversations in my flat and his anecdotes were hysterical. The only person I know who can compete in telling funny 'true' stories is Colin Welland, the playwright and actor.

One of the best after-dinner speakers I have heard is Lord Gerry Fitt. His brother George died in action with the Irish Guards in 1944. Because of this, I introduced him to the Irish Guards in Chelsea Barracks, the Royal Military Academy, Sandhurst and some Household Division units. At several dinners we attended together, Gerry was the guest speaker and he was always superb, mixing serious subjects with humour. The first time I took Gerry to dine with the 1st 'Micks', one of my officer friends in the Battalion, a non-Catholic, made it clear to me that he disagreed with me bringing him to the dinner. When Gerry finished his speech, I was rather chuffed to see that this same officer led the standing ovation. I cannot write about Gerry without mentioning his dear wife Ann and five lovely daughters. It was a joy for Mary and me to be friends of the family and share many happy occasions.

What a shame that Lord Cheshire V.C. was in poor health when he was created a Life Peer! He and his wife Baroness (Sue) Ryder were a terrific combination and together could have contributed enormously to the Lords. I was introduced to him by David Shannon, an Australian who had been a pilot on the Dambusters' Raid in the 1939/45 War. Lord Cheshire was a humble and modest man and, like his wife, extremely popular with everyone.

Prior to the visit of the King and Queen of Spain in April 1986, we were told that it would be normal 'day dress', which meant lounge suits for the men. On the morning of the visit it was raining, and the Comptroller of the Royal Household asked me to take the King's raincoat from him at the Royal Entrance and have it taken to the point of departure at Peers' Entrance. When the royal couple arrived, I was surprised to see that the King's raincoat was a plastic mac, the type you can fold up and put in a pocket! Anyhow, I complied with the earlier request and His Majesty was most gracious in his thanks. Incidentally the Queen is quite beautiful and was most tastefully dressed. Everyone was most taken with them both.

Late one evening, about 10 pm I think, the telephone rang and when I answered I was told by one of the Security Officers that a Peer had got out of a taxi at Chancellor's Gate and 'done a runner'. He had not paid the driver. The officer concerned had the Peer's name, which he passed on to me. I asked the Security man to pay the driver and then I reimbursed him

later. When I told Black Rod the following morning, he was not surprised –
as he had already heard that the person concerned 'was on drugs'.

Another story connected with a taxi driver happened at about noon one
day. The police officer on duty at Peers' Entrance telephoned to tell me that
a taxi had turned up and the Peer in the passenger seat was DEAD. Quite
rightly, the policeman had refused to accept the body and had suggested that
the driver take the Peer to Westminster Hospital. He agreed to this but
would not move until the fare was paid. I told the PC to pay the driver and
said that I would refund the cost to him. After lunch I told Black Rod and
he ordered me to commend the officer for his correct and prompt action.
This I did. There was a sequel to this story. The driver returned later in the
day to tell the officer, in a joking sort of way, that Westminster Hospital had
refused to take the body – after confirming the death – and redirected the
driver to the mortuary. The mind boggles at the thought of a taxi touring
London with a dead Peer in the back!

July each year saw the visit to the Lords of the Lord Lieutenants of
counties. Their meetings in the Moses Room were always well attended.
Major General Sir George Burns, Colonel of the Coldstream Regiment of
Foot Guards, was the Lord Lieutenant of Hertfordshire. He invariably met
me – not just in the Lords but wherever we happened to be – with the
words, 'I hope you're keeping those Peers in order,' and followed this with a
chuckle. At a Guards dinner I sat the High Commissioner for Australia next
to General Burns and afterwards Doug McClelland said to me, 'No wonder
we won the War with officers like him!'

A Russian Trade Delegation, including a Deputy Prime Minister, visited the Palace in 1981 and Black Rod asked me to give them a tour of the Line of Route. They had an excellent interpreter and the tour went very well; they asked questions and I gave them appropriate answers. However, there was not a single smile throughout the tour until we arrived in St Stephen's Hall. I, through the interpreter, pointing at the statue of 'Pitt the Younger', told them that it was alleged that he had died through alcoholism, having started at a very young age. With this the whole group of about ten burst into laughter and started to talk animatedly. I think that for the first time they had seen us as human beings. Perhaps this contributed to the destruction of the Berlin Wall!

At the end of the tour, the Deputy Prime Minister, Mrs Alexsandra Biryukova, made a speech thanking me for the guided tour and presented me with a book, *The Armoury in the Moscow Kremlin*. A day or two later I read in the papers that amongst items purchased by the delegation during its visit were 1,700,000 pairs of women's shoes, more than 50 million pairs of panty-hose, large quantities of soap, toothpaste, razor blades, cassettes and coffee. Could it be that the tour of the POW assisted in these sales?

One of the most popular Peers was Lord Elwyn-Jones, who was an ex-Lord Chancellor. Two of the Housemaids cleaned his residence when he lived on site and they adored him and his wife. Whenever he spotted me, he would stop for a gossip and wanted to know what was happening with the staff and their families. Mary Raymond, who cleaned his office, was heartbroken when he died – as were we all.

Unfortunately this chapter has to finish on a sad note: the death of the Lord Great Chamberlain in 1990. I had become very close to him, having done ten SOPs and several other state occasions with him. We had also dined together on a number of occasions and he had invited Mary and me to his home at Houghton Hall. John Gingell was Black Rod at the time and sent for me at about 2 pm – a time when he would normally be preparing for the Lord Chancellor's daily procession. He broke the news to me very gently and was as shocked and upset as I was. I like to think that the three of us had made a very good team. Without question, Hugh Cholmondeley was a really nice, decent guy with not a nasty bone in his body. I still miss him.

CHAPTER 18

The Ibbs Report and Large Works Services

IN MAY, 1990 the House of Commons Commission decided to invite Sir Robin Ibbs to undertake a review of management and decision-taking responsibilities for services to the House. With hindsight, I think that it was a mistake not to include the House of Lords in this review. My reason for saying this is that so much 'duplication' takes place, with each House doing its own (similar) thing.

There are many examples of this, but in particular I may mention cleaning, ordering of 'housekeeping' items such as uniforms for the Doorkeepers and Attendants, overalls for the Housemaids/part time cleaners, ordering of stationery, and numerous minor tasks. A good Executive Officer with a small staff could easily have dealt with these tasks. Remarkably, for such a detailed survey, the Report was published in six months. I read it in full and although some important points were missed, in general terms the Report was outstanding.

When the Report was discussed in the Commons in January 1991, I was disappointed that only three and a half hours were allowed for it to be debated. Some of the MPs seemed just to use the opportunity to snipe at certain members of staff and alleged poor services. Others even found the Report and/or debate amusing. I was surprised to read in *Hansard* that the standard of cleaning was so poor, as we had got the Lords right in the early 80s.

It is worth repeating this section of the Report, as it is in this aspect of business in the House that duplication took place; hopefully this is much improved nowadays:

HOUSE OF LORDS
The transfer to the Commission of control of the Commons works budget will affect the House of Lords. At present there is no distinction between the two Houses within the DOE Works Vote. If the House of Lords were to take over its share of the budget (as opposed to leaving control within DOE), the Upper House would require an intelligent client capability similar to that proposed for the Commons.

The PWO works programme makes no distinction between the two Houses, reflecting the reality that the Palace of Westminster is a single physical entity in which it is often not possible to assign particular items to individual occupants. This arrangement aims to safeguard, and ensure sufficient resources for the long-term maintenance requirements of the fabric of the Palace. If the Commons were to take over responsibility for its own accommodation, it would be difficult for the two Houses to operate separate works programmes.

It will be for the House of Lords to decide the extent of its participation in the new arrangements. But it would seem sensible for the proposed Director of Works and his staff to serve both the Commons and the Lords, providing the same services to the Lords, through Black Rod, as he will provide to the Commons. The Director would draw up a single works programme for approval by the authorities in both Houses. The arrangement would require co-ordination of the policy-making bodies in both Houses. The informal arrangements which currently operate in respect of other shared services may provide a model.'

As a result of the Report, as mentioned elsewhere, Henry Webber took over as Director of Works, which was a really good move. I quickly built up a good rapport with him and he helped me in many ways. Nevertheless I disagreed with one aspect of his appointment but did not know where the fault lay. To put it simply: the bureaucrats took over and there were far too many 'middle managers' appointed. They were 'Empire building' in fact! The junior staff in the Works Department started to joke about the 'inverted pyramid'. Instead of one boss at the top of the pyramid and lots of workers at the bottom, the opposite applied. They also thought it was amusing that a 'docket' was required before even the most simple job was carried out. Thank goodness I had a good relationship with most of the workmen, and got away without a docket at times. NEEDS MUST!

I sat next to Sir Robin Ibbs at lunch some time after his Report, and although he was guarded in what he said, it was obvious that he was disappointed at the way parts of it had been disregarded.

A request was made to the Works Department in 1984 to clean the throne canopy in the House of Lords Chamber. Work commenced as soon as the summer recess started and the intention was that the work was to be completed by mid-October, when the House resumed. Within no time at all, it was realized that this would not be possible. As the gilding and woodwork was cleaned, all sorts of serious problems were revealed. Previous work had been carried out in an ad-hoc and almost amateurish way. For instance, harsh methods of repair had been used, including screws, nails, tacks and even polyfilla to fill cracks. All sorts of cheap materials had been used, possibly due to shortage of time rather than poor workmanship. Another example of bad work was gilding overlapping on to woodwork. Obviously the installation of sound radio, cabling and light fittings had caused damage to prestigious areas.

The above bad news resulted in good news, as a full survey and investigation was carried out and the end product is now there for all to see: the throne canopy and surrounding area is quite magnificently beautiful and that is no exaggeration. All sorts of experiments were carried out and samples taken prior to any renovation taking place. Nothing was too much trouble for the (mainly young!) people carrying out the work, and their care and attention to detail were exemplary. They even found the Pugin recipe for oak stain, which was:- 'Boil bitumen in oil; mix the alum according to depth of colour; 2 parts – fine boiled oil, 1 part – Jan gold size, 1 part – Copel varnish'. Two types of gold leaf were used, liquid and tiny sheets out of a kind of book.

Every day for about a year scaffolding was erected in front of the throne canopy – a work of art in itself – and restoration work would take place until about 12.30 pm. On sitting days, the scaffold had to be stripped down by 1 pm to allow the Chamber to be prepared for the session. There was a certain amount of bad luck here as the televising of the Lords commenced in January 1985, and the Peers did not want the scaffold to be seen on the screens. I frequently spoke to the youngsters carrying out the work and was amazed at the dedication they showed to their work.

All the work was completed by the the end of 1986 summer recess. Black Rod was on holiday so I insisted on a proper 'handing over ceremony' with all interested parties in attendance. Fortunately a number of Peers got to hear about this and gathered in front of the throne canopy in the Chamber for my speech. I kept it short but gave high praise to those who had shown such craftmanship and zeal in their work. Those present obviously agreed, as they applauded long and hard.

Those involved in the restoration gave me a wonderful book, containing the details of every aspect of the work, which I treasure. Surprisingly, I have never seen this published but I hope it has been used by other craftsmen on similar projects. When anyone says to me that certain 'crafts' are dying, I refute this by quoting as an example the above, as well as work carried out by stonemasons and master carpenters.

Two ceilings in the Lords caused an enormous amount of problems. The first one was in the Peers' Lobby. Early in the 80s large cracks started to appear alongside the panels. The theory was that due to gas lighting, and more recently central heating, the woodwork had contracted, making them too small. A scaffold-type working platform was erected several feet below the ceiling in Peers' Lobby. Those planning the project hoped that the work would take less than a year. In the event, it took over six years. This was nobody's fault but a simple fact. As a panel was removed, to be sent away for restoration, more faults would be found in and around the place where the panel belonged. Quite rightly there were to be no short cuts on this occasion.

After the ceiling had been restored and the scaffold dismantled, the whole area of the Peers Lobby was cleaned and renovated and is now spectacular for Peers and visitors to see. Even this project was made to appear 'small fry' compared to the ceiling in the actual Chamber.

One evening when the House was sitting, a huge wooden boss fell from the ceiling, landing on the seat recently vacated by Lord Shinwell. If he had been sitting there, he would not have celebrated his 100th birthday! The House was quickly evacuated and for some time afterwards the Royal Gallery was used for sittings. Interestingly, when the staff set up the Royal Gallery for use as the Chamber, the exact floor specifications were used as in the actual Chamber. It was a tremendous achievement.

Similar methods as those in Peers' Lobby were used in erecting the scaffold beneath the ceiling in the Chamber. Once again every panel and removable item was sent away for restoration prior to being reassembled in all its beauty. Surprisingly, it was found that the heavy wooden carvings were glued together rather than bolted. Obviously this is how Barry designed it, but one wonders how no accident had occurred during the previous 120 odd years. A miracle really! During my regular trips up on to the scaffold, I saw the same craftsmanship, dedication and attention to detail that was mentioned earlier in this chapter. Everyone came out with credit. The British workman, properly led, has no equal anywhere in the world.

By far the biggest project during my time was the restoration of Victoria Tower. In an earlier chapter I rather glibly mentioned the cleaning of the outside stonework of the Palace of Westminster. For reasons that will become apparent, the Tower was left until last in the programme. To begin with, a huge scaffolding taking six months to erect, had to be put in place prior to the cleaning being commenced. Some idea of the enormity of this task is given by listing the following statistics: 68 miles of scaffold tubes were used, 125,000 fittings, weight 1,000 tonnes, as well as heavy duty structural Bailey bridges and towers. The whole of this structure was clad in protective sheeting and the Historic Archives areas connected to a mechanical ventilation and filtration system off site. This in itself was a wonderful feat of engineering.

One of the two Bailey bridges was erected over our flat on the west front of the House of Lords. For this to be carried out, the biggest crane in the country had to be hired. Mary and I were in residence at the time, and our lives were not disrupted at all. We were thrilled to watch the '8th wonder of the world' being put in position.

High pressure cold water jets were used on the stonework, as they had been when cleaning the rest of the Palace. Regilding, refurbishing and repairs to every possible area were completed and the workmen showed the same care and dedication to their work as to the other projects listed above. I made regular trips up the Tower and it was a joy to watch the craftsmen at work. Black Rod, Sir Richard Thomas, accompanied me one day and asked one of the stonemasons if this 'was just another job.' I cannot remember the exact reply, but the man concerned gave Richard a withering look and made it obvious that this was 'more than a job'!

Work on the stonecleaning had started with the New Palace Yard in 1981 and finished with the Victoria Tower between 1990 and 1993. I could spend several pages in detailing the fine work that contributed to the magnificent results, which are now there for all to see. The next time any reader is passing Victoria Tower, let him just study the artwork, including the gilding, metalwork and stonework. All those involved can be very proud of their efforts.

Until the late 1980s there was a desperate shortage of dining rooms in the Lords. This all changed due to a very brave decision taken by the then Black Rod, Air Chief Marshal Sir John Gingell. He arrived in my office unannounced one morning and asked me to accompany him. We proceeded to what can only be described as the grottiest part of the whole Palace. It was loosely described as the Furnishing Store, but in fact it was a tip or dump! All sorts of scruffy and grubby items from areas all over the Palace seemed to finish up in these three rooms. They were located underneath the Chamber of the Lords.

Sir John had what can only be described as an infectious enthusiasm. Within minutes he had convinced me that this was the site for a new dining room for Peers and their guests. Needless to say, I was more than a little dubious. A few days later Black Rod held a meeting on site with the Government Minister and me. He 'chatted up' the Minister to persuade him to allocate the appropriate cash for the work to be carried out, initially estimated at about £550,000. What Black Rod did not mention is that the associated works, such as re-routing, plumbing, electrical and other services, would almost double the cost. But who could blame him? He got what he wanted and the end justified the means.

I mentioned earlier that Black Rod's decision was a brave one. My reason for saying this is because prior to the project he met a lot of opposition. Traditionally it appeared that the Works Department had been allowed to 'squat' in the Lords area and naturally they did not want to move. They merited some sympathy, but quite honestly did not deserve to stay, as they had neglected these areas and allowed them to become run-down and dirty.

If I had not monitored the project, I would not have believed that the work on the dining room and a new kitchen could be finished so speedily. Not much more than a year after Black Rod's initiative, The Barry Room opened in all its splendour. The main room is a series of stone arches which, once restored, looked magnificent. Chandeliers, a few pictures, smart dining room furniture and some attractive plants were all that were needed to make the place look superb. Those who had known the Furnishing Store as it was thought the transformation amazing. So did I. The meals provided by Alfie Bibbiani and his staff are excellent and this new dining room is extremely popular.

Some of the associated works required in the Barry Room project were not small by any means. For example, printing presses, for use in emergencies, were in the area of the Furnishing store. These are huge and a new site – underneath Victoria Tower – had to be found. This also meant the moving of the plumbers' and carpenters' shops. So it is easy to see why the cost of the new dining facility virtually doubled. Suffice it to say that EVERYONE has benefited by Black Rod's personal idea.

Another large restoration was completed just a few days before I retired in January 1995. This was the building on the opposite side of the road to the House of Lords. During the 17th, 18th, 19th and 20th centuries, this building consisted of two houses, and had been used by all sorts of people from various parliamentary organizations. At one time the Clerk of Parliaments and Clerk Assistant in the Lords lived there. During the period from 1958 until the end of 1993 the building had been used by MPs and their secretaries, until it was returned to the House of Lords. To understate the case – the interior had become decidedly run down and rather 'grotty'.

As with other projects mentioned in this chapter, an enormous amount of research and investigation took place prior to any restoration work being undertaken. Acting on instructions from the Chairman of Committees, Lord

Ampthill, I monitored all the work taking place. Work commenced on the 21st February, 1994 and the whole programme had to be finished by the end of the 1994 Christmas recess. This may sound simple on paper, but proved to be very hard indeed. Hardly a day went by without new and serious problems arising. Stonework crumbled, floors were rotten, cabling and other plumbing had to be replaced and many other structural problems came to light. Regardless of these obstacles, things were going along quite swimmingly until the late summer of 1994, when English Heritage became involved.

I hate being critical of English Heritage, but it is hard to avoid it. They have a job to do, namely to protect such old buildings, but at times they did go 'over the top' in what they expected of the restoration team, who I thought were superb. Every sort of 'rule' was laid down on what was expected of the architects and the mechanical, electrical and structural engineers, to say nothing of the builders and decorators. Their patience was tested to the extreme.

One argument we lost to English Heritage was a personal disappointment. Prior to the takeover of 6/7 Old Palace Yard, it had been decided that my successor as the Staff Superintendent would not have his residence in the main building but would live on the top floor of this building. I had set myself the task of looking after his interests and asked for a lift; this had been agreed. This was still planned for until a meeting took place between Lord Ampthill and English Heritage that neither Black Rod nor I attended. Richard Thomas was furious when he heard this, but by then the 'die was cast'. My replacement and his wife and family suffer from this deficiency to this day. I feel guilty that I let them down!

Space does not permit me to describe the various pitfalls and problems. Imagine how delighted I was when the whole project was completed by the deadline date, and a grand opening took place on the 12th January 1995 – just days before I retired. The Lord Ampthill was kind enough to say in his speech that without the Staff Superintendent's 'oversee of the work' the building would not have been completed on time. Little did he know that I had needed to wear my Regimental Sergeant Major's hat at times. Interpreted, this means 'leadership of any kind!'

CHAPTER 19

The Queen Is Not Amused – Or Is She?

BEING A MEMBER OF THE Household Division and the Staff Super-intendent of the House of Lords brought me into contact with many people who mixed in royal circles. What is interesting is the extreme loyalty they have to the royals, in particular to Her Majesty the Queen. Whilst they would tell you interesting or amusing stories, they would never tell any embarrassing or nasty ones.

Anyone who has been in the company of the Queen at a 'private' event, will know that she has a spontaneous wit and an infectious laugh. Without question she has inherited this from her mother, who is known as Queen Elizabeth, not the Queen Mother, in royal circles. Some of the tales that follow are personal ones, but where I quote someone else they cannot be offended or upset, as they show the human side of the family and their associates.

During my tour at the Caterham Guards Depot in the late 50s, the Officers' Mess Colour Sergeant told me this story. Prince Philip was a guest at lunch having inspected the Welsh Guards. Ice cream, in the shape of a mouse, was the dessert course. The cook must have left these in the freezer until the last possible moment but did not realize this when he served it up. As HRH went to put a spoon into the 'mouse', it jumped off the plate. A deathly hush descended until Prince Philip, in a stage whisper, said 'The bloody thing is alive!' and all those in earshot erupted with laughter. There was no embarrassment.

Queen Elizabeth the Queen Mother visited the Pirbright Guards Depot in 1974 to present shamrock to the Irish Guards on St Patrick's Day. I was the catering officer at that time. During lunch the Commandant, Colonel Iain Ferguson, told me that the Royal Visitor wanted to meet the chef afterwards to thank and congratulate him. As Queen Elizabeth left the Mess, I had Sergeant Farmer positioned outside the door to the Officers Mess. I had briefed him about the court bow and the handshake and to address her as Ma-am. He did the bow and the handshake all right but due to nervousness, addressed the Queen Mum as 'Sir' on three occasions. She never even blinked. The Commandant and I looked at the heavens for help.

After the royal car had departed, I asked Sergeant Farmer why he had addressed HM as 'Sir' and he denied that he had done so. Thank goodness the beef wellington was OK!

Mentioning the name 'Farmer' reminds me of a story Cyril Phillips told me when he was the Superintendent of the State Apartments at St James's Palace. His job at receptions in the State Apartments was to accompany the senior royal as he or she walked around the various groups of guests. These would be in small half-circles of five or six people. On the occasion in question, the Queen and Cyril approached a party of five. The first two in the line were ladies and did a curtsy and extended a hand. The third in line was a great big young farmer, who also did a deep curtsy! Her Majesty turned to Cyril, opened her mouth like a fish out of water, but did not speak. Cyril remained poker-faced and said nothing so the Queen went on with greeting others in the party as if nothing unusual had occurred.

At these receptions the Queen usually wears a cape to travel to and from Buckingham Palace. As Cyril was helping HM to put the cape on prior to her departure, she thanked him for showing such discipline during the above incident. She went on to tell him that if he had spoken, she would have found it hard not to laugh. One wonders if the young man concerned knows to this day that he should not have curtsied. Incidentally, Cyril managed to put the Queen's cape on upside down more than once, and HM always enjoyed telling him this – with a twinkle in her eye.

Those fortunate enough to be honoured with an award are invariably amazed how knowledgeable the Queen is about recipients at investitures. In my own case in 1972 she knew that I had been the Regimental Sergeant Major at Mons Officer Cadet School. She said how sad she was that a place that had done such a good job had now closed down. When John Holbrook went for his 'gong', the Queen knew that his son had been involved in the bombing of the Paras at Warrenpoint and was lucky not to be killed. Other examples are too numerous to mention.

Everyone now seems to know that Queen Elizabeth is determined to live until 100 to receive a telegram from her daughter. Pray God that she does. However, what is not known is that she has a mischievous sense of fun. Sir Ralph Anstruther, late Coldstream Guards, has been Treasurer and Equerry to her for well over 40 years. I had him for lunch in the Peers' Dining Room in 1990 and he told me many lovely tales of the fun she initiated. He added how full of life she is and how she 'bounces off people' and enjoys company (and a 'tipple' at times!)

From time immemorial the Coldstreams and Grenadiers have argued about which regiment is the senior; not always in a pleasant way either. The Coldstream Guards was formed in 1650 and the Grenadiers several years later. When I was the Quartermaster of the 2nd Battalion at Windsor in 1976, Colonel Christopher Willoughby told me the most extraordinary story of the Queen Mum's sense of fun.

Occasionally the Commanding Officer of the Battalion in Victoria Barracks is invited to dine or attend receptions in Windsor Castle. He arrived in my office one morning to tell me the following. The previous evening he had been at a reception in the Castle and was talking to Queen Elizabeth about 'nothing in particular' when the Queen approached. Without a flicker of a smile, mother said to daughter: 'You can settle this argument. Colonel Willoughby is just telling me that the Coldstream are senior to the Grenadiers. What do you think?' Putting her hands up in mock horror, the Queen said 'Don't get me involved in that business' and walked away. Colonel Willoughby was speechless but the Queen Mother was highly amused, to say the least.

Another mischievous person, not a royal but with royal connections, is Colonel David Lewis, late Welsh Guards. In 1979 he was the Commandant of the Guards Depot and I was the Quartermaster. The Duke of Edinburgh inspected a passing out parade of Grenadiers and then came to lunch in the Officers' Mess. The order of dress for lunch had been changed at the last minute – all the other officers were in woollen pullovers, I was in service dress with sam browne belt. Colonel Lewis immediately pointed this out to Prince Philip, who roared with laughter.

Two weeks later the Duke of Kent inspected a passing out parade of Scots Guards and came to lunch in the Officers Mess. I went to a great deal of trouble, including ringing the Adjutant and checking the notice board in the Officers' Mess. The instructions were clear – WOOLLEN PULLOVERS. I therefore turned up in that order – only to find all the other officers in service dress. When introducing me to the Duke of Kent, the Commanding Officer pointed out what an ill-disciplined Quartermaster he had as this was the second time in two weeks that I had turned up improperly dressed for a VIP lunch. Even I laughed this time. Nobody has ever admitted that this was a 'send-up' but I am sure that it was.

True stories are better than fiction. For example in the 1980s the Nulli Secundus Club celebrated its 200th anniversary. The Queen was the Guest of Honour at dinner in the Savoy Hotel. During dinner, Lt. Colonel Dick Ridings whispered in my ear that I would be presented to the Queen after dinner. I thought he was joking and continued enjoying myself. Sure

enough, after dinner several of us were whisked away into a side room to meet the Queen. When she got to our group of five, the conversation was heavy going. The 1st Battalion had just returned from Northern Ireland and all my chums had been part of that Battalion. I waited for a break in conversation and then asked the Queen if she had a tip for the Derby the following day. I posed the question in a light-hearted manner but the Queen took me seriously and proceeded to list about a dozen horses that would not win and advised us not to back them. Obviously racing is no laughing matter.

Vernon Jewell, an ex-senior Warrant Officer in the Grenadiers, was the Chief Clerk and Accountant to the Duke of Edinburgh's Household for many years. He had a special rapport with Prince Philip, not just because of their regimental connection, but also because they both shared a similar sense of humour. HRH had a habit of leaning, half sitting, on the edge of Vernon's (who was known as Jimmy) desk and expected to be told of any gossip. To digress a bit, Jimmy usually knew when the Queen was approaching, as she could be heard cursing her corgis.

During the bread strike in the 1980s Prince Philip was in Jimmy's office complaining about having to leave for Windsor in a separate car ahead of the Queen. Jimmy made a throw-away remark that because of the strike 'you have to get the bread in, Sir'. Prince Philip went away chuckling. Some time later Jimmy, who was working at his desk, heard a slight noise at the door. Looking up he saw the Queen peering around the door. As he started to stand up, HM said something like: 'I understand Prince Philip has gone ahead to get the bread in, Mr Jewell' – and was gone! 'Oops' he thought, there goes my MVO. As it turned out, he eventually got the LVO, which was even better.

Jimmy lived alongside the Prince and Princess of Wales in Kensington Palace. During a hot summer's day Jimmy was in his garden when Prince William started to squirt water at him with the hosepipe. William was quite small at the time so Jimmy was telling him to stop it when Princess Diana appeared. She told Jimmy off for not smacking the Prince for his naughtiness. Jimmy protested that he could not smack the future King of England, to be firmly told by Diana that he had her permission to do so. No wonder 'Wills' and 'Harry' have turned out to be such smashing boys.

Writing about William reminds me of an incident I was personally involved in with him. In 1989 Lord Tanlaw asked me if I could give his son and a 'few school chums' a tour of the Palace. Despite Black Rod's misgivings when he heard that the future King was to be in the party, I agreed. This was a birthday treat for Master Tanlaw and he turned up with his father, a teacher, William's detective and about a dozen six- and seven-year-old boys.

Prince William at the birthday party of Lord Tanlaw's son, 1989.

For most of the tour the boys formed a 'crocodile' and were very well behaved. However, on arrival in the Queen's Robing Room, William and young Tanlaw became quite agitated when they spotted the small throne intended for the use of the monarch. During my talk about the Robing Room they asked several times if they could sit on the throne. For a few minutes I refused but eventually had a rush of blood to the head. Within seconds William and the birthday boy were BOTH sitting on the throne with the remainder fighting to join them. I whispered to Lord Tanlaw that I would finish up in the Tower, to which he replied, 'I may well be with you, Major Horsfall!' William promised me that he would not tell his Granny but would be telling his mother. When I told Sir John Gingell about this, there was no sympathy; in fact he roared with laughter.

As mentioned in an earlier chapter, the Gentleman Usher of the Black Rod is an officer of the Order of the Garter. At such times as the State opening of Parliament he acts as a 'messenger' for Her Majesty. A less well-known ceremonial event is the Prorogation of Parliament. This takes place at the end of a Parliament or a parliamentary year. Black Rod proceeds to the Commons in a similar way as that highlighted on television at the SOP, to summon the MPs to the Lords.

When General House was Black Rod in the early 80s, there was a really nasty incident. The Lords rose in the late evening and Prorogation was due to take place at about 10.15 pm. Black Rod heard that there might be trouble and asked me to watch points and try to help. He processed as normal with Lieutenant Commander Kemp and the Principal Doorkeeper. On arrival at the Commons door, his entry was barred by a party of left wing MPs. Three times he tried before turning about and coming back to the Lords. He was absolutely furious and reminded the Chief Whip, and anyone else in the vicinity, that he was the 'Queen's Messenger'.

Lord Hailsham, the Lord Chancellor, was heard to say 'Tell the Commons that they are being a bloody bore!' General House avoided a constitutional crisis by agreeing to try again about 45 minutes later – this time successfully. Since this incident, Prorogation has taken place early in the day following the last day of sittings in both Houses. This is a pity as many of the Peers and MPs are not present for what is a really impressive ceremony. Fortunately the cameras now capture this on television.

No superlatives can exaggerate how good the Duke of Norfolk is in his capacity as the Earl Marshal; he is full of good humour and common sense. His entry in *Who's Who* lists his many titles and duties but fails to do him justice. What I admire most is that he is a good listener and also, despite being steeped in tradition, is a moderniser. For example his views on the future of the House of Lords are most enlightening. However, in this chapter it is his sense of humour that I wish to highlight.

The Earl Marshal and I were standing at the top of the Royal Staircase waiting for the Queen to arrive for the Opening of Parliament one year. He started to talk to a barrel-chested non-commissioned officer in the Household Cavalry, telling him how smart he was etcetra etcetra. The NCO preened himself and grew taller and taller. After a while His Grace said to the trooper, 'There's only one thing wrong with you'. 'What's that, Sir?' said the Lance Corporal of Horse. 'You're too smart to be in the cavalry, you should be a Grenadier'. With that he walked over to the Gold Stick, The Lord Michael Fitzalan-Howard (his brother!), roaring with laughter and repeating what he had told the cavalryman. Lord Michael, who was the Colonel of the Life Guards, was also amused.

Of course not all is laughter and lightheartedness. Operation Marquee is the name of the procedure laid down for the Lying-in-State of a sovereign in Westminster Hall. Regrettably, as the Queen Mother nears her century, the meetings and rehearsals become more frequent. She is the most loved lady in the land and her demise will cause great sadness. One of the reasons the Staff Superintendent cannot be away at the same time as Black Rod is in case the end should come at an inappropriate time. Shades of Field Marshal Montgomery dying at a very busy time. The arrangements for a Lying-in-State were poor until the arrival in the Lord Chamberlain's Department of Lieutenant Colonel Anthony Mather, late Grenadier Guards. He dotted the i's and crossed the t's by picking the brains of anyone and everyone.

My favourite royal story is one told by the late Major Bill Nash when he was the Superintendent, Windsor Castle. On a Friday afternoon Bill had to report to the Queen on her arrival at Windsor to update her on various 'housekeeping' and other subjects. Sometimes she would have had a walkabout and at others she had not. Occasionally there was good-natured banter but mostly there was not. Usually before Bill chanced being light-hearted or flippant, he let the Queen take the lead.

One Friday afternoon the Queen had done her tour prior to seeing Bill. After updating each other on various projects, Her Majesty asked Bill who the Guv'nor was. He was puzzled by this and asked for more details. The Queen went on to explain that on arrival in Prince Philip's room, a black carpenter was working on a recess in the window where some shelving was to be fitted. She knew that the carpenter was not carrying out the work as requested by the Prince, so she told the man this. An argument developed between them which ended when the carpenter told the Queen that he'd 'have to ask the guv'nor'. Bill reassured the Queen that there was no doubt that she was the guv'nor. With that Her Majesty collapsed with laughter. Bill had intended to discipline the man concerned but changed his mind when he heard that the carpenter had told his mates that 'he had nearly turned white' at the thought of arguing with the Queen. 'NUFF SAID' thought Bill. Nevertheless, Bill picked his moment to tell this to HM.

A quickie – Prince Andrew arrived at Bill's house in the Castle grounds, with several chums, asking if there was anything to eat – they were starving. Bill sent out for 16 portions of fish and chips. They sat in his lounge to eat them, with his wife Josie providing lots of tea and bread and butter.

I almost became a member of the Royal Household staff on three separate occasions. Firstly as the Superintendent, Royal Mews, then as Superintendent, Windsor Castle and finally as a Military Knight of Windsor. In some ways I am sad that I didn't, but having had such a fabulous tour in the Lords, there can be no regrets. Two of the Military Knights who know me well have never forgiven me for turning down an appointment in 1991 – I was not ready for retirement at the time.

Jim Eastwood replaced Bill Nash when he died in post. When Jim retired, the Queen literally invited herself to his farewell party, but only on condition that Jim did not change his speech. Jim warned HM that some of the anecdotes he would tell did not show her in the best light. She insisted on 'no change' so Jim told them as they were. As each story was told, the Queen's laughter got longer and louder, belying the saying, 'The Queen was not amused'.

CHAPTER 20

Trips Abroad and Stories to Tell

ONE OF THE PROBLEMS when writing an autobiography is that there is no proper slot for many of the tales to be told. Partly to compensate for this, I am including this general chapter.

Whilst in the Army, I did a lot of worldwide travelling but Mary stayed in England, mainly to help in the education of Terry and Bob. Since leaving the Regiment, we have more than made up for this by having holidays in America, Australia, Canada, Cyprus, France, Germany, Hong Kong, Ireland, Isle of Man, Isle of Wight, Israel, Malaya, New Zealand, Singapore, South Africa, Spain, Thailand and several holiday islands. Apart from enjoying holidays abroad, I found that if I stayed in the UK I did not relax. Once anyone gets on a 'plane, there is nothing that can be done about a problem back at home.

Australia remains our favourite place and we have been there nine times on holiday. When we went there in 1981, to visit Mary's brother Bill and his family, we thought it would be a 'one off'. However, we have accumulated so many friends from 'down under' that the visits have become more and more attractive. Many of these are involved with cricket, rugby and Oz-rules football, which obviously pleases me. Also, the weather, except for June 1998, when it was awful, is a major attraction. Nowadays we exchange Christmas cards with about 100 friends abroad, mostly in Australia. The hospitality of the Australians particularly is nothing short of fantastic.

We list amongst our closest friends the ex-High Commissioner for Australia, Douglas McClelland, and several past and present Agents General for Australia's six states. These are a special breed of people, who do all sorts of good work for their country. Not only do they have to be highly efficient, but they need to have great diplomatic skills, charm and tact as well. Our list of friends is too large to repeat, but the McClellands, de Rohans, Sellers and Jackson families deserve a special mention, as we have shared many happy occasions with them.

I met Douglas through cricket and we were able to help each other in many ways, both on and off duty. Maurice and Margaret de Rohan happened to be at Australia House for a reception one evening and we hit it

The family in Sydney to celebrate the author's 60th birthday.
Left to right: Judi, Terry, Mary, the author, Bob.

off immediately. Maurice was a businessman at the time but he is now the Agent General for South Australia. He and Margaret have found it hard to come to terms with the loss of their daughter and son-in-law in the Zeebrugge shipping disaster in March 1987. Why do such terrible things happen to the very nicest of people? God does act in the most mysterious ways!

Basil Sellers and Alan Jackson are two very successful businessmen with lovely wives and smashing families. 'Generosity' should be their middle names, as they both enjoy life to the full, hosting parties and treating other people. Basil's 60th birthday party was beyond description. He took over Hampton Court Palace for the night, with the Royal Marines Band, a banquet, travel to and from the Palace on the Orient Express, a firework display, and many other special items and goodies. Similarly, Alan (Jackson) arranged a special birthday party for his wife Esme and hired a boat in Sydney Harbour for the week-end, with 80 guests staying on board overnight. These are just examples of their kindly nature.

Talking of parties reminds me of four surprise ones I have managed to spring on Mary: our 20th anniversary at Mons Officer Cadet School, our Pearl wedding on the House of Lords Terrace, our Ruby Wedding in

Wellington Barracks, and Mary's 60th, again in Wellington Barracks. I never cease to be amazed at how people 'in the know' can keep a secret. Not once did any of the 40 to 60 people who attended these parties 'let the cat out of the bag' and tell Mary.

For Keith Miller's 70th birthday in 1989 Doug McClelland put on a lunch party for 12 men in his residence. Apart from me, they were all famous and included the Bedser twins and Brian Johnson, the cricketing commentator. I sat next to David Shannon, an RAAF pilot who took part in the Dambusters' raid in the last War. He was a wonderful man and we became great friends with him and his lovely wife Anne and beautiful daughter Nikki. David had three gallantry awards before he was 23 and was very proud that the Queen Mother, when she was Queen, attended his 21st birthday party. Lord Cheshire V.C. was a great pal of his and they had a lot in common, not least their humility and modesty.

Holders of the Victoria Cross have a quality which is hard to define, an intangible quality in fact. I knew Peter Wright V.C. and there will be more about him later. This is the Citation of an Australian that we have become friends with in recent years:

Sir Arthur Roden Cutler, VC, AK, KCMG, KCVO, CBE, K. St. J.

CUTLER, Lieutenant Arthur Roden
2/5th Australian Field Regiment, A.I.F.

19th June to 6th July 1941, at Merdjayoun-Damour area, Syria

CITATION: For most conspicuous and sustained gallantry during the Syrian Campaign and for outstanding bravery during the bitter fighting at Merdjayoun when this artillery officer became a byword amongst forward troops with which he worked.

At Merdjayoun on 19th June, 1941 our infantry attack was checked after suffering heavy casualties from an enemy counter-attack with tanks. Enemy machine gun fire swept the ground, but Lieutenant Cutler with another artillery officer and a small party pushed on ahead of the infantry and established an outpost in a house. The telephone line was cut and he went out and mended this line under machine gun fire and returned to the house, from which enemy posts and batteries were successfully engaged. The enemy then attacked this outpost with infantry and tanks, killing the Bren gunner and mortally wounding other officers. Lieutenant Cutler and another manned the anti-tank rifle and Bren gun and fought back, driving the enemy infantry away. The tank continued the attack, but under constant fire from the anti-tank rifle and Bren gun eventually withdrew. Lieutenant Cutler then personally supervised the evacuation of the wounded members of his party. Undaunted he pressed for a further advance. He had been ordered to establish an outpost from which he could register the only road by which the enemy transport could enter the town. With a small party of volunteers he pressed on until finally with one other he succeeded in establishing an outpost right in the town, which was occupied by the Foreign Legion, despite enemy machine gun fire which prevented our infantry from advancing. At this time Lieutenant Cutler knew the enemy were massing on his left for a counter attack and that he was in danger of being cut off. Nevertheless he carried out his task of registering the battery on the road and engaging enemy posts. The enemy counter-attacked with infantry and tanks and he was cut off. He was forced to go to ground, but after dark succeeded in making his way through enemy lines. His work in registering the only road by which the enemy transport could enter the town was of vital importance and a big factor in the enemy's subsequent retreat.

On the night of 23rd-24th June he was in charge of a 25-pounder sent forward into our forward defended localities to silence an enemy anti-tank gun and post, which had held up our attack. This he did and the next morning the recapture of Merdjayoun was completed. Later at Damour on 6th July, when our forward infantry were pinned to the ground by heavy hostile machine gun fire Lieutenant Cutler, regardless of all danger, went to bring a line to his outpost when he was seriously wounded. Twenty-six hours elapsed before it was possible to rescue this officer, whose wounds by this time had become septic necessitating the amputation of his leg. Throughout the Campaign this officer's courage was unparalleled and his work was a big factor in the recapture of Merdjayoun.

(London Gazette: 28th November 1941)

The above tells you about his courage and gallantry but says nothing about the type of person he is. Although a giant of a man, who has achieved everything in life, he remains self-effacing, modest, of good humour and of a kindly nature. When in his company you feel that you are with someone quite special, as he has a great presence. I strongly recommend the biography of Roden Cutler, V.C. by Colleen McCullough. He is blessed with a lovely wife Joan. Amongst the appointments Sir Roden has held are:

Governor of New South Wales, and at various times the High Commissioner for Australia to the following countries:- New Zealand, Ceylon, Pakistan. He has also held various ambassadorial and ministerial posts. What a guy, what a record!

When I was introduced to Sir Roden he told me that he had met a friend of mine, Peter Wright V.C. This was when Peter and his wife Mollie

With Sir Roden Cutler V.C. and his wife, Joan, 1998.

visited Australia in the late 80s. He went on to say what a wonderful couple they were. Peter's Citation reads as follows:

2657545 W02 (Company Sergeant Major)
Peter Harold Wright Coldstream Guards

In Italy on the 25th September 1943, the 3rd Battalion Coldstream Guards attacked the Pagliarolli feature, a steep wooded hill near Salerno. Before it reached the crest, the right hand company was held up by heavy spandau and mortar fire and all the officers had become casualties.

CSM Wright, seeing his company was held up, went forward to see what could be done. Finding that there were no officers left he immediately took charge and crawled forward by himself to see what the opposition was. He returned with the information that three spandau posts were holding them up. He collected a section and put it into a position where it could give covering fire. Single handed he then attacked each post in turn with hand grenades and bayonet and silenced each one. He then led the company on to the crest but realised that the enemy fire made this position untenable. CSM Wright therefore led them a short way down the hill and up on to the objective from a different direction.

Entirely regardless of enemy fire, which was very heavy, CSM Wright then reorganised what was left of the company and placed them into position to consolidate the objective.

Soon afterwards the enemy launched a counter attack which was successfully beaten off. Later, with complete disregard of heavy enemy shell fire on the area of company headquarters and the reverse slopes of the hill and of machine gun fire from commanding slopes on the left flank of the position, he brought up extra ammunition and distributed it to the company.

It is due to this Warrant Officer's superb disregard of the enemy's fire, his magnificent leadership, and his outstanding heroism throughout the action that his battalion succeeded in capturing and maintaining its hold on this very important objective.

Although I had met Peter many times, I did not get to know him well until he visited the Guards Depot when I was the Quartermaster. The Company Commander, Major James Innes, invited him to speak to the recruits and junior guardsmen, which he did in the camp cinema at Pirbright. Having talked about the action for which he was awarded the V.C., Peter took questions from the audience. A young recruit asked him why he did what he did. Peter said in a matter of fact way: 'It was just my

With Peter Wright V.C., 1984.

The funeral of Peter Wright, V.C. The Warrant Officer is Garrison Sergeant Major 'Perry' Mason.

training – you'd probably have done the same if you'd been in my place'. Discussing the matter afterwards with James Innes, we both agreed that Peter meant what he had said. Remarkable to say the least.

Peter stayed with Mary and me at Farnborough the night of the lecture. It has been well logged that initially Peter had been awarded the Distinguished Conduct Medal and that some time later the King had this upgraded to the Victoria Cross. I asked Peter where the DCM was and he said something along the lines of 'at home in a drawer, I think'. He took some convincing that Regimental Headquarters would love to have it. I believe it is still there in RHQ until this day. Typical of this gentleman farmer's modest disposition. His funeral in 1990 told a story that is better than the written word, as there was a massive turnout of both Coldstreamers and other regiments and corps.

Talking of bravery brings me on to another special occasion hosted annually by the House of Lords – the visit of the Children of Courage. Numerous 'showbiz' stars give their time free to entertain these wonderful kids, whose shining courage in adversity is an example to us all.

On the 16th October 1834 the Palace of Westminster was destroyed by
fire and the circumstances have been well reported. What is not well known
is that soldiers from the Foot Guards stationed at Wellington Barracks
helped to put out the fire. One book I read records that '500 Coldstream
Guardsmen from the nearby barracks assisted in fighting the fire'. These
'nulli secundus' men seem to get everywhere – thank goodness!

Westminster Hall was saved due to the quick thinking of Lord Althorp,
who was heard to shout out: 'Damn the House of Commons, let it blaze
away, but save, oh save, the Hall.' Paintings displayed in the Palace now show
the soldiers and firemen doing just that.

A resumé of some other memories. Let me start with the rapport I had
with the Earl of Longford, who is nothing like the picture painted by the
tabloid press because of his links with Myra Hindley (the Moors Murderer)
and other criminals. What a talented family too – his wife Elizabeth is still
writing in her nineties, as is daughter Lady Antonia Fraser and her husband
playwright Harold Pinter. His lordship put on a luncheon party for Mary
and me before we retired in 1995 and I found his grandson (who was sitting
next to me) as 'bright as a button' and extremely pleasant.

I have made two unedited broadcasts about the POW; unedited because I
insisted on this as I did not want to give any false impressions. One of the
top interviewers in Vancouver, Canada, is Gary Bannerman. Geraldine
Jamieson is by far the best in the Isle of Man. Naturally I was worried about
these, as I had no prior warning of the questions, but in the event received
lots of praise from those who had heard the broadcasts, including some
Peers. I have replayed the tapes recently and am 'chuffed' with the results.
Self-praise is no recommendation however!

Authors who write about the Palace, or either House, fascinate me,
whether they are dealing with fiction or fact. They all see the building and
its occupants in a different way. Lord Longford's *History of the HOL* is by far
the best factual one. Lord Denham's fictional novels are great entertainment
but contain many vivid true descriptions of the Palace. Michael Dobbs'
intimate knowledge of both Houses has made his three books *House of
Cards*, *To Play the King* and *The Final Cut* more realistic than if purely
fictional. Michael and I became pals after he had written the *House of Cards*
and I was able to assist him in a small way when he was researching the
other two books. Seemingly he gained all his detailed knowledge of the
Commons when he was the 'Chief of Staff' to Margaret Thatcher during
her time as Prime Minister. His books made great television programmes.

When the late John Wells approached me in 1993 and asked me to give him a tour of the Lords because he was writing the 'modern' history of the House, I willingly agreed. He had a press photopass so within reason I could take him anywhere. We toured the House several times and John could not believe his luck when I introduced him to Lord Longford. It resulted in them spending many hours together. Through me he also met Lord Ampthill, who at the time was the Lord Chairman of Committees. Although the finished product, *The House of Lords: An Anecdotal History* contains some errors, it makes excellent and easy reading. I was embarrassed that he wrote so much about me because he never at any stage asked if he could. He MUST have had a pocket tape recorder as he NEVER made a note. John's memorial service in April 1998 was attended by too many famous people to list, but they included the future King, HRH Prince Charles.

Mary and I visited Houghton Hall, the home of The Lord Great Chamberlain, the Marquess of Cholmondeley, twice, invited once by Hugh and once by David. Despite there being a number of distinguished guests present, we were treated as the main ones at lunch, with Mary sitting at one end of the table alongside his Lordship and me at the other end with Lady Cholmondeley. They were both great fun and we were made to feel very much at home. The highlight was being shown Lord Hugh's wonderful collection of model soldiers. There are battle scenes, trooping the colour and many other items, which are very famous. Lord Cholmondeley corrected me several times when I referred incorrectly to 'toy' soldiers! Lord Hugh was a very special person and David will have a stiff task in trying to live up to his reputation.

Bomb-blast net curtains were fitted in the windows on the west front and facing south in 1985. General House hated the thought of having these in his office but eventually agreed. Mary and I never did allow them to be fitted in our flat.

Occasionally I took special friends to the top of Victoria Tower, always accompanied by a fireman. Being considerably higher than the Clock Tower, it affords a wonderful all-round panoramic view of the whole of Central London. My brother Terry discovered for the first time that he was scared of heights, despite having flown in aircraft many times. Mollie Sugden and many other visitors describe this trip to the top as one of the highlights of their lives – no pun intended!

After I had shown the High Commissioner for Tonga and his beautiful wife and daughters through the Line of Route, he described the building as the finest he had seen anywhere, including London.

During the 1980s the Lord Chancellor's Breakfast, which takes place each year on the 1st of October, was held in the Royal Gallery. The layout was brilliant and I was dismayed and disappointed when the decision was taken to move to Westminster Hall, where it is held until this day. Although the Great Hall is magnificent, it does not have the grandeur of the Royal Gallery, Presumably the change was made because of the Hall's connection with judicial trials many years ago.

The Lords of Appeal sometimes get a bad press, for example in the recent Pinochet case. This is most unfair; as I have mentioned elsewhere, they work very long hours and regularly during recesses when the House is not sitting.

There is talk of the Bishops being excluded from any revised House of Lords. This is a pity as they give some balance to proceedings. Some MPs think that they should not get involved in such subjects as the 'inner cities'. I ask, 'Why not?'

Women Peers make a huge contribution to the workings of the House and in general terms are better attenders than many of the males. Also, most of the lady members of the staff, including the Clerks, are outstanding. When the first woman was made a Clerk of the Table in the Commons, I said, as a joke, to Sir John Gingell that I could see him being replaced as Black Rod by a lady. He replied, 'Why not?' and went on to tell me about some of the first-class senior servicewomen he had served with. WATCH THIS SPACE!

When a particular Bill was going through the Lords, some ladies disagreed with certain aspects of it. They therefore decided to abseil from the gallery in the Lords into the body of the Chamber. One of the ladies landed up, literally, in the arms of Black Rod. When I next saw Air Chief Marshal Sir John Gingell, I congratulated him on his capture. He was in good humour about this but said, 'I wouldn't have minded, Peter, but she was a so-and-so lesbian!'

CHAPTER 21

Nearing Retirement and the Years After

REACHING 60 MADE ME realize that retirement would be upon me before I knew it and this proved to be the case. The ten years I had been the Staff Superintendent had absolutely flashed by. This was probably due to enjoying my work and having so many outside interests. In addition to my enthusiasm for all sports, Mary and I enjoyed live theatre and going abroad. We had also accumulated numerous wonderful friends in and around London.

Being so near to my Regiment's headquarters in Wellington Barracks meant that Mary and I were in constant touch with our friends of many years. Indeed, remarkably, either the 1st or 2nd Battalion was in Chelsea or Wellington Barracks almost continually between 1980-92. I did not feel like an 'intruder' as I had a Mess Bill number in both officers' messes, so always paid my way. I still do. With the fierce cut-back in the armed forces, the Regiment welcomes my efforts to organise reunions for past and present officers and guardsmen. By far the most successful one was of the 3rd Battalion in 1984, when almost 400 attended, including 37 officers. Major General Sir George Burns (ex-CO) and Charlie Smy (ex-RSM) were quite rightly treated like national heroes.

Reunions of a more intimate nature were the ones held by the Guards Officers Brigade Squad I trained in 1959. This squad was mentioned earlier in the book. Interestingly, Michael Heseltine has never missed one of these, no matter how busy he was. Talking of 'Tarzan', imagine how proud I was in 1984 when Mary and I were invited to watch the Sovereign's Parade at Sandhurst. At the ceremony he represented the Queen as the Inspecting Officer. He was the Secretary of State for Defence at the time. In 1986 I attended a lecture to businessmen by Michael in the Grand Committee Room in the Commons and he received a standing ovation. Did this reflect well on the 'five minute lecturettes' insisted on by Captain Dawson in 1959? I'd like to think so. Michael Crick, in his biography of Heseltine, did not make enough of this aspect of his qualities.

A most interesting thing happened to me in 1986 when I was given the Freedom of the City of London. As a Yorkshireman, I enjoyed being described as a 'citizen of London' on the magnificent scroll presented to me by the Clerk. This seems an appropriate moment to mention the ridiculous statement made by the author Beryl Bainbridge in 1999. She seems to think that people with regional dialects are either uneducated or should not be considered for prestigious posts. In recent years I have met so many 'senior' people with strong regional accents that this makes a mockery of her comments. Michael Parkinson of TV fame and I once had a conversation on this subject and we both agreed that if the diction was good, the dialect could benefit the subject being talked about.

Another nice thing happened to me in 1986 when General Sir David recommended me for an appointment as a Military Knight of Windsor. After a very tough interview at the Ministry of Defence, I was placed on the Register. What a pity the post was offered me (as it is literally 'dead men's shoes') in 1992, when I was not yet ready to retire from the Lords. Apart from my personal feelings, a new Black Rod had just been appointed and I thought I would be letting him down. Mary supported my decision to turn down the offer and Terry and Bob were delighted that we were staying in London.

There is an organisation in the POW called the 'E' Club. There are very few members and they meet twice a year to dine. Nobody seems to know who recommends someone for membership or who makes the final decision as to who is to join. At my first lunch in the mid-80s the man on my right, an ex-Royal Navy Officer, said he had waited 17 years to be invited to join. Many senior management staff never do join, and I must say that all the members I have met are great people and delightful to know.

A very sad thing happened on the 31st July 1993 due to the defence cuts. The 2nd Coldstream was reduced from Battalion strength to a Company – about 100 all ranks compared with 600. I had never served in any other Battalion in almost 34 years service, so the final parade in Chelsea barracks was a heartbreaking occasion. Some of the spectators, who had fought in action with that Battalion and lost comrades, literally cried unashamedly. Fortunately, number 7 Company, who now carry the Battalion's colours, lives up to the very highest traditions of the Regiment.

When work started on the extension to the Jubilee Line underground, we never thought that the Lords would be affected. What a shock we had when the mice changed their allegiance from the Lower House to the Upper one. Our flat was inundated with the horrible little blighters. Rentokil got nowhere in its efforts to rid us of them. The carpenters blocked up every possible entry point but still they got in. In desperation, Mary and I went to 'The Cut' open market and purchased three old-fashioned mousetraps at 50 pence each. This did the trick, as we caught/killed eight within a fortnight. Also, they knew they had met their match with Mary. On entering the kitchen, she saw one streaking across the floor and sometimes managed to stamp on it and kill it. Leeds United could do with her skills at centre forward!

Late in 1991, when John Gingell was due to retire, Lords Oxford and Caldecote told me of a surprise present the Peers were planning for his departure. Having taken advice from Lady Pru Gingell, this was to be a portable work-bench. I have seen some of Sir John's DIY work and I can understand why his wife suggested this gift. The work-bench would be delivered to my office on the day of the presentation and I was to hide it. When it arrived, I was horrified to see that on the brass plate containing the engraving the word 'Marshal' had been misspelt and had a second 'l' on the end. Lords Caldecote and Oxford 'did not think Black Rod would notice' the misspelt word and suggested that the plate could be altered afterwards. Little did they know the eyesight of an ex-pilot! Sir John spotted the error immediately and roared with laughter. As far as I know, the engraving has never been amended to this day.

I have followed with interest the career of the present Chief of the Defence Staff, Sir Charles Guthrie. Mary and I have known him since he was a young officer in the Welsh Guards. He is married to Catherine, who is the daughter of the late Lt. Colonel Claude Worrall, Coldstream Guards.

Bob and Judi's wedding day, 15 June 1991.

Catherine's two sisters also married Welsh Guardsmen, Major General Christopher Drewry and Colonel David Lewis. Their Mum is very proud of the influence her daughters have in the junior Regiment of the Household Division. As I have said before, these Coldstreamers get everywhere!

Sir Charles was on duty as an Aide-de-Camp General to the Queen at the 1994 State Opening of Parliament. I noticed him at the bottom of the Royal Staircase with the other senior officers awaiting the arrival of Her Majesty. Knowing how approachable he was, I congratulated him on being appointed the Chief of the General Staff. He placed his hand on my shoulder and said, 'Peter, I think you've done better than me'. With that he gave a chuckle and went on to ask how the family was. Typical of his manner and friendliness.

Guardsmen everywhere are very proud that for several years during the 90s the Division has provided three members of the Army Board, General Guthrie, General Sir Michael Rose and Lieutenant General Sir William Rous, both Coldstreamers. After his outstanding tour in Bosnia, General Michael became the Adjutant General and General Willie was the Quartermaster General. Coldstreamers past and present were absolutely delighted to have General Rous as our '27th Colonel' after the retirement of the late Sir George Burns.

During the late 80s and until I retired, I terribly missed Brigadier David Stileman and Ray Scott, the Yeoman Usher and Assistant Superintendent respectively. This was not just because it put much more work my way, but also because we had so many laughs and great fun together. Both of us being members of the MCC, I still see David occasionally and we share a sticky bun and 'cuppa' together. He has a wimpish sense of humour and comes out with terrifically amusing 'one liners'.

The All-Party Rugby League Group had invited me to become a member in the late 80s, and on my retirement made me their first and only life member. We have monthly meetings with guest speakers, and the annual dinners each December are an absolute treat. Members of the Group do an enormous amount of good for the game in general.

Bob had met the young lady who was to become his wife in the late 80s and they hit it off immediately. He and Judi went 'around the world' together and remained friends – not always the case, from what we gather! Mary, Terry and I took to Judi straight away and we were delighted when they became engaged on the 11th July 1990. Mary and I learned of the engagement five minutes before midnight when Judi telephoned us, waking us up to tell us that 'Bob has just proposed and I have accepted'. I'm ashamed to admit that when Judi 'phoned, my first thought was that they had crashed MY CAR. I related this story at their wedding, causing much hilarity.

Judi has turned out to be a cracking daughter-in-law and we think the world of her. She is also very clever, producing a baby girl (Jemma) for our Ruby wedding, a baby girl (Megan) for our retirement, and a son (Jack) because Bob and I wanted someone who may play soccer for Leeds United and/or cricket for Yorkshire. No kidding! As Judi has sadly lost both parents, we are more like her Mum and Dad than in-laws.

Their wedding on the 14th June 1991 was a great affair, and was followed by a champagne reception and lunch that lasted all afternoon at Le Manoir aux Quatre Saisons near Oxford. This was a joyous occasion and I was honoured to be the best man – Terry having said that I made better speeches than he. The following evening a party was held on the Terrace of the POW. Sir John Gingell had given permission for this, despite the strictly laid-down rules that functions were not to be held on Saturday evenings. Including the musical group, 93 people attended a really lovely and happy event.

Another joyous occasion was our Ruby Wedding dinner for 40 people held in the London District Sergeants' Mess, Wellington Barracks. The host for the occasion was Garrison Sergeant Major 'Perry' Mason, who had been a Guardsman in No. 3 Company, 2nd Coldstream in 1965, when I was the Company Sergeant Major. How the wheels of time turn! It was quite fortuitous for me; not just on this occasion but on many others. 'Perry' has proved to be a Sergeant Major out of the very top drawer – both in efficiency and popularity.

Even though Doug McClelland had returned home, Mary and I continued to be invited to Australia House by the New High Commissioner, Richard Smith and his wife Janice. We missed the visits to the official residence, Stoke Lodge, as these were mostly 'family affairs' and very amusing and entertaining. Doug told us several royal stories which are worth relating. When Doug took Bob Hawke to Windsor to be presented to the Queen, he briefed him about the etiquette involved. Imagine how horrified Doug was when, on arrival in the Castle, without a pause, Bob Hawke leapt out of the car, approached the Queen at a rapid rate and said 'G'day, your Majesty'. Unperturbed, HM said something like 'That's the nicest greeting I've ever had, Prime Minister'.

On Anzac Day the Queen lunched at Stoke Lodge and during the meal was told by Lorna that a new conservatory had been built on to the house. The Queen said she would like to see it and as soon as lunch finished, proceeded out there, followed by Lorna and a 'worried' Doug. A man was up a ladder making out that he was cleaning the conservatory windows. Seeing Her Majesty looking up at him, he almost fell off the ladder. One did not need to be a mastermind to realise that the window cleaner was a policeman and the Queen laughed like fury. Doug was not amused and told Lorna off afterwards for mentioning the conservatory.

Doug McClelland has continued to play an active role in public life and carry out some tasks for his government. We have benefited through this; for example when he was the Australian High Commissioner to Expo 92 in Spain, Mary and I were invited to stay with him and Lorna in Seville and we had a wonderful few days with them.

My links with the Hyatt Carlton Tower Hotel remain strong due to my close friendship with Michael Gray and Jeremy Jasper, the General Manager and Diplomatic Liaison Officer respectively. Through them I arranged a luncheon party in December 1992 for the Liverpool-based Lung Cancer Fund. This raised an enormous amount of cash for the charity. The Liverpool-based surgeon, Professor Ray Donnelly, was the inspiration behind this fund and the late Roy Castle and his widow Fiona have done more than anyone to make this a wonderful success story. I hosted a dinner in the Lords which also helped to raise cash for this very special cause.

Surprisingly, four years after retirement, Mary and I still get invited to the Hyatt Carlton Tower. My retirement party was held there in January 1995 and those who attended maintain to this day that it was the best meal, including wines and service, that they have ever had. As this included Royal Household 'seniors' as well as the House of Lords hierarchy, this is praise indeed.

Both before and since our retirement, Mary and I have kept our links with the military by attending the Queen's Birthday Parade, massed bands concerts and Beating Retreat, the Royal Military School of Music, the Royal Tournament, the Garter Ceremony at Windsor and various parades. This means that we have kept in touch with the friends of our 'youth'.

The brilliant artist June Mendoza, who painted the picture of the House of Commons in session, continues to invite us to exhibitions at the Mall Galleries. One of the thrills of my life was having lunch at the Ritz, thanks to Ron Gerard, with the one and only Terence Cuneo on the 16th February 1995. He told us that he had painted the Queen on a number of occasions and that she 'fidgeted' a lot. He kept having to ask her to resume the position she started in.

During the late 80s and early 90s my brother Terry had been in poor health, which had him in hospital several times. However, his daughter Denise arranged a wonderful surprise party for his 65th birthday on the 3rd October 1993 and he was in sparkling form. It therefore came as a shock when he was rushed into Pindersfield Hospital near Leeds on Boxing Day. I visited him in early January on my own and was shocked at how quickly he had deteriorated since October. On the 22nd January Bob, Jemma and I visited him and it was obvious that the end was near. I recall kissing him on the forehead and as I left the ward I did not look back. Bob held me whilst I wept in the corridor, with Jemma (19 months) looking up at us. It was no surprise when he died four days later. Terry was always very popular and respected and there was a huge turnout for his funeral. We all still miss him but I think I do more than most as there was only 16 months between us. R.I.P.

Throughout the book reference has been made to General Sir David House and Air Chief Marshal Sir John Gingell, and it has been obvious that they were both outstanding in the appointment of Gentleman Usher of the Black Rod and Secretary to the Lord Great Chamberlain. Unfortunately Admiral Sir Richard Thomas was unable to fulfil his early promise as he was struck down by a major illness.

When Richard Thomas and his wife Paddy arrived in early 1992, they made a terrific impression on everyone. He quickly built up an excellent rapport with the members of his own Department and many others – especially the Works Department. Sir Richard performed the same ritual whenever I took him around the Palace to meet people. When we met anyone, he did not wait for me to complete the introductions; he simply stuck out his hand, shook hands, and said 'I'm Richard Thomas, what do you do?'. He was a good listener and this made a great impression on all who met him.

From 1981 onwards, with the permission of Black Rod, I had started to give a barrel of beer to the Sports and Social Club each Christmas. This was paid for from the Lord Great Chamberlain's bookstall account, which I administered. It was for all those who used the club. When Richard Thomas heard of this, he suggested that we change the date of giving the beer to soon after the State Opening of Parliament. Somehow this got into the Press and added to his popularity and charisma. Why not? This was great P.R.!

Richard Thomas was furious when he heard that I had no natural cover or stand-in when I was away and always returned to piles of paperwork and numerous decisions to be taken. To get rid of this, he proposed phasing out the Assistant Superintendent's post and bringing in an Administration

Officer to take some of the work-load off him and to assist me. For reasons that will become apparent, this never really worked.

As soon as he arrived, he followed in the footsteps of the previous Black Rods by getting thoroughly involved in large works services and improving all aspects of the 'bricks and mortar' in the Palace. He and I also shared a common interest in various sports, especially cricket. Before starting any business, he would ask me to select a Test Match XI to see if it agreed with his team. He accused me of bias as I always had Yorkshiremen in the team! I had always called many of the staff and security force by their Christian names and he copied this style of address. This increased his popularity and broke down certain barriers. Despite his good humour and sense of fun, he had a 'short fuse' at times and was quick to reprimand wrongdoers. I was glad that I never crossed him!

Tragedy struck at the start of the 1993 summer recess. On Wednesday 28th July he and I had a good 'bang on' about things in general, discussed the recess works programme and talked about cricket – naturally! Sir Richard was in absolutely sparkling form. He told me that he would be in the Palace for a couple of meetings during the recess but otherwise would be away. The following Monday evening Mary and I were entertaining guests in the flat when the telephone rang. I could barely hear Lady Thomas as she was speaking so softly, but she told me that Richard was 'not well' and asked me to cover for him at a meeting a couple of days later.

For two or three days I was kept in the dark but eventually Lady Thomas had to admit to me that Black Rod had had a massive stroke the previous Saturday and was in hospital in Ipswich. I drove up there immediately and was shocked when I saw him. In the week or so since I had seen him, this fine figure of a man had become shrivelled up and a virtual cabbage. With great fortitude, he gripped my right hand and held me close to him so that he could whisper what had happened. He cou'd recall vividly that whilst mowing the lawn outside his 'holiday home', he had collapsed on the grass and started giggling and thinking what a bloody idiot he was for falling over. Until Paddy came rushing out to try to pick him up, he did not realize that he was ill.

The next few weeks were touch and go and I don't think I am overstating the case when I say that Richard was at death's door several times. Twice more I went to see him in Ipswich Hospital and dreaded the thought of him being transported to Midhurst in Sussex by ambulance. Lord Ampthill and I wanted to use the helicopter ambulance service but Paddy would not agree to this. When I went to see Richard in Cowdray Ward in

King Edward VII Hospital a couple of days after his move, he looked worse than ever. However he started to gain strength and was kind enough to say that my visits cheered him up. I was also impressed that he started to ask how things were going on in the House. He was VERY critical about certain people not going to see him or contacting Paddy, and gave me a couple of names of those he did NOT want to see.

Things were not helped by Lady Thomas insisting that Richard's illness was not to be advertised – in fact to be kept secret. I had to tell Malcolm Ross, the Comptroller of the Royal Household, who in turn told the Queen and the Lord Chamberlain. I also told the Marquess of Cholmondeley and he went to Midhurst to see him. By sheer bad luck, we were advertising for a new Yeoman Usher of the Black Rod in the broadsheet newspapers and the media somehow found out about Sir Richard's illness. The press, especially the *Evening Standard*, became a darned nuisance and kept on telephoning to try to get facts on the rumours of Richard Thomas's health. I even got a 'reprimand' from the Leader of the House, via the Clerk of Parliaments, for more or less telling a reporter to get lost on the 19th August.

Paddy Thomas was determined that Richard would return to work and the doctors agreed that that was part of the therapy to get him reasonably well. He returned in February despite his left arm being virtually useless and having to drag his left leg. His courage was beyond belief and a wonderful example to us all. Without question, Paddy and his lovely family helped to pull him through but his bravery shone out. About once a week I delivered him to St Thomas's Hospital for physiotherapy. Occasionally I assisted him to put on his collar and tie or fasten his shoelaces. His excellent batman, 'Jumper' Collins, did not come on duty until late AM as he was a Doorkeeper. Malcolm Honeywood and Jim Warburton helped him if I was not about.

Although Sir Richard's illness made my last 18 months in the House difficult, it was a joy to serve him. My final and long lasting memory of him was at the 1994 State Opening of Parliament, when he carried out the full duties of Black Rod impeccably. The 'dolly' television camera that goes on ahead of him when he proceeds to the Commons showed him talking and telling himself to get a move on and do his job properly. He confirmed this to me later.

Due to the circumstances described above, the newly created Administration Officer never did manage to assist me in any way whatsoever. Quite rightly, he spent most of his time in trying to make life easier for Black

Rod. Indeed in some way my work-load increased as I spent a lot of time telling him and the replacement Yeoman Usher the form. I have no idea of how the work-load is allocated nowadays.

There is a postscript to the above. Sir Richard retired for medical reasons about ten weeks after me in 1995 and died on the 13th December 1998. The obituaries in the *Times* and *Telegraph* showed what a remarkable man he was. In addition to his two knighthoods, he was made a Knight Commander of Pope Pius in 1995. At his memorial service in Westminster Cathedral, Admiral of the Fleet Sir Julian Oswald gave the most moving address about this wonderful sailor, man, husband, father and godfather. It was an honour to serve him and it is a shame that the Lords did not have him longer.

So it was we spent our fifteenth Christmas recess in the Palace of Westminster. As always, we entertained a number of visitors. My routine on Christmas Day remained the same. In the morning I visited all the police, security and Works Department staff who were on duty, armed with a few bottles of booze and nibbles. On the 30th December we held an Open House party attended by about 30 of our friends. The invitation cards included the words, 'This is to have a 'last fling' (but NOT to smash up the furniture!) prior to leaving the Lords in January'. Naturally, being well disciplined, the guests did as they were told.

The start of 1995 was hectic in the extreme to say the least. It involved handing over to my successor and parties and more parties. Our final week was both moving and great fun. On Monday the Earl of Longford held a luncheon party for us in the Peers' Dining Room and included Ron and Pat Gerard in the list of guests. On Tuesday Lord Westbury (late Scots Guards) rounded up nine Coldstreamers for lunch and amongst the guests were the Colonel of the Regiment, General Rous, the Regimental Lieutenant Colonel, Brigadier Heywood, and several Peers. On Wednesday evening the Lord Great Chamberlain held a very big party in the Peers' Dining Room to bid farewell to Mary and me. On Thursday we had Charlie and Joan Chester for dinner with John and Lorna Rigby and on Friday the Housemaids saw us off in true London style.

Richard and Paddy Thomas, the Yeoman Usher and Administration Officer, also fitted in a super evening out on the town. Goodness knows how! Our departure from the House of Lords on the Sunday morning was a hoot – not least because we were looking after Jemma (31 months) since Megan was born the same day. What a way to celebrate our retirement and oncoming old age! We were sorry to go but we had had a fabulous fifteen years.

CHAPTER 22

The Future – Reform of the Lords

IF I HAD WRITTEN THIS BOOK at the time of my retirement in early 1995, I would have produced a really good argument as to why hereditary peers should retain their places in the Upper House. Four years on I am not now sure. I have held back writing on the subject in the hope that someone would come up with a realistic and sensible solution to the question of who would replace them. This chapter will contain lots of questions and comments but no proper answer.

Labour were in opposition for 18 years, with plenty of time to produce a timetable and programme for reform of the Lords, but failed to do so. Indeed, New Labour were in power for about 18 months before they decided on a Royal Commission to make proposals, and then gives its members little more than a year to put them forward.

The make-up of the members of the Royal Commission is debatable. As a former Leader of the Lords and Commons, and with an impeccable pedigree, Lord Wakeham would appear to be ideal as the Chairman. Nevertheless, as a Conservative life peer, one would query whether he can view the whole matter impartially. The neutrality of one or two other members is also questionable. I mean no disrespect to these people, but human nature is human nature!

At present, in 1999, the Royal Commission is touring the country taking the views of 'ordinary people'. It is worth asking how many of these members of the public actually know what makes the Lords 'tick' and so efficient at present. My reason for saying this is that so much rubbish has been spoken and written about the Upper House in recent years. Unfortunately those who are not conversant with the actual building are inclined to form an opinion from the little they see on television. Also, in the main the tabloid newspapers report very little about the Lords and when they do, look for the sensational headlines and stories.

Reform of the Lords cannot be treated in isolation from what is going on elsewhere. For example, the Scottish Parliament, Welsh Assembly, proportional representation (PR), a Mayor for London and the constant undeserved sniping at the Royal Household. Many members of the public

believe that the Commons is more in need of reform than the Lords. Despite my high regard for Tony Blair, I think he is ill-advised on the whole subject of the Lords Reform. The advice given him by 'spin doctors' and others is wrong.

Seemingly, over 60 countries around the world have second chambers. I would place a bet that not one of these countries could boast of an upper house with so many experts and knowledgeable members. Both hereditary and life peers can be included in this comment. Even opponents of the make-up of the Lords as it is agree that in general the standard of debate is exceptionally high. Another factor not well known is the large part played by peers on Standing or Select Committees, some of which are with members of the Lower House. These are very demanding on the time of those involved.

Since retiring, I have written to various 'offices' with my views and comments and had replies from Tony Blair (both in Opposition and as Prime Minister), Lord Richard, Viscount Cranborne, Baroness Jay, Stephen Twigg M.P., the Ministerial Correspondence Unit and the Cabinet Office. Almost without exception, these letters said WHY the reform of the Lords and its make-up had to take place but not one of them gave a semblance of an answer to my question of what might replace the present system. Two separate letters from the constitution secretariat were sheer 'gobbledygook'! The second letter in 1998 included the following:

> 'The Government is determined to remove the hereditary peers not for motives of class or political spite but because it simply does not accept, as a

matter of principle, that in social, economic or any other terms the hereditary peers can reasonably be considered to be representative of the people of the country.'

This is an interesting point as, unless the decision is to have a fully elected Upper House, whatever replaces the present system will be just as 'undemocratic'!

In January 1999 a really good article was published in the *House Magazine*. As a result of this, I wrote to the Editor, Sir Patrick Cormack MP, asking if I could write an article for the magazine giving my views. He agreed and this is what I wrote:-

'The interview given by Lord Weatherill to Austin Mitchell and published in the *House Magazine* was the most balanced one I have heard so far on the subject of Lords reform. What a pity the whole article was not given a full publication in one of the broad-sheet newspapers! Lord Weatherill's reasoning was so good that I would like to give weight to it.

'From 1980 until 1995 I was the Staff Superintendent in the Lords. My wife worked in the Lords Library and we both lived on site and like to think that we got to know what made the place 'tick'. These years were without question the busiest ever known in the Lords. A massive amount of legislation went through at the time. Many Hereditary Peers made a huge contribution to the running of Government, as did numerous Life Peers.

'In 1980 there were about 70 cross-benchers and now there are in excess of 300. It is interesting to note that some of these were in the two major Parties in the Commons as MPs. One needs to ask why this is. Could it be that they see the Lords as being more democratic that 'the other place'? I believe that they do.

'My wife and I have a large circle of friends from all walks of life. I can think of only one who could be classed as really right wing. None are left wing though they include several Labour Life Peers. We are left of centre but like to think of ourselves as cross-benchers or independents. Reading Lord Weatherill's interview is fascinating and gives a sympathetic view to all sides of the argument. It is so obvious that his period as Speaker in the Commons has enlightened him and this needs to be passed on to others.

'The only point on which I take issue with His Lordship is calling Lady Jay 'Nice Spice'.

'The Royal Commission will need to look at the Commons as well as the Lords. For example, when the Scottish Parliament and Welsh Assembly start work, the number of MPs needs to be reduced. As Lord Weatherill says, why cannot MPs' work such as 'Surgeries' and correspondence be taken on by unpaid councillors? Also, why not ask Peers to take on constituency work where possible? Lord Fitt, who ceased to be an MP in 1983, still deals with a large amount of correspondence and telephone calls from his old constituents. I know of a number of others who do likewise.

'The term 'Working Peers' is insulting to both Hereditary and Life Peers. Some of the former become Peers when very young whilst some of the latter do so in relatively old age. In very many cases they attend the POW because they think they help in governing the country in a sensible and democratic manner. Many do not claim expenses of any sort – and this applies to both Hereditary and Life Peers.

'The last Government weakened the case for retaining hereditary Peers by calling 'three-line whips' when they were not necessary. To have 'backwoodsmen' turning up to vote on a subject they know little about and are not particularly interested in (!) is simply crazy and must cease NOW.

'The deal done by Lords Weatherill and Cranborne was remarkable and deserves to succeed. Indeed, I think that the retention of 91 Hereditary Peers is an ideal figure and should become permanent. Throughout my time in the Lords I could have named at least 50 Hereditary Peers who played a very large part in the Lords. Many of these were Ministers and/or on Committees of all sorts. Two who come to mind are Glenarthur and Lyell. As Ministers of State for Northern Ireland, they were both exemplary. I have heard this from serving soldiers as well as from people in the House.

'Regrettably, many of the Life Peers contribute nothing to the work in the Lords. Some never attend the House and when they do, it is for the wrong reason – SOCIAL! I once asked a Peer why he hardly attended the House whereas in the early 80s he did. He told me that he had been brought into the House to push through one particular bill. Having done that, he thought he had 'earned his corn' and could now take it easy. How can the Royal Commission talk about getting rid of the 'backwoodsmen' without looking at this aspect of the problem?

'I was particularly impressed by a sentence towards the end of the article by Lord Weatherill: '... in the best interest of our country'. Surely this has to be the theme of any revised Chamber. There appear to be only two realistic solutions to the problem: retain the status quo with some fine tuning, including the retention of 91 hereditary Peers. Or get rid of ALL the present Peers and have a fully elected Upper House. It is interesting to note that recently the Leader of the Conservative Opposition in the Lords has said that his party now favour a fully elected Upper House. This is as big a 'U' turn as the one by the Prime Minister with regard to the retention of some Hereditary Peers!

'Bearing in mind that the MPs are well paid and the Peers only claim expenses, the following is a valid point. Quite often the Lords sits when the Commons is in recess. There has been a recent example of this: the MPs are now on 'half term' recess to spend time with their families. The Lords continue to sit. Remarkable to say the least.

'Very little has been said or written about Committee work in the Upper House. Some Hereditary Peers devote an enormous amount of time to these. I pose the question: will a sufficient amount of Life Peers be willing to volunteer for this task should ALL the Hereditary Peers be got rid of? This is doubtful as many Life Peers have numerous interests away from the Palace of Westminster.

'An interesting comparison is how various Leaders in the House performed – bearing in mind that I speak only as an ex-member of staff. Nevertheless I did get a 'feed-back' of views from several Peers from all Parties and the cross-benchers: Baroness Young 81-83 (Life) was outstanding; Viscount Whitelaw 83-88 (newly created Hereditary) was highly respected and popular and did well; Lord Belstead 88-90 (Hereditary) was outstanding; Lord Waddington 90-92 (Life) was very good.

'Reading books about the POW gives some indication of how times have changed. *The History of The House of Lords*, written by Lord Longford in 1988, is a beautiful portrayal but gives the show away by revealing that until the late 70s the Lords was a fairly 'laid back' institution. He also had the foresight to mention the 'abuse of patronage' system in creating Life Peers. Red hot news nowadays.

'Although John Wells wrote his book *The House of Lords* in 1997 in anecdotal style, it does prove just how busy the Upper House has become in recent years. The Lords in its present form makes a massive contribution to the governing of the country – not just in acting as an amending Chamber, but by having experts in every field amongst the Peers.

'The BBC does not present the Lords in a very fair way. For example, John Cole was the Political Editor for several years, yet in his book, *As It Seemed to Me* published in 1995, he hardly mentions the Upper House. What a pity Christopher Jones has not put pen to paper, as his knowledge of the Lords was particularly good. This was proved by the wonderful television series, *The Great Palace*, in the early 80s in which Christopher made a big impact. If some of the present critics of the Lords were to watch this programme, they would probably change their views.

'Whichever decision is to be made, I very much hope that Peers such as Lord Weatherill are listened to in order to ensure a 'rounded view'. Certainly we do not want the politics of envy or bigotry. During the last few years many people have been writing articles, or speaking openly, on the subject with very little knowledge of the working of the Houses of Parliament and the Lords in particular.

'The Royal Commission has a huge job on its hands but might like to keep in mind: 'If the House ain't broken – don't mend it!'

Regrettably the above was not published despite two enthusiastic letters from Sir Patrick and high praise from Lord Weatherill. No explanation was given but I suspect it was because I criticised Lady Jay and the non-attenders amongst the Life Peers.

Some people, including me, think that we are over-governed. On top of what is written above, the bureaucrats in Brussels are issuing directives galore, often to the detriment of our parliamentary system. The question is often asked: 'Are we losing our sovereignty?' The readers can judge for themselves. The cost of the Brussels set-up is staggering – in fact almost obscene!

No two bodies seem to agree on what should replace the Lords in its present form. Amongst the suggestions are a Senate, a partly elected/partly nominated Chamber, local committees to elect or select representatives, or a fully elected Chamber. Some articles have been written with a 'tongue in cheek' attitude suggesting such nominees as Delia Smith (cook), Cilla Black (singer), Trevor Macdonald (newsreader), Cliff Richard (singer), Stephen Fry (actor), David Attenborough (wildlife expert), Sean Connery (007!), Bobby Charlton (footballer) and David Shepherd (artist). Some cynics have said they would contribute more to the Lower House!

The House of Lords is relatively cheap compared to other places around the world and certainly in comparison with the Commons. As mentioned elsewhere, many Peers claim no expenses whatever and those who do will never get rich by doing so. If figures recently published are correct, it is interesting to draw a comparison with the Scottish Parliament and Welsh Assembly. The cost of salaries for the Scottish Parliament is £5.2 million – made up of £104,399 for the Scottish First Minister and 129 MSPs who are paid £40,092 a year.

The 60 Welsh Assembly members will receive £34,438 and the First Secretary £98,745, a total of 2.1 million. The 108 members of the Northern Ireland Assembly receive £38,036 and the First Minister and Deputy First Minister £102,343 each, a total of £4.3 million.

The mind boggles at the cost of a fully elected Upper Chamber of say 500 members and everything that goes with it. This makes the saving on the demise of the Royal Yacht *Britannia* look like peanuts.

To return to the Royal Commission. Will the Report be along the lines of the Independent Commission On The Voting System produced in October 1998 by Lord Jenkins of Hillhead and four members of the Committee? Although this consisted of 90 pages, it gave no satisfactory answer to the subject of proportional representation (PR). In the report it mentions New Zealand introducing PR in 1993. Recently it has been announced that a referendum is to be carried out shortly to see if the old 'first past the post' system should be reintroduced. Interesting to say the least!

How sad that sensible suggestions from distinguished Peers are 'pooh-poohed' at and not subjected to proper discussion. The Earl of Longford, who supports Reform of the Lords, suggests that Hereditary Peers be allowed to speak in debate but not vote. The Earl Ferrers makes a fair point when he says that Hereditary Peers who are Privy Councillors should be allowed to remain in the Lords until they die. There is a tremendous amount of knowledge and expertise in both these categories. What a waste to lose them! Perhaps Lord Longford did not help his cause by saying:

'We think of ourselves as the best here. We're far more intellectual, in fact we're altogether far better, than that lot down there. If you had an elected House, what would you end up with? Second-raters, people who couldn't get into Commons, MEPs but worse'.

In 1990 there were 358 Life Peers and now there are about 523. These figures do not include the Bishops or Lords of Appeal. The latter are absolutely essential and it will be interesting to see if the Muslims, Sikhs, Hindus and Jews are given seats in a revised Chamber. The Archbishop of Canterbury supports this but not if it leads to a substantial loss in the present 26 Bishops. One of the problems is literally a lack of space in what is a relatively small debating Chamber. There is talk of taking the Lord Chancellor out of the judicial system but no suggestions so far about the Lords of Appeal.

My correspondence with The Viscount Cranborne culminated in him sending me a copy of his speech to the House of 14th October, 1998. This contained good, sound material and was what I call a 'rounded' view, and it was no surprise that he helped Lord Weatherill to set up the deal with Tony Blair which would save 92 seats for the Hereditaries. This was a complete 'U' turn by New Labour and William Hague was foolish to over-react and sack Lord Cranborne for his so-called disloyalty.

The staff are shocked at the bad feeling, and a certain amount of intrigue, in the Lords at present. Some Life Peers of all parties have defended the hereditary principal. Lord (Melvyn) Bragg admits that he went to the Lords to get rid of the Hereditaries but is now charmed with their grace and courtesy. During the two-day debate Peers from the same Party made contradictory statements. The present Lord Chancellor alienates himself on all sides by being unnecessarily aggressive. In the 'other place' 131 MPs have voted for a fully elected Upper House. At least this would get rid of accusations of cronyism. Incidentally, the patronage system does not improve on the hereditary one.

If proof were needed of the confusion caused by the Government's initiative, the month of June 1999 is a good example. In the space of 10 days the following occurred:- 4 Life Peers were created in the Queen's Birthday Honours, 36 'Working' Peers – mostly Labour – were appointed, the Queen made her youngest son an Earl (which means his wife is a Countess and any sons become Viscounts and daughters Ladies) and Lord Irvine of Laing did a 'U' turn with regard to Hereditary Peers being replaced during Phase I of the Reform of the House.

At the same time the Professor who is the Director of the Constitution Unit at University College London said that it would 'take a miracle' for the Royal Commission on House of Lords Reform to reach a solution within the year. A Conservative MP wrote a well constructed article in the *Daily Telegraph* giving sound reasons why a Senate should not replace the Lords. All these points are mind boggling and do not help New Labour's case one iota!

In researching for this book, I have read literally hundreds of articles and several Hansards about Lords Reform. There is no common thread running through these, which proves how difficult a job Lord Wakeham and his team have. After all, attempts were made to change the system almost a century ago – and have been several times since.

There is a postscript to the above. On the 27th July 1999 I attended a public hearing of the Royal Commission of the House of Lords in London. The two sessions I listened to lasted over four hours. Eleven members of the Commission, including the Chairman and only two women, were on the platform. Fifteen witnesses presented their views exceptionally well and invariably answered questions from the Commission with great ability. Their views were diverse and in some cases radical and controversial.

However, it was the views of those speaking from the floor that interested me. Amongst statements made were: not enough Catholics in the Upper House; if not fully elected, how are the poor Life Peers to be got rid of; as now half of the electorate are women, at least 50 per cent of the House should be female; a referendum is essential; the members should be selected by regions; too much bad law is on the statute book and we are now over governed at all levels; too many councils/quangos; the countryside and education get poor representation in the Lords; and finally, why is more time not allowed for real Constitutional matters?

The lady who made the best impression on all those in attendance spoke from the floor. She wanted no favours because she is black, is a woman and a local councillor. What she wanted was to be elected on MERIT and went on the 'declare an interest' in wanting to be a member of a revised Upper House!

The above is mentioned for no other reason than to prove what a difficult – yes, nigh impossible – task Lord Wakeham and his colleagues have in trying to provide a solution that will suit all parties in just a few months. I hope that I am wrong!

All aspects of the media have criticised the decision to create George Robertson a Peer for cynical political reasons. Nobody begrudges him his appointment as the General Secretary of NATO after his reasonable success as the Defence Secretary during the Kosovo crisis. This is an abuse of the Honours System and makes a mockery of the future Reform of the House of Lords. By the very nature of his new appointment, Lord Robertson will NOT be available to attend the Upper House.

Who am I, as a simple ex-Coldstream Drummer Boy, to suggest what the answer is? All I wish is that the change is for proper reasons and not just 'change for change's sake.

CHAPTER 23

Goodbye General Willie

'R ETIREMENT IS BLISS' is what General Sir David House wrote in the first Christmas card he sent to Mary and me after he left the House of Lords. I was most sceptical about this at the time but he has been proved right.

We get great joy out of our two sons and three grandchildren and do not regret staying in London after our retirement. I like my sports, especially cricket, and we both enjoy live theatre and the cinema. As the Deputy President of the London Branch of the Regimental Association, I keep in touch with past and present guardsmen.

Being in London encourages friends to come and see us and we travel quite a lot, as is obvious from comments on previous pages. Our neighbours are very nice and we have made some lovely new friends in north London. Ron and Pat Gerard in particular have made us most welcome to the area. The wonderful Agent General for South Australia, Maurice de Rohan, continues to spoil us rotten by inviting us to Australia House for the most superb parties. Having the 1st Battalion Coldstream Guards back at Windsor is a special treat. The morale and hospitality of all ranks is of the highest order and in the very best traditions of the Regiment.

I had intended ending the Epilogue in a light-hearted manner but find it impossible due to the premature death of the Regiment's 27th Colonel, Lieutenant General Sir William Rous KCB, OBE, in May 1999: just as I finished writing this book. This was a treble loss to me – as a friend, as an admirer and also because I lived in hope that he would write the foreword to this autobiography.

Before paying tribute to the General I need to go back a few years. On the 13th October 1984 Lord Westbury invited Mary, brother Terry and his wife Gladys and me to York races for the Coldstream Cup. At lunch in the Stewards room we sat at a round table of eight. The Colonel of the Regiment, General Sir George Burns, was in attendance and I sat on his right. Lord Westbury sat opposite Sir George. Towards the end of the meal, the following conversation took place:

Lord Westbury: 'Come on George – who will take over from you when you step down as Colonel?'. 'Willie, of course,' said the General. 'Willie

With Lieutenant-General Sir William Rous and Admiral Sir Richard Thomas.

who?' said his Lordship. 'Willie Rous – he's a Brigadier now but he'll be a General by then,' said Sir George with great emphasis, and went on to tell us all about Willie's qualities that fitted him for the job. Obviously this news was not intended to be kept secret, so from then I started to spread the news. What was remarkable is that whoever I told this news to showed no surprise whatsoever. It was as though the position of Colonel was 'in the stars' for Willie Rous.

So it was that when General George stood down early in 1994, having been our Colonel for twenty-eight years, General Willie moved into this demanding post. He was still a serving soldier, and a member of the Army Board, initially as the Military Secretary and then as the Quartermaster General. Despite these onerous full-time military duties, he visited RHO, the 1st Battalion and No. 7 Company regularly and inspired everyone he met. His enthusiasm was infectious but more than anything he made life fun – it was a joy to be in his company at any time. There was no pomposity in him.

Not only did the Colonel get to know his soldiers but he wanted to know all about the wives and families too. His gift with words – both written and spoken – was almost beyond belief. Prior to visiting a branch of the Association, he did his homework and in his speech mentioned members of the branch. He used no notes and invariably spoke for only fifteen minutes. He was the guest speaker at the 1997 Riding Masters, Quartermasters and

Directors of Music annual dinner and everyone present agreed that this was the best speech they had ever heard. My guest that night was Bill Pertwee and he wrote to General Willie afterwards – not just to congratulate him, but also to tell him that he should have been an actor!

Earlier in the book I wrote about gallantry in action of various soldiers and the courage in illness of Richard Thomas. During the spring and early summer of 1999 members of the Regiment saw courage of the highest order. General Willie had been taken ill the previous May and needed major surgery and various other treatments. He appeared to be recovering well and attended a number of regimental and other functions. However, those of us who saw him in March 1999 realized that he had taken a turn for the worse. He told me that he set himself target dates and what he intended doing. These included the Annual General Meeting of the Nulli Secundus Club in London and the St George's Day celebrations with the 1st Battalion at Windsor – both lengthy and tiring days.

The two dates that will be remembered by those in attendance were the 9th and 20th May; the Regiment's Black Sunday and the Presentation of New Colours respectively. At the first, General Willie attended lunch in the Officers Mess Wellington Barracks, read the lesson in the Guards Chapel, went to Horse Guards Parade, laid a wreath on the Guards Memorial, and took the salute in Wellington Barracks. He was applauded as he left the parade ground – unique on a military occasion.

At Windsor Castle on the 20th our Colonel accompanied the Queen throughout the parade and during her visit to Victoria Barracks to meet the troops and families. He was in full dress and the weather was very hot. He then stayed to have a long lunch and spoke to dozens of Coldstreamers and their guests. Someone said to me that his courage and stamina were awesome. I agreed.

Five days later General Willie passed away, R.I.P. Without question he epitomized a modern-day General. His standards were of the highest and this is what he expected of his subordinates, but there was more to it than that. Many of his qualities are listed above but I believe that the reason we all adored and respected him is because we felt he was the 'head of the family'. Not long after General Willie took over as the Colonel, his predecessor General George, told me that the 'Regiment is in good hands'. What an epitaph, what a guy! I doubt if there will ever be his like again.

So many tributes, written and verbal, have been made to the Regiment's 27th Colonel that I feel most humble writing the following:–

If General Willie intended his memorial service to be a joyous occasion he achieved his aim. What he would not have known was the attendance at the Guards Chapel. This included over a thousand people from all walks of life, representatives of the Queen, Prince Philip, Prince Charles, Princess Royal, Duke of Kent and the King of Jordan, five Field Marshals, sixty Generals, two Admirals, and numerous other high ranking officers. Interestingly, there were many wives present also.

The addresses by The Lord Shuttleworth, the Lord Zouche and General Sir Michael Rose covered every aspect of Willie's life – both serious and amusing. He was quite literally a hero to everyone. His sons James and Richard read the Lessons. However, it was the music that enraptured all those present. The choir and the regimental band were in superb form. General and Lady Rous had a huge say in the choice of music and our brilliant Director of Music arranged it beautifully. All the hymns were the well known ones and were sung with gusto and enthusiasm.

Willie himself had chosen most of the musical medley, 'My Favourite Things'. David Marshall had arranged it and the musicians played it with love:

> Lira's Theme from Dr. Zhivago; I'm Getting Married in the Morning; Two Little Boys; Forty Years On; Old Coldstream Marches; 'Theme from 'Casualty'; The Galloping Major; The Farmer's Boy; Nick Nack Paddy Wick Give a Dog a Bone; How Much is That Doggy in the Window; D'Ye Ken John Peel; A Hunting We Will Go; The Lincolnshire Poacher; La Mer; Theme from 'Sailing'; Sailing By; English Country Garden; Tambourin; Trumpet Voluntary; Memory; Rule Britannia; Land of Hope and Glory.

Finally, was there a message in the song 'Stan' Up An' Fight' from Carmen Jones sung by Michael Bundy? Knowing how General Willie thought of life, I think there was. After her husband died, Lady Rous wrote to me as follows:

'It is still hard to realize sometimes that all that fun and enthusiasm and zest for life has been ended. As you know, he was the bravest of the brave, and unselfish and uncomplaining and humorous to the end. I can never remember a single occasion when he put himself first!'

As I said above, I don't think we will ever see his like again.

Knowing the fantastic support given to Willie by his charming wife Judy, I can finish on a philosophical note:

They say that in life you make your own luck, so if this is true, I obviously married the right girl and chose, albeit via the Royal Marines, the right Regiment: NULLI SECUNDUS

CHAPTER 24

Retirement is Bliss, or Is It?

A S STATED ON PAGE 230 the first time Lieutenant General Sir David House wrote to me after his retirement in 1985 he said 'retirement is bliss!' This was my exact thoughts until the 3rd May 2004 when Mary died, R.I.P. She has been my strength and inspiration from the day I met her in late 1950. It is obvious by what was said on page xi that she made a massive contribution to this book. She was a wonderful wife, mother and grandmother. Mary was in the North Middlesex Hospital for over a month and when she came home on the 8th April our house was like a florists shop due to the kindness of many people. Terry, who now lives in Sydney, arrived home five days before Mary died and was with Bob and me when she passed away.

Just a few days before Mary died several members of her family came from Ireland to see her. She was in great form despite knowing that the end was near. Judi, Jemma, Megan and Jack saw Mary about three days before she died and she asked the grandchildren to look after granddad – WHICH THEY DO! The Marie Curie nurse and the two Enfield nurses who were with Mary to the end were wonderful.

Jim and Pat (now deceased) Mace came from Canada to see Mary. They also stayed on for the funeral on the 10th May despite it being their wedding anniversary. Ron and Pat Gerard, Harry (now deceased) and Mary Berger, Eddie and Val Norton and Keith and Jennie Sansom gave me terrific support before Mary died and they have continued to do so since. Ron and Pat continue to spoil me rotten as I have become part of their extended family. Over 300 letters and cards of condolence came from all over the world, many included the words 'nice', 'kindness', 'gentle', and 'smile' when reminiscing about Mary.

Our Lady of Lourdes Church, New Southgate, was packed on the morning of the 10th May for Mary's funeral. Father Tom Egan took the most beautiful service. Roger Swift played the organ and his wife Carol encouraged Jemma and Megan as they played 'Sandman's Lullaby' and 'Echoes' respectively on the piano. Mary's nephew Brother Seamus O'Connell gave two readings which had been selected by Sister Nora Ryan. Wilf Pickles gave a most moving eulogy and Bob gave a 'Sons Tribute' (he spoke for the whole family).

The last photograph of Mary taken at the celebration of Bill Pertwee's 50 years in show business. With Mollie Sugden. February 2004.

Well – this takes me back – all those letters we wrote to each other when I was at University and you and Dad were either in Farnborough or Londonderry. Even then I appreciated that I got more letters from home than my mates did – and phone calls, too. With your busy lives, how did you find the time? Silly question – you and Dad always find the time to do the important things in life.

To start, and to use one of your favourite phrases – altered for you – 'I have got a bone to pick with you young lady'. I asked you to hang around for my birthday but you popped off 4 days early. Naughty you. Still, you always said to me that you wanted to after 'three score years and ten' so I guess I should feel lucky that I got – we all got – an extra 30 odd months out of you.

But that's not right Mum is it? Looking at how serene and beautiful you looked in the Chapel of Rest – you were too young to die. Sorry – I must stop telling you off.

So instead I will tell all your family and friends about how pleased I was that you broke those Three Promises you made to yourself when you came to England in 1947 as a 16 year old girl. You vowed to yourself that you wouldn't marry an Englishman, wouldn't marry a non-Catholic and wouldn't marry till you were 27. Thank God that meeting Dad made you happily abandon that particular game-plan. Well done – the best thing you ever did. And, of course, the Ryan family immediately embraced Dad into its bosom.

When you told me this I said 'why 27?' You told me your aim was to have a successful working life before settling down to have a family. Well, I think even you – in all your modesty – would acknowledge that you had a successful life – at work and at play – at home and outside the home – with family and with friends.

Dad is more proud of you now than ever before – counting up the cards and letters, telling all and sundry about the 53 years you had together, He's coined, a new phrase, by the way, when speaking to me and Judi and the kids – 'we are a great team and we will get through this together . . .'.

I have been amazed by the warmth of your family and friends in recent months but then Dad uttered another of his pet phrases the other day, describing a particular friend as 'being family'.

In Southgate you leave your front door unlocked during the day – that is symbolic of the way you and Dad have always lived your lives – you are open to all. You give so much of yourselves and consequently everyone is so happy and relaxed about giving back to you.

Is there a married couple out there with quite so many friends? Wherever you have been you made new tribes of them. And they aren't transitory friendships either – they live on for decades.

And you never ask of or judge people – you accept them for what they are. So some random happy memories:

- 1973: Terry's surprise 18th birthday party in the house at Farnborough – us getting him out of the house on some ruse. He returned to a darkened kitchen to be welcomed by a motley crew of people and immediately turned on his heels trying to escape.
- 1977: you, me Dad and Terry – all sleeping in Terry's flat in St. Johns Wood – the 4 of us living in 3 different cities but all doing fine. Together for one night – you and Dad in Terry's bed and me and him sleeping on the floor – the lights off – talking and giggling all through the night – Terry telling good new jokes and Dad telling corny ones that we had heard many times before but still made us laugh.
- 1980: Dad's 50th birthday party in the garden and conservatory in Farnborough.
- 1991: the day Judi and I got married – you enjoying yourself – getting ever so slightly tipsy at Lunch but not so tipsy that you didn't fail to notice how extortionately expensive the afternoon tea and biscuits were. But after you recovered from that shock you and Dad were like little children when responding to Niki's suggestion that the entire wedding party join Judi and me for a recce of our honeymoon suite. You always did enjoy embarrassing me.

That's how you liked it – gatherings of family and friends – ideally at home with you and Dad hosting. It must have been the Irish blood in you. 'The simple things in life are the best' – was your Mantra.

And, of course, there are thousands of other stories we could tell – prompted by Dad's amazing collection of photos. Not having looked at them for some time I have just been struck by two things – you were always smiling, easily and naturally and you always looked stylish and beautiful – all those Royal Occasions you went to and you could have passed for 'one of them'.

By the way, did we really cut just half of Dad's moustache off while he was sleeping or was that something we made up or dreamt about doing?

I hope your vision of Heaven has materialised for you. If you are up there playing scrabble here are some good words for you – albeit without any Qs or Xs or Zs. They happen to describe a person who means more to me now than ever before: humble; sincere; modest; warm; caring; adventurous; gentle; loyal; cheeky; beautiful.

But most of all – you were yourself – no airs and graces for you, no matter who you were meeting.

And, of course, you had courage by the ton – hence you coming to London as a 16 year old; hence you getting through the illness in 1977 – for you, it was fun wearing a wig – and hence you getting through the last 3 months with such dignity, good humour and strength.

I am afraid we are going to keep Dad from you for some time yet – there is some unfinished business – getting the kids settled and married etc. And Dad and I are on a secret mission to convert Jack off Arsenal and over to Leeds – but keep that to yourself please.

And don't worry about the kids – if they inherit just 10% of the qualities of you/Dad/Terry and Judi they will all be made for life.

But when Dad does join you, don't worry – he will bring that phone book of yours and you can have a whale of a time together. Dad can talk for England and you can listen for Ireland.

I had better wrap things up now – Dad hasn't been as quiet as this since Leeds got relegated in the 1980s. Anyway, he will make up for it at The Wake, you can be sure of that.

Dad – on Mum's behalf – thank you – you made her life and ours richer. You were my Best Man for a good reason. Even in retirement you are a Natural Born Leader.

One final observation, Mum – it was all pre-destined for you wasn't it? When you were given that name of yours – MARY.

Well done Mum – we are all proud of you.

All my love and more, ♥

THFO

P.S. Where's my birthday present?

(written on 7 May 2004)

The church service was followed by a committal at New Southgate Crematorium. Terry and Bob chose some lovely music including 'The

Wonder of You' by Elvis Presley. Most of the congregation stayed on for the refreshments in the church hall afterwards. We invited about 40 back to the house afterwards but in the event about 70 came – nobody wanted to go home. Little did I think that brother Tony (80) and his lovely wife Anne (85) would be with Mary within a couple of years.

Mary's ashes were divided between the local crematorium and the garden of the house in Shower (Ireland) where Mary was born. Instead of flowers at the funeral we asked for donations to the North London Hospice. This totaled over two and a half thousand pounds including five hundred pounds from an Australian friend.

Memorial services were held in Sydney. Australia, excellently organised by Alan Keyes, a friend of Terry's. There were several moving Eulogies. The service in Newport, Ireland was attended by all the family (including those from the UK and Terry) Mary's nephew Charlie O'Connell gave a most moving tribute to 'Auntie Mary'.

Unfortunately a number of people named in this book have died since it was first published.

The Lord Aberdare, Sir Ralph Anstruther, Alan Barber, Eric Bedser, Pete Blaby, Derek Cessford, 'Kiwi' Clements, Arthur Clues, Denis Compton, Terence Cuneo, Maurice de Rohan, Lord Fitt, John Ghika, (brother) Tony Horsfall and his wife Anne, Colin Ingelby-Mackenzie, Sir Johnny Johnston, Bill Kirke, Bert Lees, Sir Victor Le Fanu, Lord Longford, Tony Pearson, Keith Miller, Bill Moore, Sir Jeremy Moore, Eva Nicholas, 'Trixie' Nockall, Alastair Tower, Bill Perris, Sir Philip Ward, Lord Weatherill, Lord Westbury, Denis Wilkinson and Ernie Wise.

When you see this very sad long list it is apparent why I have included a question mark after the title of this chapter. It is impossible to put into words how much I am missing Mary and many of those who have died. Anyhow I don't doubt that now they are in 'the great parade ground in the sky.' General Willie will be organising some fun and games for them!

CHAPTER 25

Postscript and Moving On

THE ARGUMENTS AND PROS AND CONS about a modern House of Lords have been made in Chapter 22. However, what a mess the Labour government has made of this and the future looks bleak. Phase one was carried out and ninety per cent of the hereditary peers were got rid of – sacked in fact! Many of these were really conscientious at attending and taking part in debates. Numerous life peers have been credited with the badly named title of 'working peers'. Some of these NEVER attend the House.

The future House of Lords has been debated many times in the Commons and numerous proposals made. When the late Robin Cook was the leader of the Commons seven different solutions were made and not one of them received the necessary 'yes vote'. At the time of going to print the 'cash for honours' argument and controversy rages on. Any one of the three Black Rods I served could have sorted this out in a day.

My successor, Major Mike Charlesworth BEM, is doing a great job as I expected. However, I feel sorry for him on two counts. Firstly, his apartment is not in the Palace of Westminster and he has a 'Line Manager'. This means that he has not got direct access to Black Rod whereas I did. The news that Michael Pownall is about to become the Clerk of Parliament is wonderful news. Of all the Clerks I dealt with he was by far the best. I visit the Lords occasionally and the Police and Security staff always makes a fuss of me.

I enjoy my monthly meetings of the All-Party Rugby League group in the House of Commons. David Hinchcliffe has retired but there are still a number of old friends including Lords Hoyle and Lofthouse. Not long before he died Lord Longford invited me for lunch in the Peers Dining Room. We covered all sorts of subjects – mainly sports which he loved. He asked me if I would like to be a Labour Peer but at my age I did not even consider it. This would have suited Edward Crofton as he always calls me 'Your Lordship'!

The armed forces, particularly the army, are having a terrible time at present with very little chance of improvements. The gaps between operational tours are getting shorter all the time. Ironically, if it wasn't for the situation in Northern Ireland improving the infantry would not have been able to operate both Afghanistan and Iraq wars at the same time. As the

Deputy President of the London Coldstream Association and organiser of the Drummers reunions I see quite a lot of the soldiers and they are terrific young men – cheerful, professional and very good company. Some have as many as eight (mainly operational) medals!

Finally, how about the family? Terry now lives in Bondi, Australia. In addition to his accounting and managerial skills he now has his own Pet Shop which sells all sorts of 'luxury' items for cats and dogs plus food stuffs. He even has two magnificent Great Danes – Phoenix and Ryan – which he insists are my grandchildren.

Bob is a very successful solicitor specialising in entertainment law. Amongst his clients is Cat Stevens (now called Yusuf Islam) and the Spice Girls are looked after by his firm. He is setting up his own company and this will be fully operational in April 2008. His wife Judi has a full time job but is always very busy looking after three very active children. Jemma (15), Megan (12) and Jack (10) are all doing well at school. Mary left some money to help with the children's education and this is being put to good use including: Jemma is learning the piano and drums; Megan is learning the piano, keyboard and saxophone; Jack is learning the electric guitar.

I have been to Australia three times since 2004, to France twice and Ireland twice. The hospitality of the Australians is phenomenal. As ever the Regiment takes a big place in my life and I continue to give talks about the Palace of Westminster and humorous anecdotes – all for charity.

As the book goes to print Ron Gerard is hosting a private lunch to entertain the Field Marshals of the British Army at the Ritz Hotel, London and the following attended – Field Marshals HRH The Duke of Edinburgh, The Lords Bramall, Chapple, Inge and Vincent, Generals the Lord Ramsbotham and the Lord Walker, Major General Currie, Brigadiers Heywood and Hunt-Davies. As a former Drummer Boy I was honoured to be included. This was typical of Ron's generous hospitality. How sad to think there is no longer a Field Marshal post in the army so those named above may be the last ever.

Needless to say, Bob and his family have been my strength since I lost Mary. So, apart from missing her I count myself very, very lucky. My only complaint is that the time passes far too quickly – but I suspect all elderly people say that! A new friend, Bill Boyle (88), agrees! Tony and Melody Parfitt have become the most wonderful friends. I cannot resist finishing with a touch of wimpish humour. Bearing in mind that the former Deputy Prime Minister, Michael Heseltine was one of my recruits I wrote to congratulate him on his peerage in 2001. This was his reply:

Dear Pete, thank you for your letter of the 23rd July. It was good of you to write.

If you'd have been in charge of the House of Lords and ran it like the Guards Depot, I'd never have gone near it!'

Every good wish

Yours ever

Michael

Postscript: This letter is framed and displayed in my loo with a picture of Michael.

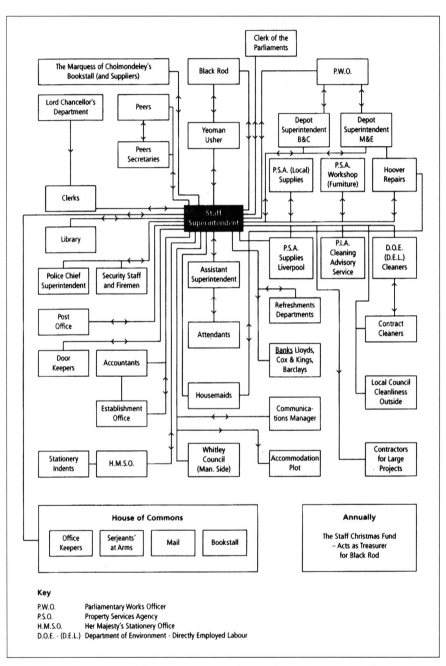

The Position of the Staff Superintendent in the Organization of the
House of Lords in 1980.

Index